Lecture Notes in Computer Science 13136

More information about this subseries at https://link.springer.com/bookseries/7410

Andrea Saracino · Paolo Mori (Eds.)

Emerging Technologies for Authorization and Authentication

4th International Workshop, ETAA 2021
Darmstadt, Germany, October 8, 2021
Revised Selected Papers

 Springer

Editors
Andrea Saracino 🆔
Consiglio Nazionale delle Ricerche
Pisa, Italy

Paolo Mori 🆔
Institute of Informatics and Telematics
Pisa, Italy

ISSN 0302-9743   ISSN 1611-3349 (electronic)
Lecture Notes in Computer Science
ISBN 978-3-030-93746-1   ISBN 978-3-030-93747-8 (eBook)
https://doi.org/10.1007/978-3-030-93747-8

LNCS Sublibrary: SL4 – Security and Cryptology

This Springer imprint is published by the registered company Springer Nature Switzerland AG
The registered company address is: Gewerbestrasse 11, 6330 Cham, Switzerland

Preface

This book contains the papers selected for presentation at the 4th International Workshop on Emerging Technologies for Authorization and Authentication (ETAA 2021), held in Darmstadt Germany, on October 8th, 2021, and co-located with the 26th European Symposium on Research in Computer Security (ESORICS 2021).

The workshop program included 11 full papers focusing on the workshop topics, in particular: new techniques for biometric and behavior-based authentication, and authentication and authorization in the IoT and in distributed systems in general, including the smart home environment.

We would like to express our thanks to the authors who submitted their papers to the fourth edition of this workshop, thus contributing to making it again a successful event, despite the difficulties associated with a fully virtual event. We acknowledge the sponsorship and promotion done by the EU-Funded H2020 SIFIS-Home project (GA number: 952652).

Last but not least, we would like to express our gratitude to the members of the Technical Program Committee for their valuable work in evaluating the submitted papers.

October 2021

Paolo Mori
Andrea Saracino

Organization

Workshop Chairs

Paolo Mori   Consiglio Nazionale delle Ricerche, Italy
Andrea Saracino   Consiglio Nazionale delle Ricerche, Italy

Technical Program Committee

Benjamin Aziz	University of Portsmouth, UK
Francesco Di Cerbo	SAP Lab, France
Damiano Di Francesco Maesa	University of Pisa, Italy
Giacomo Giorgi	Consiglio Nazionale delle Ricerche, Italy
Vasileios Gkioulos	Norwegian University of Science and Technology, Norway
Jens Jensen	Science and Technology Facilities Council, UK
Erisa Karafili	University of Southampton, UK
Georgios Karopulos	JRC, Italy
Mirko Manea	HPE Italia, Italy
Eleonora Losiouk	University of Padova, Italy
Silvio Ranise	University of Trento and Fondazione Bruno Kessler, Italy
Marco Rasori	Consiglio Nazionale delle Ricerche, Italy
Francesco Santini	University of Perugia, Italy
Marco Tiloca	RISE, Sweden

Contents

WYK: Mobile Device Authentication Using the User's Address Book

Mehari Msgna$^{(\boxtimes)}$, Sokratis Katsikas, and Vasileios Gkioulos

Norwegian University of Science and Technology (NTNU),
Teknologivegen 22, 2815 Gjøvik, Norway
{mehari.g.msgna,sokratis.katsikas,vasileios.gkioulos}@ntnu.no

Abstract. Authenticating a user the correct way is paramount to IT systems, where the risk is growing more and more in number and complexity. This is specially important in mobile phones, where a number of applications require continuous device authentication following the *Point-of-Entry* user authentication. Existing common approach in systems that require strict security rules and regulations is to use a *One-Time-Password (OTP)*. Usually the OTP is generated using a special hardware device or another application that is synchronised with the back-end system. Another approach is to use SMS based activation/approval codes such as used by Telegram, Facebook, Twitter and other social media platforms. However, this approach has three major drawbacks: (1) it requires active user participation/interaction which could be annoying if repeated continuously, (2) SMS messages can be accessed by service provider's employees, and (3) it does not consider the authenticity of the device from which the services are being accessed. The later is particularly serious as access sessions can be hijacked by malicious entities. In this paper, we investigate the possibility of using the user's address book (contacts list) to continuously authenticate the device to ensure the services are only accessed from the mobile phone that belongs to the legitimate user. We call this authentication the *Who-You-Know (WYK)* scheme. For our research, we developed three components, the *WYK-Mobile-Service*, *WYK-API-Server* and a *Mobile-Demo-Application*. The *WYK-API-Server* exposes a set of authentication server APIs and the *WYK-Mobile-Service* consumes these APIs to authenticate the device every time the mobile applications are launched and make a request to the API server. Finally, the *Mobile-Demo-Application* will extract user's data from the server if the device is successfully authenticated.

Keywords: Device authentication · Mobile authentication · Address book

1 Introduction

Authenticating a user on a mobile phone is an essential task as users store sensitive personal information (such as photos, text messages and call history data), financial details (like banking application and their associated data) and other

© Springer Nature Switzerland AG 2021
A. Saracino and P. Mori (Eds.): ETAA 2021, LNCS 13136, pp. 1–16, 2021.
https://doi.org/10.1007/978-3-030-93747-8_1

essential applications' data. Smart phones implement two separate authentication mechanisms. These are the native device and application authentication mechanisms. The native device authentication, is part of the device's operating system/platform. The aim is to verify the user's identity before accessing any software or hardware features of the mobile device. On the other hand, application authentication aims to verify users before they are allowed to access the applications features.

Different devices and applications employ different authentication mechanisms depending on their security requirements. Some of the common native device authentication approaches in mobile phones are Personal Identification Number (PIN), passwords, graphical patterns and biometrics data (such as fingerprint and facial). These native authentication approaches are often used when users launch the device and they require the user's active participation. However, the main problem with PIN and password approaches is that users usually choose a simple combination that can be easily guessed by imposters to gain access into the user's device [1]. On the other hand, graphical patterns leave traces of oily residues on the screen that can easily be repeated to unlock the target device [2]. The use of biometrics is considered as the most secured among these authentication mechanisms [3]. However, according to [4], biometrics are hard to keep secret, stolen biometrics pose lifelong security risks to users as they cannot be reset and re-issued. Furthermore, transactions authenticated by biometrics across different systems are linkable and traceable back to the individual identity (in other words they don't preserve the user's privacy). These authentication mechanisms, have three major challenges. Firstly, device activity is permitted on an all-or-nothing basis, depending on whether the user successfully authenticates at the beginning of a session. This ignores the fact that tasks performed on a mobile device have a range of sensitivities, depending on the nature of the data and services accessed. Secondly, users are forced to re-authenticate frequently due to the bursty nature that characterizes mobile device use. Owners react to this by disabling the mechanism, or by choosing a weak "secret". Thirdly, these mechanisms only authenticate the user not the device from which the services are accessed.

In addition to the devices' native authentication, mobile applications use the popular username-password combination to authenticate their users. However, the use of biometrics is also recently getting a lot of acceptance. The common challenge of mobile application authentication is the user's identity is only verified only one time during the application setup process. To compensate for this most security critical applications perform a one-time-password for consecutive interactions with the application features [5]. However, still the user is not continuously authenticated during these transactions and offer little towards transparent user authentication [6]. As a solution a number of continues authentication mechanisms are proposed over the years [7–9]. The common factor among these mechanisms is that they aim to track the user's usage patterns and then use it to continuously verify the identity of the user throughout the application session. However, their usability is often glossed over. Usability along with security is another important factor that plays a pivotal role in evaluating user authentication schemes. This leads to an important question, how to trade-off between security and usability? [10]. The usability of an authentication mechanisms is one of the dominant attributes that influence users' acceptance of a particular authentication scheme [11]. Even though, continuous authentication sounds secure and attractive, it has not been practically implemented due to usability factor.

In this paper, we investigate a novel mobile device authentication mechanism based on the uniqueness of an address book. An address book is ubiquitous among all mobile devices and considered be unique to each person. In addition to that, an address book is dynamic, which is an important characteristic for authentication mechanisms. In our work we investigate the possibility of using this entity (an address book) to successfully and continuously authenticate the mobile device from which services are accessed. This mechanism can be used, in conjunction with the existing authentication mechanisms, to address the above mentioned challenges. Furthermore, it can also be used to bind services to devices.

The rest of the paper is organised as follows. Section 2 provides an explanation of the different ways and mechanisms of entity (a user, device or a process) authentication. This is followed by Sect. 3, which presents a survey of published authentication mechanisms particularly for mobile device platforms. Section 4 provides a detailed discussion of the proposed WYK authentication mechanism. This includes a detailed discussion of the proposed protocols, such as the *Initialization*, *Update* and *Authenticate* protocols . Section 5, gives a full analysis and implementation of the proposed WYK authentication mechanism. Analysis details include how often address books changes and a proof-of-concept implementation of it. Finally, Sect. 6 concludes the paper and offers future recommendations.

2   Authentication on Mobile Devices

An entity authentication, as defined bu NIST [12], is the process of providing assurance about the identity of an entity interacting with a system. An entity (user, device or process) authentication is performed in different ways by different systems. All of them, however, have to have an identification and verification information. In this section, we discussed the nature of these information and the different, yet commonly deployed, authentication mechanisms on mobile devices.

2.1   Ways to Authenticate a User

Ways a computer system authenticates a user are broadly categorized into three categories [13], these are the "what-you-know", "what-you-have" and "what-you-are".

1. **What-you-know:** The "What-you-know" is a category of authentication mechanisms that uses a secrete knowledge (an information that a legit user only knows) to verify the identity of the claimant. The most widely used "what-you-know" authentication mechanisms are the use of PINs, passwords or graphical patterns. For such mechanisms to work, the users set up the

secret knowledge prior to using the authentication mechanism, which is commonly known as the enrollment process. Two of the most common challenges of such a mechanism are (1) the selected secret knowledge must be easily rememberable, and (2) it must be difficult for others to easily guess it.

2. **What-you-have:** The "what-you-have" category refers to authentication mechanisms that use physical devices that the legitimate user possesses. Such mechanisms use smart cards, special hardware tokens or even mobile phones to verify the identity of the user. Usually, these devices store a unique identification/verification information that is then presented to the verifier by bringing them into contact or simply into proximity with it.

3. **What-you-are:** The mechanisms that fall into the last and third category, "what-you-are", relies on the measurement of the users physiological characteristics, such as fingerprint, facial and other biometric features. On smartphones, physiological traits, like facial features and fingerprints, can be collected using the built-in hardware, i.e. camera and finger scanners. However, other forms of biometric data, such as iris or retina scan require special hardware modules. Similarly, behavioral biometric data, such as gait, swipe, touch, and voice can be profiled unobtrusively, by collecting user data using various built-in mobile phone sensors (such as accelerometer, gyroscope, magnetometer, proximity sensor, touch screens, and microphone) [14].

2.2   Authentication Mechanisms

Researchers and solution providers have been investigating on how to use and/or combine the different ways of authentication (discussed in Sect. 2.1) in order to design and develop different authentication solutions for different application scenarios. Some of the most common authentication mechanisms are:-

1. **One-Shot Authentication:** One-shot authentication is a type of authentication mechanism in which users' credentials are verified only at the beginning of the session [15]. This is a simple process where the user claims an identity and provides his or her credentials, and the identity claimed is only accepted, by the verifying system, upon successful verification of the provided credentials. On smartphone, such credentials can be a secret knowledge (like PINs, passwords, graphical patterns, etc.) or biometric data (fingerprints, facial, voice, etc.). Under such mechanism the session remains valid until the user or the system closes it.

2. **Repeated Authentication:** Periodic authentication is simply the variant of "one-shot authentication" in which idle timeout duration is set, for closing the session, automatically [7,15,16]. If a user remains inactive for more than the idle timeout duration, the device locks itself. Once the session closed, new session is created by re-authenticating the user again.

3. **Continuous Authentication:** As the name implies, continuous authentication mechanisms are developed to authenticate a legitimate owner throughout the entire session. Unlike the *one-shot* or *repeated* authentication continuous authentication mechanisms, continue to verify the identity of the user after a

successful point-of-entry authentication until the session ends. If any anomaly is detected by the device, the session will be stopped and all existing granted access will be terminated, immediately, and the device requests for an explicit re-authentication [7–9].

4. **Transparent Authentication:** Transparent authentication is a concept that stresses more on the procedure of collecting and analysing user authentication identifiers [17]. Specifically, if the system performs authentication steps in the background, without requiring explicit user cooperation [17,18]. This concept is also called implicit or unobtrusive authentication systems.

5. **Multifactor Authentication:** Multifactor authentication utilizes the concept of combining 2 or more authentication ways, that is, e-mail verification, OTP via SMS, phone call to the predefined numbers, push notification to the paired device, smart tokens, and so on, along with the usual method of authentication [19,20]. A very common practice is registering ones mobile number with service providers, and whenever the corresponding user accesses that service for sensitive operation, for example, online banking, service provider sends the one-time passcodes (OTPs) via SMS, getting assured that a legitimate user has requested access to that service.

3 Related Work

As mentioned above, smartphone operating systems and platforms come with native authentication mechanisms, such as the use of PINs, passwords and graphic patterns. Even though these mechanisms provide the first line of defence in authenticating users, they have a number of drawbacks. In addition to the drawbacks discussed above, they are also vulnerable to shoulder surfing. To address this, Alexander De Luca et al. [21], proposed the use of the back of the mobile device to input authentication patterns. Although such approach protects the device from shoulder surfing attacks, it still inherits the same drawbacks as the other native authentication mechanisms.

To address these inherited challenges and drawbacks a number of behavioural biometrics based continuous authentication mechanisms are proposed [7,22,23]. In their paper, Özlem Durmaz Incel et al. [22] discussed the use of behavioral biometrics to complement the usual point-of-entry authentication. In their work, users' behavioural biometrics (interactions with the touch screen, such as micro-movements, pressure, finger movements, etc.) were collected using mobile phones integrated sensors (such as accelerometer, gyroscope, and magnetometer) and then used to continuously authenticate the user. Their experiment yield a 99% true positive recognition rate (TPR) and 3.5% equal error rate (EER). Their continuous authentication method was implemented on a live banking application and authentication data was collected from 45 users of the bank. In another but similar work, Pin Shen Teh et al. [23] user touch screen dynamics is used to reduce user impersonation, in case the built in 4 digit PIN was compromised, from a 100% to merely 9.9% by applying both the 4 digit PIN authentication and touch screen dynamics together. Similarly in [7] they have used touchscreen gesture data to continuously authenticate mobile phone users. Even though these mechanisms open the possibility of using behavioral biometrics as authentication information among mobile users, the challenges are: (1) these mechanisms only target to verify the identity of the users not the devices, and (2) their practical usability is often glossed over.

Another approach to authenticate devices that has been proposed and discussed in the literature is the use of mobile phone together with additional sensor devices to authenticate a target device. In [24], the authors proposed the use of body area network to provide device-to-device authentication. In their work, they utilized devices worn on the same body to collect acceleration patterns to continuously authenticate the devices. Similarly, in [25] the authors investigate a proximity based IoT device authentication that uses movement of near by host mobile device. These approaches, however, inherit the same challenges as the behavioral biometrics mechanisms discussed above regarding their usability. Essentially they collect and analyse similar information and will have similar challenges.

Recently, a different approach have gained momentum in the device authentication arena and that is the used blockchain to verify devices at real-time [26–29]. The basic mechanics of this approach is to store immutable device information, such as serial numbers, in an open and yet secure digital ledger and, then use it to authenticate the devices on demand. Although such approach is resistant to unauthorised changes and certainly solves the usability issue of the mechanisms discussed above, it requires prior device registration. This could lead to practical issues when users change their devices. Another security weakness of this approach is its use of static authentication information. This could possibly introduce a security vulnerability into the system as it could lead to false positive results if the information used falls in the hands of malicious actors.

4   WYK Authentication Scheme

An address book (contacts list) is expected to be unique. This is mainly because of the different contact circles (family, work, friends, foreign correspondents, etc.) in one's address book. In this paper we investigate the possibility of using this unique address book to authenticate mobile devices on demand. A mobile phone's address book maintains an extensive data about one's contacts. This data is split into two sets: (1) raw information (such as name and phone number), and (2) call information (like last time a contact was called/texted, number of calls & texts exchanged, etc.). In our proposed solution we utilised both sets of address book information. The proposed device authentication scheme involves the following three main components:

1. **WYK-API-Server:** this is an API server that implements the device authentication logic. The API server stores the device's unique authentication information extracted from the address book. Depending on the privacy requirement the API server may also store other personal information and

share it with the applications during and/or post authentication. The server exposes all device authentication functions as a RESTFul APIs for the other entities to consume.

2. **WYK-Service:** this is a mobile service locally installed on the target mobile device. This mobile service acts as a gateway between the API server and the target applications. Up on completion of device authentication, the *WYK-Service* broadcasts the authentication result to all the applications that registered for this service.

3. **Mobile Application:** this entity is a mobile application that requires device authentication service.

The scheme defines at three authentication phases, the (1) Initialization, (2) Update and (3) Authentication phase. Before we dive into the details of the protocols, it is worth mentioning all the protocol messages are tunnelled within https link to provide confidentiality and integrity of exchanged messages.

4.1 Phase 1: Initialization

The initialization phase, the first phase, is performed when the *WYK-Service* is installed on the target mobile phone. The primary purpose of this phase is to setup the mobile device and the *WYK-API-Server* for future authentication tasks. During installation, the service generates its pair of asymmetric keys (Pub_k^m, Prv_k^m). The Pub_k^m is the public and Prv_k^m the private key. After the keys are generated, the target device then executes the initialization protocol as illustrated in Fig. 1.

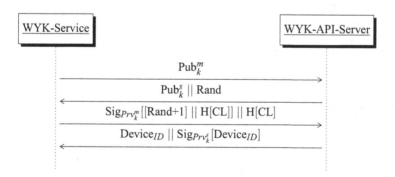

Fig. 1. Initialization protocol of the WYK Service

The protocol is started by the *WYK-Service* sending its public key (Pub_k^m) to the *WYK-API-Server*. Then the server responds by generating a random challenges $(Rand)$ and sending it back along the server's public key (Pub_k^s). At this point both entities have each other's public keys. The *WYK-Service* then increments the random challenge, compute hash value of the address book, sign them and send them to the *WYK-API-Server*. Up on successful verification of the signature, the server generates a unique identity, signs it and forwards it to the service. The protocol is then concluded by the service verifying the signature and initializing the *WYK-Service* with the received unique ID.

4.2　Phase 2: Update

One of the challenges of using the device's address book is its dynamic nature. User's address book changes often and when it does the *WYK-Service* and the *WYK-API-Server* need to keep track of the changes. The update phase is a synchronization process between the service and the API server.

As illustrated in Fig. 2, whenever the address book data is changed, the service computes new address book hash value, signs it by concatenating it with the old hash value and sends them to the server along with the unique device id (established during the initialization phase). The server then verifies the signature by using the new hash value received from the service and the old hash value in its database. If the signature is valid. the server updates its database with the new hash value, otherwise rejects the update request. Finally, notifies the service about the update result.

Fig. 2. WYK scheme update protocol

4.3　Phase 3: Authentication

This phase is the device authentication phase. At this stage, the *WYK-Service* and *WYK-API-Server* have their public key pair, each other's public key, unique device identity information ($Device_{ID}$) and hash value computed over the device's address book ($H(CL)$). As illustrated in Fig. 3, the authentication phase is triggered by mobile application requesting to authenticate the device.

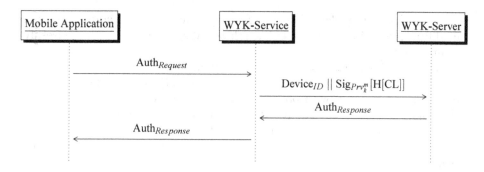

Fig. 3. WYK scheme authentication protocol

Up on reception of the request, the service forwards the device ID and signed address book hash value to the server. The server verifies the signature and the received hash value. If it is valid logs the request and responds with authentication response ($Auth_{Response}$). The *WYK-Service* then concludes the authentication process by relaying the authentication response to the requesting mobile application.

5   Implementation and Analysis

In our research we have worked on two different types of implementation of the proposed WYK scheme. Firstly, we have implemented it on Android platform which has three separate entities of the scheme. Secondly, analysis of the proposed scheme is presented against criteria to evaluate the scheme's suitability for authentication purposes.

5.1   Proof of Concept Implementation

The proof-of-concept implementation has three separate entities and these are: *WYK-API-Server*, *WYK-Service* and a *Mobile-Application*. The *WYK-API-Server* is a back-end component of the system that has a simple database (mySQL [30]) and an application server that exposed four API end-points. The database stores authentication data such as address book hash value, unique identity number, hash update time and device authentication time. On the other hand, the application server implements the proposed scheme's protocols and exposes them as restful APIs. The APIs are:

– */wyk/api/v1/user/initialize*: is called only once at the beginning of the scheme. It generates unique identity for the device and populates the database with the initial address book hash value.

- */wyk/api/v1/user/update*: this API is called when ever the address book is modified. Accordingly it updates the relevant database fields with the freshly computed hash value.
- */wyk/api/v1/user/authenticate*: this end-point is called when ever device authentication is required. It performs the authentication as defined in the protocol and responds with positive or negative authentication result.
- */wyk/api/v1/user/info*: finally, this end-point, returns the update and authentication request log when invoked. This API can only be invoked after successful devices authentication and only returns data belonging to a particular device. The aim of this API is to simulate how application may use the proposed scheme.

The *WYK-API-Server* is implemented using Golang [31] and screenshot of the application running is presented in Fig. 4.

The *WYK-Service* is a mobile application that consumes the APIs exposed by the *WYK-API-Server*. This entity is basically a background mobile service implementation that provides a link between the mobile device and the back-end server. It also provides a service intent link to applications on the target device. For instance, when an application is launched, it sends device authentication intent to the service and the service invokes the authenticate end-point with the required data, and broadcasts back the result. It also implements a content observer class to keep track of changes to the address book data set. Whenever change is detected the service updates the back-end server by calling the update end-point. Similarly, when the service is installed and started for the first time it initializes the back-end server as described earlier. Screenshot of the service is presented in Fig. 5.

The last entity in our proof-of-concept implementation is the *Mobile Application*. The mobile application was designed to demonstrate how the device authentication scheme can be used. When the application is launched, it first requests device authentication and waits for the result. The result is received via a broadcast receiver. Up on a successful authentication result, the application then proceeds to the next screen and fetch log data (hash value update and authentication request time) that belongs only to the target device. Again screenshot of our mobile application is shown in Fig. 6.

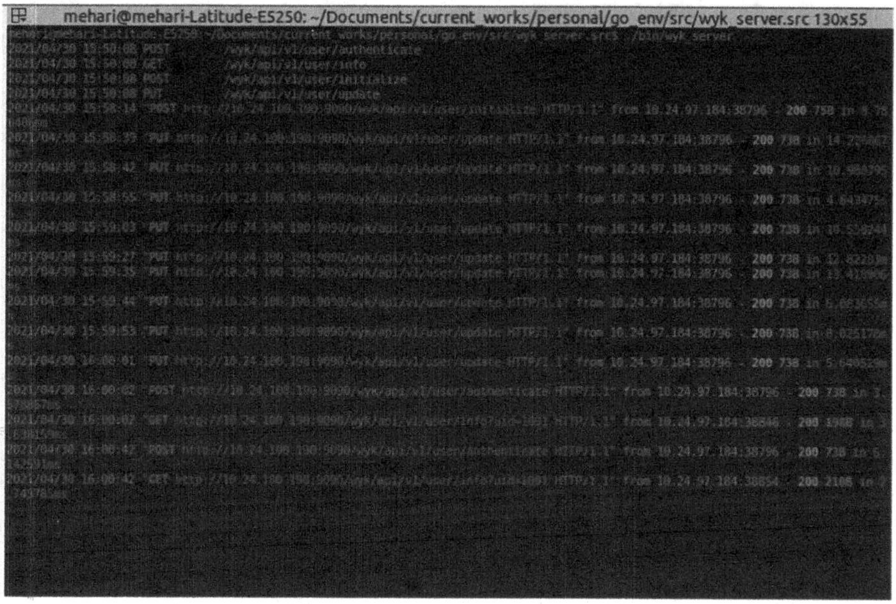

Fig. 4. WYK API Server.

5.2   CasperFDR: Formal Verification

Another implementation is the casper-fdr implementation of the proposed protocols. Casper is a program that will take a description of a security protocol in a simple, abstract language, and produce a CSP description of the same protocol [32,33]. The CSP description is then fed into the FDR [34] for security analysis. FDR is used to either find attacks on protocols, or to show that no such attack exists, subject to the assumptions of the Dolev-Yao Model [35] (i.e. that the intruder may overhear or intercept messages, decrypt and encrypt messages with keys that he knows, and fake messages, but not perform any cryptographic attacks on the underlying protocols). The casper-fdr implementation was, primarily, done to see if there can be a man-in-the-middle attack against key protocol messages, such as address book hash. The FDR tests showed the hash of the address book is protected from MITM attacks throughout the protocol run.

5.3   Analysis

Any authentication scheme have an identification and verification information. The only requirement for an identification information is to be unique within the realm of the authentication system. Example of an identification information is email address, user name, etc. However, the verification information must satisfy a number of criteria to be considered as a viable solution. Our proposed WYK authentication scheme is evaluated against the following criteria.

Fig. 5. WYK Service.

1. **Universality:** Universality refers to a basic question of "how many of the target devices have the required authentication data/information?". The WYK scheme uses mobile phone address book as its verification information which is present in 100% of smartphones regardless of the type and model of the device.

2. **Stability:** Stability refers to whether the authentication information is static or changes over time. Some of the most popular authentication information, like PIN, passwords and cryptographic keys, are static. This however, can be a vulnerability if the authentication information is easy to guess or falls into the wrong hands. Thus, the need to change them regularly or introduce a challenge-and-response into the authentication schemes that use them to introduce dynamism. An address book is a dynamic data set that has two parts: (1) the raw contacts data (like name, number, etc.) and, (2) generated data (such as last time it was changed, last time a particular contact was contacted, how many times, etc.). This makes it a dynamic data set that changes multiple times a day. Sometimes, during our test, a given address book changed up to 40 times a day, which meant new authentication information was computed 40 times during that day.

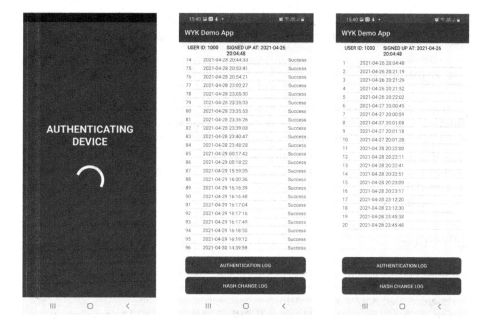

Fig. 6. A mobile application that consumes the device authentication service.

3. **Collectability:** Another critical question that needs answering when evaluating an authentication mechanism is "how easy is the information to collect?". This hugely affects the usability of the mechanism. Sometimes an information can fulfill all the requirements but proves impractical if it can't be collected and processed by the target devices. The WYK scheme only requires a read access to the device's address book and processing it is quite trivial as it only means executing a cryptographic hash algorithm.

4. **Performance:** Does the information have achievable authentication accuracy, speed and memory requirements? Although such metrics can vary from device to device based on their computational capacity, WYK scheme takes less than 5 s to compute the hash (on Samsung Galaxy S20 with an address book with 800+ entries). Verifying the hash is typically done in milliseconds.

5. **Acceptability:** Acceptability is another critical evaluation point that determines the success of any authentication scheme. Anything that requires access to contacts list can create unease among users. However, the proposed scheme only computes a hash value over them. The fact that hash values are irreversible should comfort users that there won't be any privacy issues for using our scheme.

6. **Forgery Resistance:** Last but not least is the question of "how easy is it to replicate the required authentication information and fool the system?". The WYK scheme uses the address book in its entirety to extract the authentication hash value. Thus, it would take someone to replicate the entire address book of a target. However, since it is dynamic and changes depending on the

calling and/or SMS patterns of the user, an adversary must replicate the state of a given address book at particular time to successfully fool the system.

6   Conclusion

This paper has explored a novel approach of using mobile address book, which is ubiquitous among mobile phone devices, as a dynamic authentication information to provide device authentication service. Our proposed scheme have three protocols to manage the device authentication life-cycle. In our work we have implemented the proposed authentication scheme on Android platform to provide a working principle of the scheme. Finally, we have provided analysis of the scheme against a number of authentication mechanism evaluation points.

References

1. Patel, V.M., Chellappa, R., Chandra, D., Barbello, B.: Continuous user authentication on mobile devices: Recent progress and remaining challenges. IEEE Signal Process. Mag. **33**(4), 49–61 (2016)
2. Aviv, A.J., Gibson, K.L., Mossop, E., Blaze, M., Smith, J.M.: Smudge attacks on smartphone touch screens. In: Miller, C., Shacham, H. (eds.) 4th USENIX Workshop on Offensive Technologies, WOOT 2010, Washington, D.C., August 9, 2010. USENIX Association (2010)
3. Mayron, L.: Biometric authentication on mobile devices. IEEE Secur. Privacy **13**(03), 70–73 (2015)
4. Azimpourkivi, M., Topkara, U., Carbunar, B.: A secure mobile authentication alternative to biometrics. In: Proceedings of the 33rd Annual Computer Security Applications Conference, pp. 28–41, Association for Computing Machinery, New York (2017)
5. Hazhirpasand Barkadehi, M., Nilashi, M., Ibrahim, O., Fardi, A.Z., Samad, S.: Authentication systems: a literature review and classification. Telemat. Inform. **35**(5), 1491–1511 (2018)
6. Abuhamad, M., Abusnaina, A., Nyang, D., Mohaisen, D.A.: Sensor-based continuous authentication of smartphones' users using behavioral biometrics: a survey. CoRR, abs/2001.08578 (2020)
7. Feng, T., et al.: Continuous mobile authentication using touchscreen gestures. In: 2012 IEEE Conference on Technologies for Homeland Security (HST), pp. 451–456 (2012)
8. Traore, I., Ahmed, A.A.E.: Continuous Authentication Using Biometrics: Data, Models, and Metrics. University of Victoria, Canada (2011)
9. Frank, M., Biedert, R., Ma, E., Martinovic, I., Song, D.: Touchalytics: on the applicability of touchscreen input as a behavioral biometric for continuous authentication. IEEE Trans. Inf. Forensics Secur. **8**(1), 136–148 (2013)
10. Braz, C., Robert, J.-M.: Security and usability: the case of the user authentication methods. In: Proceedings of the 18th International Conference of the Association Francophone d'Interaction Homme-Machine, Montreal, Quebec, Canada, 18-21 April 2006, pp. 199–203 (2006)
11. Theofanos, M.F., Micheals, R.J., Stanton. B.C.: Biometrics systems include users. IEEE Syst. J. **3**(4), 461–468 (2009)

12. NIST. Computer security resource center. https://csrc.nist.gov/glossary/term/entity_authentication
13. Schneider, F.B.: Something you know, have, or are. https://www.cs.cornell.edu/courses/cs513/2005fa/NNLauthPeople.html
14. Forsblom, N.: Were you aware of all these sensors in your smartphone? (2015). https://blog.adtile.me/2015/11/12/were-you-aware-of-all-these-sensors-in-your-smartphone/
15. Gupta, S., Buriro, A., Crispo1, B.: Demystifying authentication concepts in smartphones: ways and types to secure access. Adv. Person. Mobile Serv. **2018**(2018)
16. Bertino, E., Bettini, C., Ferrari, E., Samarati, P.: An access control model supporting periodicity constraints and temporal reasoning. ACM Trans. Database Syst. **23**(3), 231–285 (1998)
17. Crawford, H., Renaud, K.: Understanding user perceptions of transparent authentication on a mobile device. J. Trust Manag. **7** (2014)
18. Buriro, A., Crispo, B., Zhauniarovich. Y.: Please hold on: unobtrusive user authentication using smartphone's built-in sensors. In: 2017 IEEE International Conference on Identity, Security and Behavior Analysis (ISBA), pp. 1–8 (2017)
19. Michaluk, K., Nickinson, P., Ritchie, R., Rubino, D.: The future of authentication: Biometrics, multi-factor, and co-dependency (2021). https://www.androidcentral.com/talk-mobile/future-authentication-biometrics-multi-factor-and-co-dependency-talk-mobile
20. Stanislav, M.: Two-Factor Authentication. IT Governance Ltd., Berlin (2015)
21. De Luca, A., et al.: Back-of-device authentication on smartphones. In: Proceedings of the SIGCHI Conference on Human Factors in Computing Systems, CHI 2013, pp. 2389–2398 (2013)
22. Incel, D.Ö., et al.: DAKOTA: sensor and touch screen-based continuous authentication on a mobile banking application. IEEE Access **9**, 38943–38960 (2021)
23. Teh, P.S., et al.: Strengthen user authentication on mobile devices by using user's touch dynamics pattern. J. Ambient. Intell. Humaniz. Comput., **11**(10):4019–4039 (2020)
24. Schürmann, D., Brüsch, A., Sigg, S., Wolf, L.: Bandana - body area network device-to-device authentication using natural gait. In: 2017 IEEE International Conference on Pervasive Computing and Communications (PerCom), pp. 190–196 (2017)
25. Zhang, J., Wang, Z., Yang, Z., Zhang, Q.: Proximity based IoT device authentication. In: IEEE INFOCOM 2017 - IEEE Conference on Computer Communications, pp. 1–9 (2017)
26. Shen, M., et al.: Blockchain-assisted secure device authentication for cross-domain industrial IoT. IEEE J. Select. Areas Commun. **38**(5), 942–954 (2020)
27. Khalid, U., Asim, M., Baker, T., Hung, P.C.K., Tariq, M.A., Rafferty, L.: A decentralized lightweight blockchain-based authentication mechanism for IoT systems. Clust. Comput., **23**(3), 2067–2087 (2020)
28. Gong, L., Alghazzawi, D.M., Cheng. L.: BCoT sentry: A blockchain-based identity authentication framework for IoT devices. Information **12**(5) (2021)
29. Chen, F., Tang, X., Cheng, X., Xie, D., Wang, T., Zhao, C.: Blockchain-based efficient device authentication protocol for medical cyber-physical systems. Secur. Commun. Netw. **2021** (2021)
30. MySQL. Mysql: The World'd Most Popular Open Source Database. https://www.mysql.com/
31. Golang. Go. https://golang.org/
32. Lowe, G.: Casper: a compiler for the analysis of security protocols. In: Proceedings 10th Computer Security Foundations Workshop, pp. 18–30 (1997)

33. University of Oxford: Department of Computer Science. Installing casper. http://www.cs.ox.ac.uk/gavin.lowe/Security/Casper/installation.html, 2021
34. University of Oxford. Fdr4 - the CSP refinement checker. https://cocotec.io/fdr/
35. Herzog, J.: A computational interpretation of Dolev-Vao adversaries. Theor. Comput. Sci. **340**(1), 57–81 (2005)

Future-Proof Web Authentication: Bring Your Own FIDO2 Extensions

Florentin Putz[(✉)] [ID], Steffen Schön [ID], and Matthias Hollick [ID]

TU Darmstadt, Darmstadt, Germany
{fputz,sschoen,mhollick}@seemoo.de

Abstract. The FIDO2 standards for strong authentication on the Internet define an extension interface, which allows them to flexibly adapt to future use cases. The domain of establishing new FIDO2 extensions, however, is currently limited to web browser developers and members of the FIDO alliance. We show how researchers and developers can design and implement their own extensions for using FIDO2 as a well-established and secure foundation to demonstrate innovative authentication concepts or to support custom deployments. Our open-source implementation targets the full FIDO2 stack, such as the Chromium web browser and hardware tokens, to enable tailor-made authentication based on the power of the existing FIDO2 ecosystem. To give an overview of existing extensions, we survey all published FIDO2 extensions by manually inspecting the source code of major web browsers and authenticators. Their current design, however, hinders the implementation of custom extensions, and they only support a limited number of extensions out of the box. We discuss weaknesses of current implementations and identify the lack of extension pass-through as a major limitation in current FIDO2 clients.

Keywords: Security · Authentication · Key management · Hardware token · Passwordless · WebAuthn

1 Introduction

Stronger forms of authentication than passwords can protect online accounts from phishing attacks and mitigate the impact of data breaches. The FIDO2 standards [8] are now implemented in all major web browsers and allow users to securely log in to websites without passwords, using either a hardware security key (e.g., a YubiKey [28]) or a built-in authenticator in modern smartphones or laptops. Website operators can easily implement support for FIDO2 using the WebAuthn JavaScript API [25], which also supports custom extensions to implement special use cases.

Extensible web standards such as X.509 [2] or TLS [3] have played a key role during the advancement of the Internet so far. A standards organization such as the IETF cannot predict all possible future use cases of the standard beforehand, but custom extensions provide flexibility to the otherwise fixed specification and

© Springer Nature Switzerland AG 2021
A. Saracino and P. Mori (Eds.): ETAA 2021, LNCS 13136, pp. 17–32, 2021.
https://doi.org/10.1007/978-3-030-93747-8_2

prevent fragmentation via the creation of new competing standards to satisfy new use cases. The behavior of a protocol can then be modified without the effort to get the modifications accepted into the main standard.

Why Extend FIDO2? At its core, FIDO2 is a well-established and secure platform for accessing public-key credentials, with little restrictions imposed on the authenticator. In the future, however, innovative authentication approaches might require modifications to the standard, e.g., by transmitting or receiving additional information to the authenticator. FIDO2 extensions can be used to support new uses cases, implement additional features, and mitigate shortcomings of the standard.

The potential of FIDO2 extensions becomes clear by looking at the extensions that have been proposed so far: A major weakness of FIDO2 is the lack of efficient recovery options, which has been criticized in previous user studies [1, 5,15]. Yubico proposed a new FIDO2 extension to address this problem, by implementing an efficient way to automatically register backup credentials, which can be used in case the authentication token gets lost [30].

Developers and researchers can also use FIDO2 extensions to prototype and demonstrate new authentication designs within the existing FIDO2 ecosystem on real-world web browsers. Companies can use FIDO2 extensions to adapt the protocol for tailor-made authentication in internal deployments.

Web browsers, however, currently do not support any third-party FIDO2 extensions. Furthermore, there is no clear development path to implement custom extensions in current web browsers. Even FIDO2 extensions which do not require any special processing by the web browser need explicit browser support instead of automatically being forwarded to the authenticator. Although extensions are an important part of any standard, the extensibility of the FIDO2 standards unfortunately has not received much attention as of today. This calls for a detailed analysis of FIDO2 extensions:

- As our core contribution, we show how to design and implement tailor-made authentication based on the power of the existing FIDO2 ecosystem (Sect. 5). Our source code and additional documentation is available at https://seemoo. de/s/fido2ext.
- We survey all publicly known FIDO2 extensions by manually inspecting the source code of major web browsers and authenticators (Sect. 3 and Sect. 4).
- We describe limitations of current FIDO2 extension implementations and identify the lack of extension pass-through as a major weakness that inhibits the development of innovative FIDO2 extensions (Sect. 6).

2   Background

2.1   FIDO2

Strong and passwordless authentication has been standardized by the FIDO industry alliance and the World Wide Web Consortium (W3C) in form of the

FIDO2 standards [8]. The top part of Fig. 1 shows the FIDO2 system model, consisting of relying party (RP), client, and authenticator. In essence, FIDO2 is a challenge-response protocol, which RPs such as websites can use to access public key credentials, managed for the user by an authenticator. The authenticator can be embedded into the client device or attached as an external hardware token via USB, NFC, or Bluetooth. It mainly supports the following two operations:

1. `authenticatorMakeCredential`: The authenticator generates a new key pair, binds it to the requesting RP, and returns the public key and optionally an attestation signature. Websites use this operation to implement account registration.
2. `authenticatorGetAssertion`: The authenticator returns an assertion signature over a challenge from the RP. Websites use this operation to implement account login.

The client (e.g., a web browser) forwards the RP's requests to the authenticator, which stores all key material. FIDO2 consists of two specifications, WebAuthn (Web Authentication) [25] and CTAP (Client to Authenticator Protocol) [6], which succeed the older Universal 2nd Factor (U2F) standard [7]. All major web browsers implement FIDO2 [17] and there exists a large ecosystem of commercial hardware tokens, e.g., Yubico's YubiKey [28].

2.2 FIDO2 Extensions

The FIDO2 authentication protocols WebAuthn and CTAP2 can be extended to support special use cases. Figure 1 shows the general protocol flow of a FIDO2 extension, as specified by §9 of the WebAuthn specification [25]. The RP initiates an extension request with the client, which then processes the request and responds to the RP. WebAuthn distinguishes between different types of extensions. An extension is always a *client extension*, as it involves communication with the client. The extension specification defines the form of the JSON *client extension input/output* and what kind of *client extension processing* the client needs to perform to transform the inputs to the outputs.

If the extension also involves processing on the authenticator, it is additionally an *authenticator extension* and defines the form of the concise binary object representation (CBOR) *authenticator extension input/output* and what kind of *authenticator extension processing* the authenticator needs to perform to transform the inputs to the outputs. In this case, the client also needs to know how to convert the JSON *client extension input* to the CBOR *authenticator extension input*, and how to convert the CBOR *authenticator extension output* back to the JSON *client extension output*.

FIDO2 extensions also are *registration extensions* and/or *authentication extensions*, depending on which part of the protocol they affect. We describe further implementation details in Sect. 5.

Each FIDO2 extension has an extension identifier string, which can be registered in the IANA "WebAuthn Extension Identifiers" registry [12]. This registry

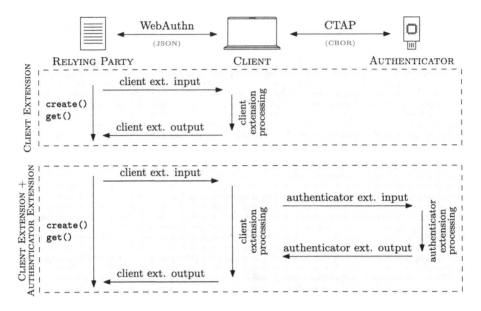

Fig. 1. Protocol flow of FIDO2 extensions. Extensions can communicate between RP, client, and authenticator *(top)*. An extension is always a client extension *(middle)* but can also additionally be an authenticator extension *(bottom)*.

has been defined and established by RFC 8809 [11] and contains an up-to-date list of all currently registered WebAuthn extension. We describe all currently available FIDO2 extensions in Sect. 3.

Authenticators supporting CTAP 2.1 must implement the `hmac-secret` extension and the `credProtect` extension if they support some form of user verification (§9 in CTAP2 [6]). Clients can use the CTAP `authenticatorGetInfo` method to detect which extensions an authenticator supports. We give an overview of which FIDO2 extensions are supported by popular browsers and authenticators in Sect. 4.

2.3   Extension Pass-Through

In general, clients and authenticators do not need to support any WebAuthn extensions and can simply ignore them as they are all optional. RPs must therefore be prepared to deal with any subset of requested extensions being ignored, as this must never fail the WebAuthn transaction. To increase compatibility with unknown extensions, clients can choose to directly pass through extension inputs to the authenticator and outputs to the RP, without any additional client processing. The WebAuthn standard defines conversion rules between JSON and CBOR to facilitate this [26]. Authenticators must be prepared to ignore such inputs in case such a direct pass-through results in invalid inputs.

To increase compatibility, extensions that do not require special client processing should define the authenticator input and outputs in such a way that direct pass-through results in semantically correct values. Clients that implement pass-through facilitate innovation as they allow extensions to work when only the authenticator explicitly supports them.

3 Survey: Existing FIDO2 Extensions

Our survey on FIDO2 extensions consists of two parts: (1) This section is the first part, where we identify all extensions that have been published so far. (2) Section 4 is the second part, where we determine which clients and authenticators support these extensions. Table 1 shows the results of our survey.

Most extensions are specified in the FIDO2 standards themselves ("standard extensions"), such as the hmac-secret extension for using a symmetric key with a FIDO2 credential [6]. Additionally, there are three non-standard extensions which are not specified in the official FIDO2 standards. First, there is Yubico's recovery extension [30], which has a separate specification but no web browser implementation yet. Second, there is Google's caBLE extension [19], which is part of the Google Chrome browser but has no public specification. Third, there is the googleLegacyAppIdSupport extension [13], which is implemented in some browsers but has no formal specification yet. We briefly introduce the standard extensions and then go over the non-standard extensions in more detail, as they are currently less well-known.

3.1 Standard Extensions

We refer to the extensions defined in the FIDO2 standards as *standard extensions*. At the time of writing, the IANA registry [12] contains eight registered extension identifiers, which are all specified in WebAuthn Level 1 [24]. WebAuthn Level 2 defines three additional extensions and also plans to register them (§12.4 in [25]). Furthermore, CTAP 2.1 defines five extensions and plans to register them as well (§14.1 in [6]). One of them is the hmac-secret extension, which allows requesting a symmetric secret from an authenticator to encrypt and decrypt user data. This extension can support new use cases where a static secret is necessary, such as disk encryption or unlocking password managers like KeePass. The other standard extensions enable features such as compatibility with legacy Universal 2nd Factor (U2F) credentials, specifying a credential protection policy, or storing arbitrary data associated with a credential. The FIDO2 standards contain further information on each extension as well as a formal specification.

3.2 Recovery Extension (Yubico)

Recovery and backups still are open problems within the FIDO2 standards, as the current best practice of manually registering multiple tokens on each RP has low usability. Yubico aims to solve this problem using the `recovery` extension, which currently has a draft specification available online [30]. This extension allows automatically registering a backup authenticator for recovery purposes without needing to have the backup authenticator physically available at the time of registration, so that it can be permanently stored at a secure location. Their proposal is based on a key agreement scheme where the primary authenticator generates nondeterministic public keys, but only the backup authenticator can derive the corresponding private keys. This enables a usable recovery process while maintaining the FIDO2 privacy protections of unlinkable public keys. Frymann et al. generalized the procedure to Asynchronous Remote Key Generation (ARKG) and proved the cryptographic security of such protocols [9].

3.3 CaBLE Extension (Google)

Google proposed caBLE (Cloud-Assisted Bluetooth Low Energy), which allows using a smartphone as a FIDO2 roaming authenticator via BLE [19,20]. The caBLE protocol consists of two phases: A pairing phase using a QR code, which encodes a nonce to derive key material. Afterwards, the smartphone broadcasts advertisements via BLE, which the web browser recognizes to initiate a handshake phase to establish a CTAP2 channel. There is no public specification available for caBLE and it is currently implemented only in the Chrome web browser and in Android smartphones via the proprietary Google Play Services. The Chromium implementation hints at a WebAuthn registration extension with client input `cableRegistration` and an authentication extension with client input `cableAuthentication`. The communication with the smartphone is not implemented using the standard FIDO2 extension API, but using a custom CTAP2 transport instead.

3.4 GoogleLegacyAppIdSupport Extension (Google)

Google proposed the `googleLegacyAppIdSupport` extension [13] to provide compatibility with some Android factory images, which only support the U2F JavaScript API and cannot be patched with WebAuthn support. Google Chrome plans to deprecate the U2F API, but credentials created using WebAuthn are normally not backwards compatible with the U2F JavaScript API. This extension allows creating WebAuthn credentials which work with both WebAuthn and U2F, by using a hard-coded U2F `AppID` specific to Google Accounts, limited to `*.google.com` domains.

4   Survey: Compatibility of FIDO2 Extensions

While the first part of our survey identified all currently known FIDO2 extensions, this section contains the second part of our survey, where we determine the client and authenticator support for all FIDO2 extensions. Since it is standard compliant for a client to ignore any extensions, the currently available feature

Table 1. FIDO2 extension compatibility as of July 2021.

Identifier	Chrome	Edge	Firefox	Safari	libfido2	python-fido2	Windows Hello	YubiKey 5	SoloKey	OpenSK	Specification	Reference	IANA Registration?
appid	✓	✓	✓	✓	✗	✓	-	-	-	-	WebAuthn2 §10.1	[25]	✓
appidExclude	✓	✓	✗	✗	✗	✗	-	-	-	-	WebAuthn2 §10.2	[25]	✗
authnSel	✗	✗	✗	✗	✗	✗	✗	✗	✗	✗	WebAuthn1 §10.4	[24]	✓
biometricPerfBounds	✗	✗	✗	✗	✗	✗	✗	✗	✗	✗	WebAuthn1 §10.9	[24]	✗
credBlob	✓	✓	✗	✗	✓	✓	✓	✗	✗	✗	CTAP2 §12.2	[6]	✗
credProps	✓	✓	✗	✗	✗	✗	-	-	-	-	WebAuthn2 §10.4	[25]	✗
credProtect	✓	✓	✗	✗	✓	✓	✓	✓	✓	✓	CTAP2 §12.1	[6]	✗
exts	✗	✗	✗	✗	✗	✗	✗	✗	✗	✗	WebAuthn1 §10.5	[24]	✓
hmac-secret	✓	✓	✓	✗	✓	✓	✗	✓	✓	✓	CTAP2 §12.5	[6]	✗
largeBlob	✓	✓	✗	✗	✗	✗	✗	✗	✗	✗	WebAuthn1 §10.5	[24]	✗
largeBlobKey	✓	✓	✗	✗	✓	✓	✗	✗	✗	✗	CTAP2 §12.3	[6]	✗
loc	✗	✗	✗	✗	✗	✗	✗	✗	✗	✗	WebAuthn1 §10.7	[24]	✓
minPinLength	✗	✗	✗	✗	✗	✓	✓	✗	✗	✗	CTAP2 §12.4	[6]	✗
txAuthSimple	✗	✗	✗	✗	✗	✗	✗	✗	✗	✗	WebAuthn1 §10.2	[24]	✓
txAuthGeneric	✗	✗	✗	✗	✗	✗	✗	✗	✗	✗	WebAuthn1 §10.3	[24]	✓
uvi	✗	✗	✗	✗	✗	✗	✗	✗	✗	✗	WebAuthn1 §10.6	[24]	✓
uvm	✓	✓	✗	✗	✗	✗	✗	✗	✗	✗	WebAuthn2 §10.3	[25]	✓
caBLE	✓	✓	✗	✗	✗	✗	✗	✗	✗	✗		[19]	✗
googleLegacyAppIdSupport	✓	✓	✗	✓	✗	✗	✗	✗	✗	✗		[13]	✗
recovery	✗	✗	✗	✗	✗	✗	✗	✗	✗	✗		[30]	✗

trackers for web browser WebAuthn implementations do not indicate support for individual extensions. Table 1 gives an overview of FIDO2 extension support for popular web browsers, client libraries, and authenticators. In the following, we explain our methodology and results in more detail.

4.1 Web Browsers

There is no automatic way to query all extensions supported by a web browser, so we need to manually inspect each browser's source code to see which FIDO2 extensions they implement. We checked the Chromium source code[1] (which forms the base of Google's Chrome browser and Microsoft's Edge browser), the Gecko source code[2] (which corresponds to Mozilla's Firefox browser), and the WebKit source code[3] (which forms the base of Apple's Safari browser).

---

[1] Chromium version *canary 93.0.4570.0* → Google Chrome 93, Microsoft Edge 93.

[2] Gecko version version *nightly 91.0a1* → Mozilla Firefox 91.

[3] WebKit version *611.2.7.1* → Apple Safari 14.1.1.

Table 1 shows all WebAuthn and CTAP2 extensions currently supported by these browsers. Chrome supports 11 FIDO2 extensions, including the non-standard caBLE extension, while Firefox and Safari only support two extensions each. All browsers support the `appid` extensions for compatibility with legacy U2F credentials.

Extension pass-through is an important feature that allows FIDO2 clients to transparently forward extension inputs and outputs between RP and authenticator, even for unknown extensions. The WebAuthn specification notes that extension pass-through can "facilitate innovation, allowing authenticators to experiment with new extensions and RPs to use them before there is explicit support for them in clients." [26]. While inspecting the web browser source codes, however, we noticed that no web browser currently supports extension pass-through. This makes it very difficult to establish custom extensions, as users will not be able to use them.

4.2   Client Libraries

Yubico's `python-fido2` library [27] can be used to implement custom FIDO2 clients that interface with CTAP authenticators. It currently supports six FIDO2 extensions as of version 0.9.1. This library is especially interesting for researchers and developers as it provides an easy interface for implementing custom CTAP2 extensions. Yubico also provides the C library `libfido2` [29] for interacting with FIDO2 authenticators, with bindings available to many other languages. This library supports four different FIDO2 extensions as of version 1.7.0.

4.3   Authenticators

To query the extensions supported by different FIDO2 authenticators, we use the `authenticatorGetInfo` CTAP2 request to retrieve a list of supported extensions in the `extensions` response field. As not all extensions are specified to announce themselves this way, we also manually inspect the authenticator's source code if available. We looked at Yubico's YubiKey 5 NFC, YubiKey 5C NFC, the open source Solo[4] C implementation (which powers the SoloKey, the NitroKey, and the OnlyKey), and Google's open source OpenSK[5] authenticator implementation written in Rust. All tokens only support the `credProtect` and the `hmac-secret` extensions.

In addition to these roaming authenticators, it is also possible to use platform authenticators. Microsoft provides Win32 headers for communicating with the Windows Hello platform authenticator and with roaming authenticators in general [18]. The actual implementation of these APIs is proprietary, but developers can use these headers to support FIDO2 authentication on Windows. As of `WEBAUTHN_API_VERSION_3`, Windows implements three FIDO2 extensions. It also partially implements `hmac-secret`, but obtaining the secret is not supported yet.

---

[4] Solo version 4.1.2.
[5] OpenSK version 1.0.0.

4.4 Summary

The survey in the last two sections shows that FIDO2 extensions have the potential to solve major weaknesses of the FIDO2 standards, such as the lack of efficient recovery options. Support of these extensions by web browsers, clients, and authenticators is currently weak, however, as shown in Table 1. Some extensions defined in the FIDO2 standards have no support at all. Extension pass-through would improve the compatibility of FIDO2 clients with current and future FIDO2 extensions, which would facilitate researchers and developers to create their own extensions, to add new features or to solve shortcomings of FIDO2.

5 Design and Implementation of Custom Extensions

In order to showcase the possibilities of FIDO2 extensions and the required steps to implement one, we define a proof-of-concept extension that we implement on all parts of the FIDO2 stack: RPs (web applications), clients (browser and non-browser), and authenticators. Implementing a custom FIDO2 extension is not straightforward and often undocumented, so we try to facilitate the process for other researchers and developers. We start by defining our extension and then describe the process of implementing this extension for each affected component. Our source code as well as supplemental material is available online[6].

There are two primary requirements for our proof-of-concept extension. First, it should use all capabilities that FIDO2 extensions offer, namely inputs, outputs, and usage in both registration (`makeCredential`) and authentication (`getAssertion`). Second, it should be simple in order to allow readers to focus on the implementation of an extension in general instead of the functionality of our example. Thus we choose to define and implement the `greeter` extension, which implements a concept that is well known in communications.

Definition 1 (Greeter Extension). *The `greeter` extension is an authenticator extension, which allows the authenticator to respond to the RP with a greeting message. We define an input string, which is the name of the sender (e.g., "John"). We also define an output string, which is the greeting message (e.g., "Hello John"). This extension requires no special client extension processing, as the client can simply pass through all inputs/outputs to/from the authenticator. The authenticator extension processing consists of constructing the greeting message from the input string and returning it. Our greeter extension uses the identifier `greeter` in both CTAP and WebAuthn.*

5.1 Relying Party

The RP initiates the FIDO2 authentication protocol and can include extensions in its requests. To demonstrate this, we implement our FIDO2 extension in a proof-of-concept web application, which uses the native browser

---

[6] Online repository with our source code and additional documentation on how to implement your own FIDO2 extensions: https://seemoo.de/s/fido2ext.

JavaScript WebAuthn APIs supported by all modern browsers [16]. The process of using extensions for registration (`makeCredential`) and authentication (`getAssertion`) is very similar. To register a credential using the browser API, we use `navigator.credentials.create()`. This function takes a parameter object with the `publicKey` member in case of WebAuthn.

The `publicKey` object accepts an `extensions` attribute that contains the extension identifier including inputs: `extensions: {"greeter": "John"}`. In this case we do not use a backend to generate the challenge and various other values. In practice, those values should not be computed on the client side. After the extension was successfully processed by browser and authenticator, the outputs of the extension can be accessed using `credential.getClient` `ExtensionResults()`, which returns an object with the extension identifiers as keys and the respective extension outputs as values.

5.2   Web Browser

Web browsers are the most common FIDO2 client and are next in the FIDO2 stack. They receive the authentication request from the RP and communicate with the authenticator. As web browsers do not currently support FIDO2 extension pass-through, we need to modify the browser to support our custom extension. We have implemented the `greeter` extension in the Chromium browser, as it is the foundation of the most popular web browser on the market, Google Chrome. Unfortunately, Chromium does not implement FIDO2 extension support in a modular way, which means that we need to modify different components of the browser stack in order to implement support for our `greeter` extension. Chromium does not provide any documentation for this, so we had to find out the correct approach by inspecting the implementation of other FIDO2 extensions in the source code.

Figure 2 shows how Chromium processes and sends FIDO2 extensions to authenticators. Let us assume a web application with the JavaScript code described in the previous section. Chromium's rendering engine Blink contains the V8 JavaScript engine, which runs this code and dispatches the command `navigator.credentials.create()` to the corresponding Blink module implementing this Web Platform API. This command is part of the general Credential Management API[7], which gets called first. This gets treated as a WebAuthn request in `CredentialsContainer::create()`, because we specified `publicKey` in the code above.

The JavaScript request contains a parameter object following the `PublicKey` `CredentialCreationOptions` WebIDL specification. This object also contains the client extension inputs according to `AuthenticatorExtensionsClient` `Inputs`, which we need to modify to include our own extension input. In Chromium, these parameters from JavaScript get converted into Mojo structures in `authenticator.mojom`[8], which are used for IPC between different

---

[7] Chromium Credential Management API *(Blink)*: `third_party/blink/renderer/` `modules/credentialmanager/`.

[8] Chromium WebAuthn Mojo *(Blink)*: `third_party/blink/public/mojom/webauthn/`.

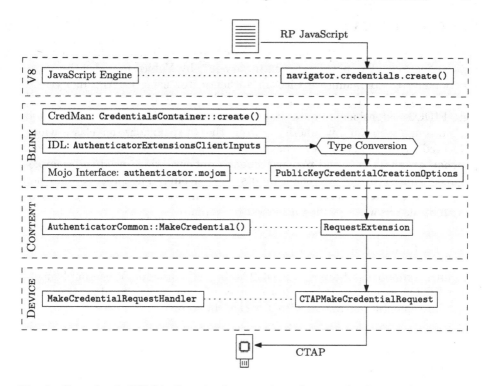

Fig. 2. Chromium's FIDO2 client implementation, showing the data and processing flow for sending extensions to an authenticator.

parts of Chromium. In our case, the relevant Mojo structure is `PublicKey` `CredentialCreationOptions`. We need to change both the Mojo structure and the converter from IDL to Mojo. Afterwards, the call arrives at `Authenti` `catorCommon::MakeCredential()` inside Chromium's `content` layer[9]. We need to modify this function to include our extension as a `RequestExtension`. This function then calls the `MakeCredentialRequestHandler` inside Chromium's `device` layer[10]. We modify the `CTAPMakeCredentialRequest`, which converts our request into a CTAP message. Afterwards, this gets sent to the authenticator, which responds back to us.

The response path is similar and traverses back to the `content` layer and finally to the `Blink` layer, where the client extension output gets converted into the WebIDL `AuthenticationExtensionsClientOutputs` and passed back to the V8 JavaScript engine.

---

[9] Chromium Web Authentication *(content)*: `content/browser/webauth/`.
[10] Chromium CTAP *(device)*: `device/fido/`.

5.3   Client Library

Besides browsers, it is also possible to implement a FIDO2 client in desktop applications. The `python-fido2` library [27] by Yubico provides the client functionality to communicate with an authenticator using CTAP2 in Python. Although not officially documented, the library can be extended with custom FIDO2 extensions due to its modular design. We have implemented our custom extension by inheriting from the `Ctap2Extension` class, which is located in `fido2/ctap2/extensions.py`. There are two abstract methods, `process_create_input` and `process_create_output`, which need to be implemented in order to use extension inputs and outputs. The subclass does not have to be registered anywhere, as `Fido2Client` considers all subclasses of `Ctap2Extension` when parsing a request or response.

5.4   Authenticator

The final component involved in FIDO2 is the authenticator. When implementing a FIDO2 extension, there are a number of open source hardware security token implementations available that we can build on:

– SoloKeys Solo 1 [21]
– SoloKeys Solo 2 [23]
– Google OpenSK [10]

While Solo 2 is still in early development and thus might not be suitable yet, Solo 1 and OpenSK are in a state that can be used to implement custom extensions. We have implemented the `greeter` extension in Solo 1, but describe the process for both Solo 1 and OpenSK. Neither project has a modular software architecture for implementing FIDO2 extensions, as all extensions are hard-coded at different code locations across the CTAP stack. Solo 1, however, provides documentation on how to implement custom extensions [22]. For OpenSK, we figured out the correct approach by inspecting the implementation of other FIDO2 extensions in the source code. In general, when implementing an extension for an authenticator, three modifications are required independent of the CTAP implementation:

– Announcing the support for the extension in the CTAP 2 `getInfo` function.
  - In Solo: `ctap_get_info()`.
  - In OpenSK: `process_get_info()`.
– Parsing and processing the extension inputs.
  - In Solo: `struct CTAP_extensions`, `ctap_parse_extensions()`.
  - In OpenSK: `struct MakeCredentialExtensions`,
    `MakeCredentialExtensions::try_from()`,
    `create_make_credential_parameters_with_cred_protect_policy()`.
– Building the extension outputs.
  - In Solo: `ctap_make_extensions()`.
  - In OpenSK: `process_make_credential()`.

6 Discussion

6.1 Extension Pass-Through

In the previous sections, we showed that FIDO2 extensions can address short-comings of the current FIDO2 standards and allow them to easily adapt to new use cases. In practice, the applicability of FIDO2 extensions is limited due to browser design decisions. In order to facilitate the development and usage of innovative FIDO2 extensions, we argue that web browsers should pass-through unknown extensions to authenticators, as the WebAuthn specification suggests [26].

Some custom FIDO2 extensions might pose the risk of exposing too much fine-grained data to RPs, which would allow them to discriminate between authenticators. This is the reason why Chromium does not support the official uvi and uvm extensions [14]. This potential problem can be approached by letting the user opt-in to pass-through custom FIDO2 extensions, e.g., via a configuration option in chrome://settings/securityKeys or via the permission API that is already used for camera or microphone access.

6.2 Supporting FIDO2 Extensions via Browser Extensions

Apart from supporting pass-through, web browsers can also facilitate the development of innovative FIDO2 extensions by making it easier to implement them. As we have shown before, Chromium's support for FIDO2 extensions is currently hard-coded in many different parts of the browser stack. This could be improved using a modular architecture. Another interesting approach would be to allow implementing custom FIDO2 extensions as regular web browser extensions. Chromium already has an extensive web extensions API, which could be extended with an API for FIDO2 extensions. This would also facilitate the use case of internal company deployments, as it is already possible in an enterprise setting to provision web browsers with a set of extensions.

6.3 Outlook

Without support for custom FIDO2 extensions in web browsers, it is unlikely that FIDO2 extensions will be utilized to a similar extent than X.509 or TLS extensions (see Sect. 7). The domain of developing new FIDO2 extensions currently is rather limited to developers of web browsers or members of the FIDO Alliance, like Google is already doing with their caBLE extension. Third-party developers have difficulties of implementing and testing their custom FIDO2 extensions in web browsers. In practice, the primary use case of custom extensions is probably not the public Internet but rather internal deployments with a limited target audience. In this case, the argument of possible authenticator discrimination is not applicable anymore as these internal deployments already have custom authentication policies in place.

The previously mentioned restriction on the usage of custom extension might also explain the limited support for implementing custom extensions in FIDO2 authenticators and clients. Documentation is often limited, if available at all. The software architectures are not designed to be modular with regards to FIDO2 extensions. One instance of a well designed modular extension architecture is the `python-fido2` client library, although it still requires modification of the internal source code and lacks public documentation.

7   Related Work

FIDO2 is not the first protocol that allows the definition of extensions in order to extend the capabilities of the specified protocol. There are a number of other protocols or data formats that support extensions and successfully integrate them in real world usage, two of which we describe in more detail:

- **X.509 Certificates:** In the context of public key infrastructures, the use of X.509 [2] certificates is very common. X.509 allows the inclusion of additional fields in certificates, revocation lists, etc. through extensions. In practice, these extensions are heavily used to address issues that cannot be solved using the specification alone. An example is the subject alternative name extension, which allows the declaration of additional identities of the certificate subject, as the basic certificate only allows a common name.
- **TLS:** The transport layer security protocol provides a secure communication layer for otherwise insecure protocols such as HTTP. Since TLS 1.2 [3], additional data can be communicated in the handshake of the protocol using extensions [4]. These can, for example, be used to let clients specify the domain of the requested resources in addition to the IP address using the server name indication extension. In the modern web, servers often do not only serve a single domain but a number of domains. If different certificates are used for the different domains, the server cannot know which certificate to include in the response without the server name indication extension.

In summary, extensible protocols are easier to adapt to new use cases, which prevents fragmentation. This is especially important for authentication protocols such as FIDO2, which so far have not managed to get widespread adoption to replace passwords.

8   Conclusion

In this paper, we showed that the extensibility of the FIDO2 standards is an important feature to remain flexible and future-proof. We demonstrated how to design and implement new FIDO2 extensions in web browsers, client libraries, and authenticators. This allows researchers and developers to use the existing FIDO2 infrastructure as a secure foundation for custom authentication deployments or for demonstrating new authentication approaches with real-world browsers and hardware. We surveyed all existing FIDO2 extensions and determined their respective support by web browsers and authenticators. A small number of extensions have widespread support, but most extensions have only minimal support or no support at all.

Current FIDO2 client implementations limit FIDO2's extensibility due to missing features and complex software architectures. We also showed that web browsers should (1) implement a configuration option that enables FIDO2 extension pass-through, and (2) consider extending the regular web browser extensions API to allow implementing custom FIDO2 extensions as, e.g., Chrome extensions. Both steps would empower researchers and developers to create their own extensions.

Acknowledgements. This work has been funded by the LOEWE initiative (Hesse, Germany) within the emergenCITY center. We thank the anonymous reviewers for reviewing this paper and for their helpful comments.

References

1. Ciolino, S., Parkin, S., Dunphy, P.: Of two minds about two-factor: understanding everyday FIDO U2F usability through device comparison and experience sampling. In: Fifteenth Symposium on Usable Privacy and Security (SOUPS 2019), pp. 339–356. USENIX Association, Santa Clara, August 2019
2. Cooper, D., Santesson, S., Farrell, S., Boeyen, S., Housley, R., Polk, W.: Internet X.509 public key infrastructure certificate and certificate revocation list (CRL) profile. RFC 5280, RFC Editor, May 2008. http://www.rfc-editor.org/rfc/rfc5280.txt
3. Dierks, T., Rescorla, E.: The transport layer security (TLS) protocol version 1.2. RFC 5246, RFC Editor, August 2008. http://www.rfc-editor.org/rfc/rfc5246.txt
4. Eastlake, D.: Transport layer security (TLS) extensions: Extension definitions. RFC 6066, RFC Editor, January 2011. http://www.rfc-editor.org/rfc/rfc6066.txt
5. Farke, F.M., Lorenz, L., Schnitzler, T., Markert, P., Dürmuth, M.: "You still use the password after all" – exploring FIDO2 security keys in a small company. In: Sixteenth Symposium on Usable Privacy and Security (SOUPS 2020), pp. 19–35. USENIX Association, August 2020
6. FIDO Alliance: Client to authenticator protocol (CTAP), June 2021. https://fidoalliance.org/specs/fido-v2.1-ps-20210615/fido-client-to-authenticator-protocol-v2.1-ps-20210615.html
7. FIDO Alliance: FIDO U2F raw message formats, April 2017. https://fidoalliance.org/specs/fido-u2f-v1.2-ps-20170411/fido-u2f-raw-message-formats-v1.2-ps-20170411.html
8. FIDO Alliance: FIDO2: Moving the world beyond passwords using WebAuthn & CTAP, June 2020. https://fidoalliance.org/fido2
9. Frymann, N., Gardham, D., Kiefer, F., Lundberg, E., Manulis, M., Nilsson, D.: Asynchronous remote key generation: an analysis of Yubico's proposal for W3C WebAuthn. Association for Computing Machinery, New York, October 2020. https://doi.org/10.1145/3372297.3417292
10. Google: OpenSK. https://github.com/google/OpenSK (2020)
11. Hodges, J., Mandyam, G., Jones, M.B.: RFC 8809: Registries for web authentication (WebAuthn). RFC 8809, RFC Editor, August 2020. https://www.rfc-editor.org/rfc/rfc8809.txt

12. IANA: Web authentication (WebAuthn) registries, August 2020. https://www.iana.org/assignments/webauthn/webauthn.xhtml
13. Kreichgauer, M.: Intent to deprecate and remove: U2F API (cryptotoken)(2021). https://groups.google.com/a/chromium.org/g/blink-dev/c/xHC3AtU_65A
14. Langley, A.: Re: issue 1097972: support WebAuthn uvi & uvm extension, June 2020. https://bugs.chromium.org/p/chromium/issues/detail?id=1097972#c3
15. Lyastani, S.G., Schilling, M., Neumayr, M., Backes, M., Bugiel, S.: Is FIDO2 the Kingslayer of user authentication? A comparative usability study of FIDO2 passwordless authentication. In: 2020 IEEE Symposium on Security and Privacy (SP), pp. 842–859. IEEE Computer Society, May 2020. https://doi.org/10.1109/SP40000.2020.00047
16. MDN: Web authentication API. https://developer.mozilla.org/en-US/docs/Web/API/Web_Authentication_API (2021)
17. MDN: Web authentication API: Browser compatibility, March 2021. https://developer.mozilla.org/en-US/docs/Web/API/Web_Authentication_API#Browser_compatibility
18. Microsoft: Win32 headers for WebAuthn (2021). https://github.com/microsoft/webauthn
19. Mooney, N.: Addition of a network transport (2020). https://github.com/w3c/webauthn/issues/1381
20. Protalinski, E.: You can now use your android phone as a 2FA security key for google accounts. VentureBeat, April 2019. https://venturebeat.com/2019/04/10/you-can-now-use-your-android-phone-as-a-2fa-security-key-for-google-accounts
21. SoloKeys: Solo 1: open security key supporting FIDO2 & U2F over USB + NFC (2018). https://github.com/solokeys/solo
22. SoloKeys: Tutorial: writing an extension for the solo stick (2020). https://github.com/solokeys/solo/blob/b86f0ee4e563f0b5ceb69770a6d6f64e42a688b6/docs/tutorial-getting-started.md
23. SoloKeys: Solo 2 monorepo (2021). https://github.com/solokeys/solo2
24. W3C: Web authentication: An API for accessing public key credentials - level 1. W3C recommendation, March 2019. https://www.w3.org/TR/2019/REC-webauthn-1-20190304/
25. W3C: Web authentication: An API for accessing public key credentials - level 2. W3C recommendation, April 2021. https://www.w3.org/TR/2021/REC-webauthn-2-20210408/
26. W3C: Web authentication: An API for accessing public key credentials - level 3. W3C first public working draft, April 2021. https://www.w3.org/TR/2021/WD-webauthn-3-20210427/
27. Yubico: python-fido2, March 2018, https://github.com/Yubico/python-fido2
28. Yubico: Discover YubiKey 5. strong authentication for secure login, July 2021.https://www.yubico.com/products/yubikey-5-overview
29. Yubico: libfido2, July 2021. https://developers.yubico.com/libfido2
30. Yubico: webauthn-recovery-extension. https://github.com/Yubico/webauthn-recovery-extension (2021)

Heartbeat-Based Authentication on Smartwatches in Various Usage Contexts

Dmytro Progonov[1,2]($\boxtimes$) and Oleksandra Sokol[1]

[1] Samsung R&D Institute Ukraine, Samsung Electronics, Kyiv, Ukraine
{d.progonov,o.sokol}@samsung.com
[2] Igor Sikorsky Kyiv Polytechnic Institute, Kyiv, Ukraine

Abstract. Today wearable devices, such as smartwatches, become significant part of our life. Despite of rich functionality, computational and device geometry constraints limit the possibility of their usage for strong user-friendly authentication, such as fingerprint or face recognition. As an alternative, the physiology and behavior based solutions were proposed. They utilize on-board sensors for capturing user-specific features that are hard to forge, such as fine motions patterns, gait etc. Nevertheless, these solutions require usage of high-precision sensors and are focused on a single usage context, that may be inappropriate for mass-market products. Thus a suitable alternative is needed for on-device sensitive information processing in any usage context.

In our study we consider user authentication on modern smartwatches by heartbeat signals analysis. We proposed extended set of heartbeat signals features based on Discrete and Continuous Wavelet Transforms for reliable user authentication in various usage contexts. Performance evaluation of state-of-the-art Enamamu's and proposed solutions has shown that suggested method allows achieving the same or even better authentication accuracy (0.2% FAR and 3.7% FRR) for fixed usage context (during still standing). Effectively mitigation with motion artifacts by proposed method gives an opportunity to outperform state-of-the-art solutions in case of user authentication during walking (0.2% FAR and 23% FRR for proposed solution, and 2% FAR and 45% FRR for state-of-the-art solution).

Obtained results make proposed method fall into Tier 2 Class 3 of Android Tiered Authentication Model. This makes smartwatch suitable for standalone usage in security-sensitive scenarios such as payments without companion device (mobile phone).

Keywords: User authentication · Wearable devices · Heartbeat signals

© Springer Nature Switzerland AG 2021
A. Saracino and P. Mori (Eds.): ETAA 2021, LNCS 13136, pp. 33–49, 2021.
https://doi.org/10.1007/978-3-030-93747-8_3

Acronyms

ATAM	Android Tiered Authentication Model
BCG	Ballistocardiogram
CWT	Continuous Wavelet Transform
DT	Decision Tree
DWT	Discrete Wavelet Transform
ECG	Electrocardiogam
FAR	False Acceptance Rate
FRR	False Rejection Rate
HBA	Heartbeat-based authentication
HBS	Heartbeat signals
kNN	K-nearest neighbors
NB	Naïve Bayes
PPG	Photoplethysmogram
PTA	Pan-Tompkins algorithm
RF	Random Forest
SAR	Spoof Acceptance Rate
SCG	Seismocardiogram

1   Introduction

These days wearables have become one of the main drivers for mobile companion devices market. Smartwatch format of wearable devices has drawn special attention, since these devices allow for combining classic design of watches with rich functionality and variety of embedded sensors. While being always on owner's hand, smartwatches add new human-to-machine interface for messaging, healthcare applications, contactless payments and many other use cases.

Typically a smartwatch is paired with user's smartphone. It extends its functionality with a variety of biometric sensors, such as heart rate monitor, pulse oximeter, hand motions, to name a few. During the last years several startup companies have proposed solutions for using smartwatch as an independent device for processing user's sensitive data [7, 20]. As an example, we may mention Keyble solution by Italian startup FlyWallet presented at CES-2021 show [4]. The Keyble provides several means of biometric authentication to enable contactless payments and digital services. Moreover proposed solution is consistent with industry standards, such as EMVCo, FIDO2, OATH and Mifare. Another example is B-Secur HeartKey solution for smartwatch [20]. HeartKey solution provides transparent health monitoring, though it can ultimately be incorporated into any device or platform that requires heart rate biometrics [5]. Also, the technology can be used for secure biometric heartbeat-based authentication in a variety of settings. It can effectively mitigate alterations of heart beat rhythm caused by changes of usage context, such as a person starts walking after still standing.

Reliable user authentication for smartwatches introduced by these solutions enables a wide range of new use cases, including smartphone-free contactless payments, access control to enterprise services etc. Special interest is paid to Heartbeat-based authentication (HBA) methods that allow for reliable user recognition and liveness checking without any external trusted devices or dedicated user actions.

The majority of proposed solutions in the domain of heartbeat-based authentication, such as B-Secur HeartKey [20], are aimed at using costly and high-precision sensors for accurate tracking of heartbeats, which may be unrealistic for mass-market devices. Our study focuses on applicability of HBA technology for mass-market modern smartwatches. As an example, we considered the Samsung Galaxy Watch3 device that includes Electrocardiogam (ECG) and Photoplethysmogram (PPG) sensors for capturing heartbeat signals.

The main contribution of paper may be summarized as follow:

1. Proposed method for accurate non-continuous person authentication by Heartbeat signals in various usage context (during different physical activities). The method is based on complex analysis of Heartbeat signals (HBS) by usage of several wavelet transformations. This allows effectively suppressing distortions of Heartbeat signals caused by person's movements during signals capturing.
2. The performance analysis of state-of-the-art and proposed methods for HBS-based user authentication in various usage context. This provides estimation of error levels in real situations instead of commonly used open datasets that relates to fixed usage context.

The rest of this paper is organized as follows. The notations are presented in Sect. 2 correspondingly. The main features of the authentication security framework are described in Sect. 3. The review of modern solution for heartbeat-based user authentication on smartwatches is presented in Sect. 4. Proposed technology for heartbeat-based user authentication is described in Sect. 5. Results of performance evaluation of proposed method are reported in Sect. 6. Section 7 concludes this paper.

2 Notations

In **boldface** we indicate high-dimensional arrays, matrices, and vectors. Their individual elements will be denoted by the corresponding lower-case letters in *italic*. Calligraphic font is reserved for sets. If nothing extra specified, we assume that an element x from a set $\mathcal{X}$ is sampled according to uniform distribution.

Biometric data (a sample) is presented as a vector of real numbers $\mathbf{b} \in \mathbb{R}^n$. Threshold values are denoted as T with corresponding indices.

Percentile of array $\mathbf{x}$ at level of $\alpha\%$ is denoted as $F_\alpha(\mathbf{x})$. Operator $F_w^{\mathrm{med}}(\cdot)$ is used for one-dimensional median filtering with w-elements moving windows.

3 Background

Modern authentication security frameworks for mobile devices support several authentication modalities and define a corresponding set of granted privileges

(Tiers). As an example, Android Tiered Authentication Model (ATAM) [21] splits authentication modalities into three Tiers and specifies how much every of them is trusted by defining allowed usage scenarios and fallback timeouts:

– "what you know" factors (Primary Tier) is the most trusted in sense that a user is only required to re-enter a primary modality (such as PIN, password or an unlock pattern) in order to use the device;
– "what you are" factors (Secondary Tier), primarily biometric and behavioral authentication;
– "what you have" factors (Tertiary Tier) which are environmental-based (Trusted Place, Trusted Device) and are out of scope of this paper.

The Secondary Tier is split into three security classes, namely Strong, Weak and Convenience (Table 1) that reflect the length of time before the device falls back to the primary authentication, as well as the allowed application integrations. Every class is specified with error metrics levels, such as False Acceptance Rate (FAR), False Rejection Rate (FRR) and Spoof Acceptance Rate (SAR) [22].

Table 1. Three classes from Secondary Tier ("What you are") of ATAM [21]. Here IdT is idle timeout period, InA is incorrect attempts number.

Class	Requirements	Capabilities			Constraints	
		Device unlock	Application integration*	Keystroke integration**	Fallback timeout	More constraints
Class 3 (Strong)	SAR: 0%–7% FAR: 1/50K FRR: 10% Secure pipeline	+	+	+	72 h	–
Class 2 (Weak)	SAR: 7%–20% FAR: 1/50K FRR: 10% Secure pipeline	+	+	–	24 h	IdT: 4 h or InA: 3 attempts
Class 1 (Convenience)	SAR: >20% FAR: 1/50K FRR: 10% (In)secure pipeline	+	–	–	24 h	IdT: 4 h or InA: 3 attempts

(*) App integration means exposing an API to apps (e.g., via integration with BiometricPrompt/BiometricManager, androidx.biometric, or FIDO2 APIs)
(**) Keystore integration means integrating Keystore, e.g., to release app auth-bound keys

Most of proposed biometrics-based authentication methods fall into the Secondary Tier (Table 1), such as fingerprints, facial and iris recognition to name a few. Typically, these methods include two-steps procedure of user authentication: first, capturing a reference template, and then comparing the template and new biometrics received from pretended user during authentication transactions.

Considered HBA technology for smartwatches falls into the Secondary Tier as well (Table 1). The technology is non-intrusive: it does not require any additional actions from the user, since HBS are captured continuously and transparently. Also, we gently argue that it may be suitable for Class 2 (Strong) due to strong connection between heartbeat parameters and person's physiology (heart's volume, arteries and veins sizes) which are unique for every individual. This makes these signals suitable for reliable user authentication [32].

Note that spoofing attacks against HBA systems do exist. Plausible case might include adversarial use of dummy with engine tuned to person's pulse. In this case possible defences might consist of liveness detection using other non-pulse data (such as accelerometer). And fallback to the primary authentication after N incorrect authentication attempts as recommended by ATAM [21].

4   Related Works

As an example of commercial solution that uses HBS for authentication, let us mention smartwatch by Nymi [7] and Flywallet [6], as well as B-Secur HeartKey SDK for wearables [20]. The Nymi proposed using smartwatch as a secondary token after initial (strong) multifactor authentication on a trusted device, such as a smartphone. A person wears smartwatch during authentication procedure. Captured ECG signals are used as a liveness indicator. This allows for using smartwatch as a token to provide access to restricted areas/resources within the company. Finally, de-authentication procedure is triggered by taking off the smartwatch from user's wrist.

The Flywallet extends Nymi's concept to secure usage of a smartwatch with contactless payments and third-party digital services [4]. The Flywallet's smartwatch includes Secure Element chip that stores and processes sensitive data (biometrics, payment card tokens, and access credentials) on-device. As it is for Nymi, the heartbeat signals are used as liveness indicators during authentication by Flywallet's Keyble solution [6]. The Flywallet does not sell their devices directly to the public but distributes them through partners (banks, e-money institutions, insurance companies), that makes it difficult to evaluate performance of their solution in real-life scenarios.

In contrast to Nymi and Flywallet, The B-Secur startup proposed ECG-based technology for user identification, authentication and health monitoring in automotive [20]. The main idea is tracking driver's health related parameters during trip and detect early potentially dangerous cardiac changes. Recently, B-Secur HeartKey solutions were certified by U.S. Food and Drug Administration for medical usage [5], namely B-Secur's HeartKey algorithms for Signal Conditioning, Heart Rate, and Arrhythmia Analysis. The effectiveness of HeartKey solution is based on mitigation of specific alterations of heart beat rhythm caused by changes of usage context, for example person starts walking after still standing.

The HBS parameters significantly depend on heart anatomy's features as well as features of blood vessels, which complicates capturing and reproducing these signals. For solving this task, several approaches were proposed [34]:

- Electrocardiogam (ECG) – is based on analysis of heart's electrical activity using a set of electrodes placed on skin;
- Photoplethysmogram (PPG) – analyze differences between emitted lights reflection due to vessels filling with blood;
- Ballistocardiogram (BCG) – takes into account body movements upward with each heartbeat;
- Seismocardiogram (SCG) – uses body vibrations induced by the heartbeats.

The majority of researches are focused on ECG, PPG and SCG (through accelerometer and gyroscope) for authentication based on heart beat. This is caused by availability of corresponding sensors in modern wearable devices Apple Watch [3], Fitbit Sense [1], and Samsung Galaxy Watch3 [9]. The BCG is not widely used on wearable devices due to insufficient accuracy of motion sensors (accelerometer and gyroscope) for tracking such negligible body movements.

Considered solutions for HBA on smartwatches rely on methods developed for on-device heartbeat signals processing. These methods can be divided into the following groups according to the features used:

- *Fiducial points based methods*—are aimed at detection specific points in HBS that can be used for time alignment and feature extraction;
- *Spectral transformation based methods*—involve specific transformation of HBS for robust extraction of user-specific features in various usage scenarios;
- *Artificial neural networks based methods*—utilizes generalization ability of convolutional neural networks for user's heart-related parameters variability mitigation in various usage contexts.

The first group of methods is closely related with medical research of Heartbeat signals [13,33]. These methods are based on detection of specific (fiducial) points inside ECG or PPG signals that correspond to specific part of heartbeat cycle. The examples of such fiducial points is well-known P-QRS-T complex on ECG for a single heartbeat [34], or Systolic/Diastolic peaks ratio for PPG signals [33]. Utilization of fiducial points allows for achieving high robustness against alterations of these signals caused by moving artifacts, for example negligible hands movements during signal capturing. This requires HBS capturing in predefined usage context, for example users are sitting or still standing, that may be inappropriate for real cases.

Methods from the second group leverage the ability of spectral transformations to compactly represent signals in frequency domain. As an example, a method proposed by Chun et al. [15] can be mentioned. It is based on Short Time Fourier Transform of HBS. This allows for mitigating signals variability while preserving low-computational complexity. The limitation of this approach is the necessity to pre-select a window function for capturing a user-specific features of HBS.

An example of methods from the third group is the model proposed by Patil et al. [29]. It combines learning capability of neural models and the multi-resolution analysis of wavelets [29]. It allows for achieving up to 98.78% accuracy of detection specific features in HBS related to heart disease. Nevertheless, this approach requires utilization of huge datasets for tuning neural network that may be inappropriate for authentication systems.

To overcome these obstacles, multiresolution wavelet analysis methods are proposed, such as Discrete Wavelet Transform (DWT) and Continuous Wavelet Transform (CWT). State-of-the-art works in this domain concentrate on the case when users are sitting or still standing during HBS capturing [16,17].

The purpose of this work is performance analysis of advanced non-continuous HBA systems in real cases when users may start authentication procedure in any usage context (for example, during walking). To the best of our knowledge, our work is the first one that considers performance of HBA system in such cases.

5 Heartbeat Signals Estimation on Smartwatches

User authentication by biometric-based systems is performed in several steps [30]. During the first stage liveness detection with other sensors (such as accelerometer data) can be used to check if authentication should be performed, such as whether the watch is worn by a person. On the second stage, signals from sensors are collected and preprocessed to reduce sensor-specific noise and to mitigate possible distortions (for example, artifacts caused by person's movements). Next stage is aimed at segmentation of prepared signals into separate heartbeats and further extraction of user-specific features from them. Finally, extracted features are passed to classifier that compares them with a stored template to make decision about user's authenticity.

These stages are aimed at learning user-specific features from noised signals captured by sensors of mobile device. During research we consider the case of HBS extraction with ECG sensors as one of the most accurate methods for heartbeat signal estimation. Therefore, let us describe data processing pipeline for ECG sensor in more details.

In most cases, preprocessing of HBS takes into account the information about sensor parameters (noise level), user's physical activity and influences of in-body (internal) processes [32]. Noise level is sensor-specific parameter that can be easily estimated with known spectral [31] and statistical [26] methods. Information about physical activity (usage context) can be evaluated with motion sensors or provided by mobile device platform (for example, by Android Activity Recognition API [2]). The most challenging task is estimation of HBS distortions caused by internal (hidden) processes, such as illness, stress, influence of hormones. These processes may lead to drastic changes of both amplitude and shape of Heartbeat signals.

Known methods for removing of HBS distortions caused by mentioned factors can be categorized into the following groups:

1. *Averaging-based methods*—variability of HBS is suppressed by averaging over a set of preprocessed (normalized) signals [10].
2. *Filtering-based methods*—take specially designed filters for adaptive distortion suppression [24].

3. *Approximation-based methods*—represent the task of distortion removal as a constrained convex optimisation problem [18], for example signal smoothing with nonlinear splines [14].
4. *Transformation-based methods*—based on transformation of HBS into domain where distortions can be easily removed, such as frequency domain for Fourier Transform.
5. *Methods based on component analysis*—rely on fully data-driven mechanism that represent HBS as a mixture of several components [12,25].
6. *Model-based methods*—variability of heartbeat signals is included into statistical model [23], for example variance of signal's samples amplitudes.

HBS distortions removing method selection strongly depends on prior information about features of used sensors and on available computational resources. Due to acceptable trade-off between distortion removal effectiveness and computation complexity, filtering and transformation-based methods are applied in most cases, especially for wearable devices. For de-noising ECG-based estimations of heartbeats signals, the median and Savitzky-Golay filters were used. The former one allows for effective suppression of impulse noises in captured signals, while the latter one smoothes signals for additive noises suppression.

Segmentation of prepared HBS into separate beats (pulses) involves methods of correlation analysis, or specific methods, such as Pan-Tompkins algorithm (PTA) [28]. Correlation-based methods are aimed at applying moving window for revealing similar patterns in prepared signals that are time consuming operations. The Pan-Tompkins algorithm can be divided into three steps: signal filtering for noise and linear trends suppression, signal's derivative calculation and moving window integration. Low complexity of PTA makes it suitable for using in battery-constrained devices such as smartwatches.

For segmentation of preprocessed (de-noised) ECG-based estimations of Heartbeat signals and further extraction features from them, we developed Algorithm 1 and Algorithm 2 respectively.

Here, usage of statistics over wavelet transform coefficients corresponds to the state-of-the-art solution for HBA on smartwatches proposed by Enamamu et al. [17] (see Algorithm 2). Feature of proposed solution is simultaneous usage of both DWT and CWT raw coefficients for mitigation with possible HBS alterations during persons movements (Fig. 1).

Finally, features extracted from HBS, namely raw DWT coefficients, are processed with a pre-trained binary classifier. Decision about user authentication is done according to the results of prepared features classification. Also, utilization of several spectral transformation by proposed methods allows effectively suppressing wide-band sensor-specific noise by preserving high accuracy of tracking band-limited HBS.

Algorithm 1: Extraction Heartbeat signals from ECG-sensor signal

---

Data: biometric sample $\mathbf{b} \in \mathbb{R}^n$, frequency range $\mathcal{F} = [f_{\min}; f_{\max}]$ (Hz) for normal heart rate, threshold value T_A

Result: set $\mathcal{X} = \{\mathbf{x}_i\}_{i=1}^k$ of extracted one-period heart beat

Initialize set $\mathcal{X} = \emptyset$;

Get Fourier spectrum of signal $\mathbf{b} : \dot{\mathbf{S}} = \text{FFT}(\mathbf{b})$;

Get frequency $f_{\max} = \arg\max_{f \in \mathcal{F}}(|\dot{\mathbf{S}}|)$ Estimate duration of heart beat $d = 1/f_{\max}$ (sec);

Initialize $b_{\min} = \emptyset, b_{\max} = \emptyset$;

for $(i = 2, \ldots, (n-1))$ **do**

  if $(b_i < (-T_A)) \wedge (b_{i-1} > b_i < b_{i+1})$ **then**

    Set $b_{\min} = i$;

  else if $(b_i > T_A) \wedge (b_{i-1} < b_i > b_{i+1})$ **then**

    Set $b_{\max} = i$;

  if $(b_{min} \neq \emptyset) \wedge (b_{max} \neq \emptyset)$ **then**

    if $((b_{max} - b_{min}) \geq d)$ **then**

      Append interval $\hat{\mathbf{b}} = \{b_i\}_{i=b_{min}}^{b_{max}}$ to set $\mathcal{X}$;

    Update $b_{\min} = \emptyset, b_{\max} = \emptyset$;

Algorithm 2: Feature extraction from HBS by Wavelet Transform

---

Data: biometric sample $\mathbf{b} \in \mathbb{R}^n$, DWT decomposition level n, DWT and CWT with basic functions $\mathcal{W} = \{\phi(\cdot), \psi(\cdot)\}$

Result: set of DWT-coefficients $\mathcal{D}$ and the corresponding statistics $\mathcal{S}$, set of CWT-coefficients C

Initialize sets: $\mathcal{D} = \emptyset, \mathcal{C} = \emptyset, \mathcal{S} = \emptyset$;

for $i = 1, \ldots, n$ **do**

  Get $\mathbf{C}$ CWT-coefficients of $\mathbf{b}$ at i^{th} decomposition level;

  Get approximation $\mathbf{A}$ and detail $\mathbf{D}$ DWT-coefficients of $\mathbf{b}$ at i^{th} decomposition level;

  Append $\mathbf{C}$ to set $\mathcal{C}$;

  Append $\mathbf{A}$ and $\mathbf{D}$ to set $\mathcal{D}$;

  for c *in* $\{\mathbf{A}, \mathbf{D}\}$ **do**

    Append minimum and maximum values of $\mathbf{c}$ to $\mathcal{S}$;

    Append mean, median and standard deviation values of $\mathbf{c}$ to $\mathcal{S}$;

    Append energy (sum of squared values) of $\mathbf{c}$ to $\mathcal{S}$;

    Append maximum (minimum) deviation from mean value of $\mathbf{c}$ to $\mathcal{S}$;

    Append median absolute deviation value of $\mathbf{c}$ to $\mathcal{S}$;

---

6 Experiments

Proposed solution was implemented on Samsung Galaxy Watch3 smartwatch. The solution was tested in various scenarios such as user is sitting, still standing or walking. Each usage scenario was evaluated independently: person walking is

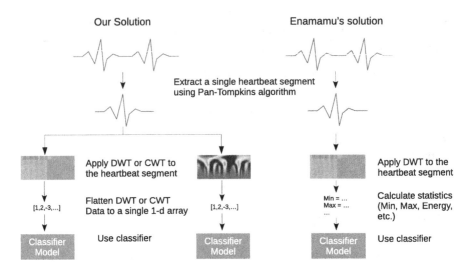

Fig. 1. Simplified version of the mentioned algorithms.

evaluated only with other people also walking, still-standing people evaluated with other people also standing, etc.

In this work we considered the case of authentication without prior identification. So we trained a one-vs-all model for each user and each usage scenario (walking, standing, etc.). Using a single model to identify any user is theoretically possible, but requires much more data to train than the one available in existing sources.

Time performance was evaluated by processing HBS data on a Samsung Galaxy S8 phone paired with smartwatch. We are glad to report that, on average, it takes only 6.8s to apply PTA, spectral transformations and to classify each extracted heartbeat from 1 minute recording using a Decision Tree. Assuming that we do not want to analyze each heartbeat all the time, we can conclude that performance overhead is negligible. Both our solution and method proposed by Enamamu et al. [17] can be added to device without disturbing a user.

Extraction of heartbeat from ECG-signals was done according to Algorithm 1 with the following parameters: threshold $T_A = 2.0$, $\mathbf{F} = [0.8; 1.5]$ (Hz). Heartbeat's features were extracted using DWT with well-known families of wavelets, such as Daubechies, bi orthogonal, Meyer to name a few. Also, application of CWT for feature extraction has been considered. The CWT gives an opportunity to process a signal with shorter time step in comparison with DWT. This allows for revealing more information about singularities (jumps and gaps) in considered ECG-signals. Decomposition level for mentioned wavelet transforms was varied from 1 to 4 with step 1.

Classification stage includes testing of proposed solution with widespread classifiers, such as K-nearest neighbors (kNN), Random Forest (RF), Decision Tree (DT) and Naïve Bayes (NB). False Acceptance Rate (FAR) and False Rejection Rate (FRR) were used as accuracy metrics. All classifiers were applied to all types of features on each dataset.

Performance analysis was done on collected and open datasets of ECG-signals. Collected dataset includes an estimation of these signals for six users (25 logs-per-user with 30 heartbeat-per-log on average for each usage context) captured by Samsung Galaxy Watch3 smartwatch. At least 20 ECG-signals with predefined duration (30 s) were collected for each person in four physical activities that correspond to widespread usage contexts: lying, sitting, still standing and walking. Time interval between ECG samplings for different activities were at least 30 min. Also, the proposed solution was tested on open datasets taken from public PhysioNet service [8]:

- *Combined measurement of ECG, Breathing and Seismocardiograms* [19] – the dataset includes measurements of 20 presumably healthy volunteers. During the measurement, the participants were asked to be still and awake in supine position on a conventional bed. Approximately, 867 signals per-user were captured.
- *Wilson Central Terminal ECG Database* [27] – the dataset includes ECG signals recorded from 92 patients (65 males and 27 females, 14 signal-per-user on average) with standard I – III Leads.

Proposed solution was compared with state-of-the-art DWT-based method proposed by Enamamu et al. [17]. The Enamamu's solution is based on usage statistical parameters of Discrete Wavelet Transform coefficients (such as mean, variance, range) ECG-signals as features during user authentication.

Evaluation was done according to well-known 10-times cross-validation procedure by splitting dataset into training (90%) and testing (10%) sets. These sets have been composed from logs (data collection sessions) instead of using individual extracted HBS. It was done that particular way because Heartbeat signals from the same log share the same statistical features. This may negatively impact the generalization ability of authentication system thus leading to incorrect (over-optimistic) estimation of error level for considered solutions in various usage contexts.

Accuracy analysis of mentioned solutions was done for two cases: initial and pre-processed sets of ECG-signals. The pre-processing stage is aimed at mitigation with variability of HBS by selection of sub-set of signals with minimum cross-distance. The cross-correlation was used as the distance metric.

For convenience, the mean authentication errors after cross-validation are presented in paper. These values were obtained after averaging over all persons from same datasets. It should be noted low standard deviation of error values (up 15% from mean error level for each person) that confirms high performance of considered solutions. Also, the FAR and FRR values for Class 3 Secondary Tier of ATAM (see Table 1) are presented for comparison with obtained results.

Performance analysis of proposed and state-of-the-art Enamamus solutions was performed in several stages. At the first stages, it was considered the authentication accuracy of proposed solution by usage of open and collected datasets. The FAR and FRR estimations for this case are presented in Table 2.

Usage of pre-selection stage allows significantly decreasing error levels for all considered datasets: from 2.5 times for in-house dataset to 42 times for open

Table 2. Error levels for proposed and Enamamu solutions by usage of ECG-signals from open and in-house databases. The minimal and maximum values of FAR and FRR for each solution are marked with green and red colors respectively.

Data-base	Used features	Decom-position level(-s)	Configuration	FAR	FRR	Configuration	FAR	FRR
			Processing all signals			Signal preselection		
	Class 3 of ATAM [21]	–	–	<0.002	<10.0	–	<0.002	<10.0
Wilson Central Terminal ECG dataset	Raw DWT coefficients	1	bior1.5 + kNN	0.17	5.99	bior1.5 + NB	0.76	5.74
		2	bior1.5 + kNN	0.19	3.71	dmey + NB	2.03	3.16
		3	bior1.5 + kNN	0.25	5.94	bior1.5 + NB	0.69	3.95
		4	dmey + NB	2.85	3.50	bior1.5 + NB	0.94	4.36
	Raw CWT coefficients	1-1	mexh + NB	9.39	17.49	mexh + NB	6.31	10.21
		1-2	mexh + NB	6.85	16.34	mexh + NB	4.16	11.58
		1-3	mexh + NB	5.21	16.17	mexh + NB	2.53	6.52
		1-4	mexh + kNN	0.19	16.17	mexh + NB	2.95	9.07
	Statistics over DWT coefficients	1	bior1.5 + NB	8.25	6.08	bior1.5 + NB	4.53	5.04
		2	bior1.5 + NB	9.33	2.56	dmey + NB	5.86	2.95
		3	bior1.5 + NB	8.13	4.13	bior1.5 + NB	3.61	2.08
		4	dmey + NB	7.87	3.43	dmey + NB	4.24	3.83
ECG, Breathing, Seismocardiograms dataset	Raw DWT coefficients	1	bior1.5 + NB	1.62	6.23	bior1.5 + RF	0.00	0.46
		2	bior1.5 + NB	1.59	9.43	bior1.5 + RF	0.00	0.32
		3	bior1.5 + NB	1.61	7.85	bior1.5 + RF	0.00	0.29
		4	bior1.5 + NB	1.45	7.59	bior1.5 + RF	0.00	0.42
	Raw CWT coefficients	1-1	mexh + DT	0.13	14.12	mexh + kNN	0.00	0.07
		1-2	mexh + DT	0.13	8.98	mexh + RF	0.00	1.11
		1-3	mexh + DT	0.13	12.24	mexh + RF	0.00	0.79
		1-4	mexh + DT	0.13	13.64	mexh + RF	0.00	1.16
	Statistics over DWT coefficients	1	bior1.5 + RF	0.06	28.72	bior1.5 + RF	0.02	2.29
		2	bior1.5 + RF	0.05	26.88	bior1.5 + RF	0.01	2.11
		3	dmey + DT	0.24	24.14	bior1.5 + RF	0.01	1.11
		4	bior15 + NB	8.82	12.30	dmey + RF	0.00	0.68
Collected ECG-signals dataset (supine position)	Raw DWT coefficients	1	dmey + RF	0.24	27.93	dmey + RF	0.23	19.26
		2	dmey + RF	0.22	26.40	bior1.5 + RF	0.11	18.63
		3	dmey + RF	0.24	24.56	dmey + RF	0.32	13.87
		4	dmey + RF	0.22	23.36	dmey + RF	0.32	14.92
	Raw CWT coefficients	1-1	mexh + RF	0.13	23.09	mexh + RF	0.14	11.88
		1-2	mexh + RF	0.15	23.01	mexh + RF	0.45	13.20
		1-3	mexh + kNN	2.26	20.53	mexh + RF	0.17	12.16
		1-4	mexh + RF	0.15	20.71	mexh + RF	0.26	11.54
	Statistics over DWT coefficients	1	dmey + RF	2.20	40.37	dmey + RF	2.39	29.64
		2	dmey + RF	2.00	38.17	dmey + DT	6.07	25.76
		3	dmey + RF	1.54	35.35	dmey + RF	1.49	25.62
		4	dmey + RF	1.30	34.29	dmey + RF	1.76	22.15

datasets (see Table 2). It should be noted that in real application pre-selection can be performed by ignoring pulses that do not satisfy some quality criteria, such as having anomalous min or max values, or improper P-QRS-T structure.

Note that usage of proposed solution allows for achieving near state-of-the-art error level for the majority of considered datasets (see Table 2). In contrast, Enamamu's solution has shown quite high error level (up to 10 times higher FAR in most cases). This can be explained by capturing of proposed method the richer set of features (the whole set of DWT and CWT coefficients) in comparison with using just their statistical description. This makes proposed solution to be a good candidate for implementation in Tier 2 Class 3 of ATAM [21] (see Table 1).

On the next stage, the error levels for various usage contexts were analyzed. The FAR and FRR values for considered user's physical activities for Enamamu's and proposed solution are presented in Table 3.

Pre-selection of HBS drastically (up to 5 times) reduces both FAR and FRR values at various usage contexts (see Table 3) as it has been shown for different datasets (Table 2). Also, proposed solution allows decreasing error level up to 4 times in comparison with Enamamu's solution by using of HBS this procedure.

Also, the accuracy of considered solutions remains acceptable in wide range of usage contexts (near 0% FAR and near 10% FRR)—while lying, sitting and still standing (Table 3). In case of users walking, the FAR and FRR values increase up to 4 times, especially for Enamamu's solution. This can be explained by negatively impact of motions artifacts on HBS (changes of shapes of signals, see Fig. 2).

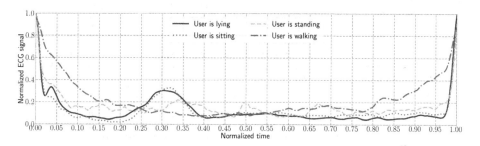

Fig. 2. Examples of R-to-R complexes of ECG signals for the same user from in-house dataset in different usage contexts.

Captured signals represent the ECG after R-to-R complex cropping. ECG-signals for lying, sitting and still standing activities are characterized by peaks after main pulse (T-complex for ECG-signal, Fig. 2). The time position of T-complex is about 0.27 for lying user state, and close to 0.33 for sitting and still standing. In case of user walking, the amplitude of the T-complex in negligible due to influence of motion artifacts. Nevertheless, the shape of leading and trailing pulses (R-complex) for all cases remains similar which makes them appropriate for user identification with proposed technology even in case of strong motion artifacts.

Table 3. Error level for proposed and Enamamu solutions by usage of ECG-signals captured on smartwatch in various usage context. The minimal and maximum values of FAR and FRR for each solution are marked with green and red colors respectively.

Data-base	Used features	Decomposition level(-s)	Configuration	FAR	FRR	Configuration	FAR	FRR
			Processing all signals			Signal preselection		
	Class 3 of ATAM [21]	–	–	<0.002	<10.0	–	<0.002	<10.0
Users are lying	Raw DWT coefficients	1	dmey + RF	0.24	27.93	dmey + RF	0.23	19.26
		2	dmey + RF	0.22	26.40	bior1.5 + RF	0.11	18.63
		3	dmey + RF	0.24	24.56	dmey + RF	0.32	13.87
		4	dmey + RF	0.22	23.36	dmey + RF	0.32	14.92
	Raw CWT coefficients	1-1	mexh + RF	0.13	23.09	mexh + RF	0.14	11.88
		1-2	mexh + RF	0.15	23.01	mexh + RF	0.45	13.20
		1-3	mexh + kNN	2.26	20.53	mexh + RF	0.17	12.16
		1-4	mexh + RF	0.15	20.71	mexh + RF	0.26	11.54
	Statistics over DWT coefficients	1	dmey + RF	2.20	40.37	dmey + RF	2.39	29.64
		2	dmey + RF	2.00	38.17	dmey + DT	6.07	25.76
		3	dmey + RF	1.54	35.35	dmey + RF	1.49	25.62
		4	dmey + RF	1.30	34.29	dmey + RF	1.76	22.15
Users are sitting	Raw DWT coefficients	1	dmey + kNN	2.19	19.94	bior1.5 + kNN	1.36	6.66
		2	bior1.5 + kNN	2.11	20.66	bior1.5 + kNN	1.39	7.64
		3	bior1.5 + kNN	2.23	20.75	bior1.5 + RF	0.20	8.82
		4	dmey + RF	0.45	21.46	bior1.5 + RF	0.28	8.93
	Raw CWT coefficients	1-1	mexh + RF	0.23	21.09	mexh + RF	0.08	8.95
		1-2	mexh + kNN	2.13	17.87	mexh + RF	0.08	8.35
		1-3	mexh + kNN	2.17	17.23	mexh + RF	0.21	11.19
		1-4	mexh + kNN	2.14	16.52	mexh + RF	0.08	8.39
	Statistics over DWT coefficients	1	dmey + RF	2.30	37.86	bior1.5 + RF	1.48	27.23
		2	bior1.5 + RF	2.26	34.85	dmey + RF	1.36	26.17
		3	dmey + RF	1.55	33.55	bior1.5 + RF	1.25	23.96
		4	dmey + RF	1.40	31.31	dmey + RF	0.95	18.79
Users are still standing	Raw DWT coefficients	1	bior1.5 + RF	0.26	24.27	dmey + RF	0.28	10.00
		2	dmey + RF	0.26	22.93	bior1.5 + RF	0.13	11.05
		3	dmey + RF	0.26	21.32	bior1.5 + RF	0.58	8.89
		4	dmey + RF	0.26	20.17	dmey + RF	0.31	8.94
	Raw CWT coefficients	1-1	mexh + RF	0.33	18.88	mexh + RF	0.08	8.94
		1-2	mexh + kNN	2.05	15.49	mexh + RF	0.36	10.89
		1-3	mexh + kNN	1.92	13.62	mexh + RF	0.13	9.09
		1-4	mexh + kNN	1.95	14.27	mexh + RF	0.33	8.81
	Statistics over DWT coefficients	1	bior1.5 + RF	1.84	37.11	bior1.5 + RF	1.28	22.75
		2	dmey + RF	1.63	34.75	dmey + RF	1.45	20.90
		3	dmey + RF	1.47	32.00	dmey + RF	0.99	16.72
		4	dmey + RF	1.50	28.70	dmey + RF	0.88	14.25
Users are walking	Raw DWT coefficients	1	dmey + DT	8.02	32.12	bior1.5 + DT	6.46	25.33
		2	dmey + DT	7.79	31.39	bior1.5 + RF	0.55	32.41
		3	dmey + DT	7.19	29.07	bior1.5 + RF	0.58	31.10
		4	dmey + DT	7.21	29.79	dmey + DT	5.47	24.82
	Raw CWT coefficients	1-1	mexh + RF	0.37	32.96	mexh + RF	0.47	25.81
		1-2	mexh + RF	0.34	32.88	mexh + RF	0.36	24.50
		1-3	mexh + kNN	3.29	28.13	mexh + RF	0.46	25.89
		1-4	mexh + RF	0.45	31.17	mexh + RF	0.23	23.04
	Statistics over DWT coefficients	1	bior1.5 + DT	11.55	49.73	bior1.5 + DT	9.77	47.31
		2	bior1.5 + RF	2.43	59.41	bior1.5 + RF	2.36	49.30
		3	dmey + RF	2.17	56.69	bior1.5 + DT	10.01	43.18
		4	dmey + RF	2.07	54.04	dmey + RF	2.03	45.37

7   Conclusion

Heartbeat-based user authentication is convenient and reliable biometric continuous authentication method suitable for wearable devices [11,32]. It allows to avoid the need of adding additional sensors such as fingerprint or camera to wearable device. Also it does not require any dedicated actions from the user and is suitable for battery- and CPU-constrained devices.

Modern solutions for heartbeat authentication are based on utilization of high-accuracy sensors for capturing these signals that may be inappropriate for mass-market products. Our study focuses on accuracy analysis of state-of-the-art HBS-based authentication methods in modern smartwatches, such as Samsung Galaxy Watch3, as well as authentication accuracy in various usage context (user's physical activities). We proposed to use spectral features based on Discrete and Continuous Wavelet Transforms for user authentication by Heartbeat signals. Proposed and state-of-the-art Enamamu's solutions were compared on both publicly-available open datasets, and our own in-house collected proprietary dataset of ECG-signals in various usage contexts (user's physical activities).

For this research we considered case when both initial enrollment and authentication happens on a single device (or device pair watch+phone), so biometric information is not shared between distinct devices.

Result of accuracy evaluation has shown that our proposed method achieves comparable results with the state-of-the-art solutions on open datasets (0.2% FAR and 3.7% FRR on Wilson Central). Also it is also capable of mitigating motion artifacts of ECG that gives an opportunity to outperform state-of-the-art solutions in this context (0.2% FAR and 23% FRR for proposed solution, compared to 2% FAR and 45% FRR for state-of-the-art solution on walking user data). Obtained accuracy measurement confirms that our suggested method falls into Tier 2 Class 3 of Android Tiered Authentication Model [21], thus allows a smart watch to be used as a standalone biometric authentication factor for sensitive operations such as payments (without trusted companion mobile phone).

For the future, we plan to investigate heart beat based user identification with a single model, heartbeat biometric data anonymization, and user authentication on many devices using shared biometric key based on fuzzy extractors.

References

1. Advanced Health Smartwatch — Fitbit Sense. https://www.fitbit.com/global/us/products/smartwatches/sense. Accessed 08 Dec 2020
2. Android Activity Recognition API (ActivityRecognitionClient). https://developers.google.com/android/reference/com/google/android/gms/location/ActivityRecognitionClient. Accessed 21 Apr 2020
3. Apple Watch Series 4 - Technical Specifications. https://support.apple.com/kb/SP778?locale=en_US. Accessed 08 Dec 2020
4. CES 2021: Wearable Device with Biometric Authentication. https://www.eetimes.eu/ces-2021-wearable-device-with-biometric-authentication/. Accessed 02 Mar 2021

5. FDA Approves Wearable Biometrics Algorithms for Medical Use. https://findbiometrics.com/fda-approves-wearable-biometrics-algorithms-medical-use-72202101/. Accessed 02 Mar 2020

6. Flywallet: Keyble Overview. https://www.flywalletpay.com/en/. Accessed 02 Mar 2021

7. Nymi: Product Overview. https://www.nymi.com/product. Accessed 04 Dec 2020

8. PhysioNet: The Research Resource for Complex Physiologic Signals. https://physionet.org/. Accessed 09 Mar 2021

9. Specs — Samsung Galaxy Watch3. https://www.samsung.com/global/galaxy/galaxy-watch3/specs/. Accessed 08 Dec 2020

10. Acharya, U.R., Joseph, K.P., Kannathal, N., Lim, C.M., Suri, J.S.: Heart rate variability: a review. Med. Biol. Eng. Comput. **44**(12), 1031–1051 (2006). https://doi.org/10.1007/s11517-006-0119-0

11. Aston, P.J., Christie, M.I., Huang, Y.H., Nandi, M.: Beyond HRV: attractor reconstruction using the entire cardiovascular waveform data for novel feature extraction. Physiol. Meas. **39**(2), 024001 (2018). https://doi.org/10.1088/1361-6579/aaa93d, https://www.ncbi.nlm.nih.gov/pmc/articles/PMC5831644/

12. Blanco-Velasco, M., Weng, B., Barner, K.: ECG signal denoising and baseline wander correction based on the empirical mode decomposition. Comput. Biol. Med. **38**(1), 1–13 (2007). https://doi.org/10.1016/j.compbiomed.2007.06.003, https://europepmc.org/article/med/17669389

13. Cao, Y., Zhang, Q., Li, F., Yang, S., Wang, Y.: PPGPass: nonintrusive and secure mobile two-factor authentication via wearables. In: IEEE INFOCOM 2020 – IEEE Conference on Computer Communications. IEEE, July 2020

14. Chouhan, V., Mehta, S.: Total removal of baseline drift from ECG signal. In: International Conference on Computing: Theory and Applications. IEEE, March 2007

15. Chun, S.Y., Kang, J.H., Kim, H., Lee, C., Oakley, I., Kim, S.P.: ECG based user authentication for wearable devices using short time Fourier transform. In: 39th International Conference on Telecommunications and Signal Processing (TSP). IEEE, June 2016

16. Enamamu, T.S., Clarke, N., Haskell-Dowland, P., Li, F.: Transparent authentication: utilising heart rate for user authentication. In: 12th International Conference for Internet Technology and Secured Transactions (ICITST). IEEE, December 2017

17. Enamamu, T., Otebolaku, A., Marchang, J., Dany, J.: Continuous m-health data authentication using wavelet decomposition for feature extraction. Sensors (Basel) **20**(19), 5690 (2020). https://doi.org/10.3390/s20195690, https://pubmed.ncbi.nlm.nih.gov/33036135/

18. Fasano, A., Villani, V., Vollero, L.: Baseline wander estimation and removal by quadratic variation reduction. In: Annual International Conference of the IEEE Engineering in Medicine and Biology Society. IEEE, September 2011

19. Garcia-Gonzalez, M.A., Argelagos-Palau, A., Fernandez-Chimeno, M., Ramos-Castro, J.: A comparison of heartbeat detectors for the seismocardiogram. In: International Conference on Computing in Cardiology. IEEE, September 2013

20. Goodwin, A.: B-Secur HeartKey tech unlocks your car with unique rhythm of your heartbeat. https://www.cnet.com/roadshow/news/b-secur-ekg-heartkey-tech-unlocks-car-with-heartbeat/. Accessed 04 December 2020

21. Google: Lockscreen and authentication improvements in android 11 (2020). https://android-developers.googleblog.com/2020/09/lockscreen-and-authentication.html

22. Google: Measuring biometric unlock security (2020). https://source.android.com/security/biometric/measure
23. Islam, S., Alajlan, N.: Model-based alignment of heartbeat morphology for enhancing human recognition capability. Comput. J. **58**(10), 2622–2635 (2015). https://doi.org/10.1093/comjnl/bxu150, https://ieeexplore.ieee.org/document/8205626/authors#authors
24. Jane, R., Laguna, P., Thakor, N., Caminal, P.: Adaptive baseline wander removal in the ECG: comparative analysis with cubic spline technique. In: Proceedings Computers in Cardiology. IEEE, October 1992
25. Luo, Y., et al.: A hierarchical method for removal of baseline drift from biomedical signals: application in ECG analysis. Bioinform. Biomed. Inform. **2013** (2013). https://doi.org/10.1155/2013/896056, https://www.hindawi.com/journals/tswj/2013/896056/
26. Marselli, C., Daudet, D., Amann, H.P., Pellandini, F.: Application of Kalman filtering to noise reduction on microsensor signals. In: Proceedings du Colloque interdisciplinaire en instrumentation, pp. 443–450, November 1998
27. Moeinzadeh, H., Gargiulo, G.: Wilson Central Terminal ECG Database (version 1.0.1). PhysioNet, https://doi.org/10.13026/f73z-an96
28. Pan, J., Tompkins, W.J.: A real-time QRS detection algorithm. IEEE Trans. Biomed. Eng. **BME-32**(3), 230–236 (1985). https://doi.org/10.1109/TBME.1985.325532, https://ieeexplore.ieee.org/document/4122029
29. Patil, D.D., Singh, R.P.: ECG classification using wavelet transform and wavelet network classifier. In: Dash, S.S., Naidu, P.C.B., Bayindir, R., Das, S. (eds.) Artificial Intelligence and Evolutionary Computations in Engineering Systems. AISC, vol. 668, pp. 289–303. Springer, Singapore (2018). https://doi.org/10.1007/978-981-10-7868-2_29
30. Sancho, J., Alesanco, A., García, J.: Biometric authentication using the PPG: a long-term feasibility study. Sensors **18**(5), 1525 (2018). https://doi.org/10.3390/s18051525, https://www.ncbi.nlm.nih.gov/pmc/articles/PMC5981424/
31. Tan, C., Wang, Y., Zhou, X., Wang, Z., Zhang, L., Liu, X.: An integrated denoising method for sensor mixed noises based on wavelet packet transform and energy-correlation analysis. J. Sens. **2014** (2014). https://doi.org/10.1155/2014/650891, https://www.hindawi.com/journals/js/2014/650891/
32. Wang, L., et al.: Unlock with your heart: heartbeat-based authentication on commercial mobile phones. In: ACM on Interactive, Mobile, Wearable and Ubiquitous Technologies. ACM, September 2018
33. Zhao, T., Wang, Y., Liu, J., Chen, Y., Cheng, J., Yu, J.: TrueHeart: continuous authentication on wrist-worn wearables using PPG-based biometrics. In: IEEE INFOCOM 2020 – IEEE Conference on Computer Communications. IEEE, July 2020
34. Zipes, D.P., Libby, P., Bonow, R.O., Mann, D.L., Tomaselli, G.F.: Braunwald's Heart Disease: A Textbook of Cardiovascular Medicine. Elsevier, New York (2018)

Quantum Multi-factor Authentication

Hazel Murray[1]($\boxtimes$)(iD) and David Malone[2](iD)

[1] Munster Technological University, Cork, Ireland
Hazel.Murray@mtu.ie
[2] Maynooth University, Maynooth, Ireland
David.Malone@mu.ie

Abstract. We present a quantum multi-factor authentication mechanism based on the hidden-matching quantum communication complexity problem. It offers step-up graded authentication for users via a quantum token. In this paper, we outline the protocol, demonstrate that it can be used in a largely classical setting, explain how it can be implemented in SASL, and discuss arising security features. We also offer a comparison between our mechanism and current state-of-the-art multi-factor authentication mechanisms.

1 Introduction

Multi-factor authentication (MFA) is of increasing importance for the security of individual accounts and infrastructures. However, many multi-factor mechanisms come with security or usability drawbacks. For example, though widely used, using SMS to send security codes is an insecure form of MFA since phone numbers are easily clone-able and SMS messages may be redirected [20]. In addition, in the near future, some authentication mechanisms using public-key cryptography, such as certificates and some hardware devices, may face challenges from quantum computing.

In this work, we suggest a quantum multi-factor authentication mechanism based on an established quantum scheme suggested for use in the banking sector by Gavinsky [6]. The proposed mechanism offers advantages over classical multi-factor authentication schemes by using quantum principles in order to protect against duplication and eavesdropping attacks. It also offers an ingrained ability to offer high and low levels of assurance with the same token, based on the current needs, trust and actions of the verifier and user. Benefits in comparison to other quantum mechanisms include the fact that there is no need for a quantum communication channel for each authentication, the verifier only needs to store classical strings rather than quantum registers, the token can be reused for multiple authentications of the same user, and a secure classical channel is not a hard requirement.

1.1 Brief Summary of Mechanism

The proposed mechanism involves a quantum MFA token which is issued by an organisation to a user. This token contains k quantum registers which correspond

© Springer Nature Switzerland AG 2021
A. Saracino and P. Mori (Eds.): ETAA 2021, LNCS 13136, pp. 50–67, 2021.
https://doi.org/10.1007/978-3-030-93747-8_4

to a list of k classical strings held by the organisation. The relationship between the classical and quantum bits is defined by an established quantum communication complexity problem known as the Hidden Matching Problem (HMP) [1]. Communication complexity describes the problem where two entities each hold information, one holds data x and the other holds data y. They wish to perform some computation using the two pieces of information but neither wishes to reveal their data to the other. In our case, Alice holds a quantum token which contains k quantum registers, and the verifier holds the k corresponding classical strings. Without either revealing their data to the other, the verifier can verify that Alice holds the correct token.

Informally, the authentication steps in the protocol involve: 1. the verifier and Alice agreeing which of the k registers should be measured. 2. The verifier then tells Alice which basis should be used for the measurements. 3. Alice will return a pair of values (a, b) to the organisation which correspond to the outcome of each measurement. 4. Using the results from Alice, the stored classical strings, and knowledge of what basis was used, the Hidden Matching Problem allows the organisation to verify that Alice does indeed hold the token.

Below we list some of the key security and utility features:

- The level of assurance depends on the number of measurements the verifier requests. This means that a single token has an ingrained ability to offer high and low levels of assurance based on the current needs, trust and actions of both verifier and user. This is valuable in a multi-factor mechanism, where a goal is to increase the assurance provided by a first factor.
- When a quantum register is selected for measurement it can not be used again. This means that there is a trade-off between the lifetime of the token and the level of assurance requested each time. This natural lifetime of an authentication token can be a valuable security feature. It also means that measurement results from a previous authentication have limited value to an attacker and therefore a secure communication channel is not a hard-requirement for the authentication.
- The quantum registers chosen for measurement are mutually agreed between verifier and user, so neither has complete control over the registers used.
- Despite being a quantum protocol, the authentication exchange does not require a quantum communication channel between user and verifier as only the measurement requests and results need to be communicated between them. This makes it viable for integration in largely classical settings.
- Also, in this mechanism the organisation only needs to hold classical strings rather than quantum registers. This is an important improvement, as holding quantum registers corresponding to each user who wants to authenticate would lead to significant overhead for an organisation.
- The security of the scheme is based on the premise of a zero-knowledge proof, where the user can prove that they hold the token without revealing the token. Unlike other schemes, there are no requirements for auxiliary classical cryptography.

- However, it is important to note that, at the time of writing, the short length of time quantum memories can hold qubits means a true hardware implementation is not currently possible.

The remainder of the paper is organised as follows. In Sect. 2 we give background on the development of quantum authentication protocols to date. In Sect. 3, we present the quantum preliminaries necessary for the understanding of the mechanism. In Sect. 4, we present the quantum multi-factor authentication protocol and the associated SASL mechanism. This section also includes an informal security analysis and explanation and discussion about the token lifetime. In Sect. 5, we discuss the proposed mechanism in relation to current state-of-the-art multi-factor authentication. Section 6 includes a discussion and we conclude in Sect. 7

2   A Brief Review of Quantum Authentication

As with classic authentication, a distinction exists between message authentication and identity authentication. In this paper, we are concerned with identity authentication, that is, Alice authenticates her identity to the server, usually using a pre-agreed secret. For example, in authentication using passwords, the password for Alice is agreed at the beginning of the communication exchanges, and then for each subsequent authentication, the user provides the password. Quantum authentication protocols will typically use quantum states as the pre-agreed secret and a user can then authenticate using these, usually through some type of measurement strategy. We will now describe the development of some of these quantum identity authentication mechanisms that have been proposed.

Quantum authentication protocols can be roughly divided up into four kinds: those based on entangled pairs, those based on a quantum key distribution (QKD), those based on superposition, and those based on a quantum computation complexity problem. To the best of our knowledge, ours is the first based on the last option. Here we will discuss the other three with reference to their positives and negatives.

Quantum Authentication via Entangled Qubits. In 2000, Zeng and Guo [26] introduced an identity authentication quantum protocol based on symmetric cryptography and EPR pairs (maximally entangled quantum states of two qubits) which have been previously shared. In their protocol, there must exist a pre-agreed key K_1. They will use this key to decide which basis to use for measurements. When Alice wants to secretly communicate with Bob, Alice and Bob set up a quantum channel which consists of a source that emits EPR pairs. Alice receives one half of each entangled pair and Bob receives the other. Alice performs a series of measurements (according to their key) on her half of the EPR pairs. Bob, in his turn, measures his half with the same key and also performs a random series of measurements M. If eavesdropping occurred, Alice and Bob can detect it using the random series of measurements, and then can identify each other by comparing the measurements done using their shared key. These results are exchanged via classical symmetric key cryptography. As it still requires classical cryptography and a secure classical channel it is not necessarily secure from quantum computing attacks.

This scheme was preceded by a similar scheme by Barnum [2]. It was also developed on by Li and Zhang in 2004 [14], Li and Barnum in 2006 [13] and Ghilen et al. in 2013 [7]. All these schemes require quantum communication channels. Li and Barnum's protocol requires no previous key to be shared between the parties, just entangled qubits. It also does not require any classical communication but does still need quantum communication of the qubits at each authentication. Ghilen et al.'s protocol [7] allows the state ϕ^+ to be represented as binary bit "0" and the state ψ^- to be represented as binary bit "1", and thus includes key agreement as part of the protocol.

In 2020, Sharma and Nene [21] proposed an entanglement-based two factor authentication scheme which combines the measurement of entangled qubits with a biometric-based secret to achieve authentication. We will discuss this scheme in more detail in Sect. 5 where we compare our mechanism to the current multi-factor state-of-the-art.

Quantum Authentication via QKD and Classical Cryptography. Quantum key distribution is the most established form of quantum cryptography. It allows two parties to mutually agree a security key. The most famous example is the BB84 protocol [3] which is widely deployed. In this protocol Alice begins by sending polarized photons, set using one of two bases, to Bob. Bob observes the received photons and randomly chooses which basis he will measure with respect to. Alice and Bob then use a classical channel to determine which data bits should be discarded by exchanging information about the bases they used for the measurements. They can now use the results which were measured using the same basis as their shared key.

Dušek [4] proposed an authentication scheme where the BB84 QKD is used to share an identification sequence. After Alice and Bob share these secret codes, they use a classical channel. They send parts of the identification sequence to each other to demonstrate that they have it. However, an additional authentication is required because the BB84 needs authentication before the parties start communicating.

Kuhn [11] proposed a new authentication scheme which used both QKD and classical cryptography. It requires a trusted server who holds a shared secret key with both Alice and Bob. If Alice wants to authenticate Bob, this protocol can then be used. The trusted server sends a stream of authentication bits via QKD on a quantum channel to Alice and Bob, such that Alice and Bob each get one part of a pair of entangled qubits. On a secure classical channel, the trusted server tells them which basis to measure each bit with respect to. Alice can then send the results of a portion of her measurements to Bob to authenticate herself. The remaining bits are kept and used as a shared secret key. A positive feature of this protocol is that the trusted server does not learn the shared secret key between Alice and Bob that is used for their future communication.

Quantum Authentication via Superposition. Quantum authentication protocols which rely on the sharing of entangled qubits have practical drawbacks. In particular, they are not very scalable, as a verifier would need to maintain qubits in a superposition state for each user who needs to authenticate. In response to this, quantum authentication schemes which rely on superposition rather than entanglement were put forward as a solution.

In 2017, ho Hong et al. [10] proposed an authentication protocol which uses single photon states. The two parties, Alice and Bob, have a pre-agreed secret string. If Alice wishes to authenticate to Bob, she encodes the classical secret string into corresponding quantum registers. She then sends these to Bob. Bob can measure these and, if the output matches the stored string corresponding to Alice, then Alice is authenticated. The authors compare this scheme to the verification of a password using a password hash. This protocol offers good efficiency, however, errors in the transmission or generation of the photons will mean this mechanism will fail. In 2019, Zawadzki [25] addressed the information loss to eavesdroppers problems which also existed in the protocol. However, in 2021, González-Guillén et al. [8] identified an attack on Zawadzki's algorithm and demonstrated that it was insecure.

Quantum Authentication via Communication Complexity. As mentioned, the scheme we propose for multi-factor authentication (inspired by Gavinsky [6]) is based on the quantum communication complexity problem known as the Hidden Matching Problem [1]. The organisation is able to issue Alice with a token which she can then use for future authentication. Alice never needs to pass quantum bits but instead sends to the results of certain measurements as they are requested by the organisation. The organisation is able to verify that Alice holds the correct token based on these responses. It takes the form similar to a zero-knowledge proof and therefore and eavesdropper learns very little from multiple observations of the protocol.

One important distinction between our scheme and the above schemes is that the verifier does not need to hold the quantum states, which can become unmanageable for a large number of users. The verifier, in our scheme, need only store classical bits which can be reused for multiple authentications of the same user. A second distinction is the ability to offer differing levels of security within the scheme. This is particularly useful for application to multi-factor authentication (MFA), as MFA is often used as step-up authentication when risky actions are attempted by a user.

3   Quantum Computing Properties and Preliminaries

Quantum computing has the theoretical power to break certain modern cryptography [16]. In 1994, Peter Shor [22], developed a quantum algorithm which threatens public key cryptographic systems which are often used in multi-factor authentication devices [12]. In 1996, Grover's algorithm was developed, which reduced the effectiveness of symmetric key cryptographic systems [9]. Without these classical cryptographic mechanisms, many of our secure authentication protocols become vulnerable.

Though quantum computing has revealed weaknesses in current cryptographic mechanisms, it also holds the possibility of unlocking solutions that exceed the bounds of our current computational capabilities. Quantum mechanical systems have properties that are at odds with our general understanding of classical physics and here we will give a brief overview of the properties we utilise.

Qubit. In classical computing, all computation is done using bits which can be either 0 or 1. A qubit is the quantum equivalent to this classical bit but has a number of important properties. These are included below.

Superposition. The first property is *superposition*. This describes the fact that a qubit can take the value of 0 and 1 or both at the same time. This gives quantum computers the capacity, in some sense, to complete computations in parallel and where n classical bits allow n computations, n qubits can allow 2^n computations.

Measurement. The second property is *measurement*. In classical mechanics, looking at something does not change its state. In quantum mechanics, a qubit can be in a *superposition* of both 0 and 1 at the same time and when measured it must *collapse* to either 0 or 1. The state of a quantum bit is represented by a wave function, where $|0\rangle$ is the 0 wave function, $|1\rangle$ is the 1 wave function, and $\alpha\,|0\rangle + \beta\,|1\rangle$ is a superposition. If we measure a wave function then there is a probability $|\alpha|^2$ of measuring 0 and $|\beta|^2$ of 1. Therefore, the result we get is probabilistic and not predetermined.

Basis. When we take measurements, we measure a particular property of the qubit. Similar to how measuring speed and weight of a classical object will result in different results, so too will measuring a qubit with respect to different *bases*. We take advantage of this and it allows the mechanism to take a form similar to a zero-knowledge protocol since measurement with respect to one basis will give no information regarding the correct measurement when done with an orthogonal basis. This means that we can offer security for the mechanism even when a secure communication channel is not available. In this paper, we assume a qubit can be measured using two particular *bases*.

Entanglement. According to Einstein, *entanglement* is the 'spooky' property of quantum mechanics. Let's say we *entangle* two qubits and move them to opposite sides of the globe. If we measure one of the qubits then we know that we will get the same measurement for the second, entangled, qubit. Imagine we take the first qubit and measure it using a momentum basis and get 1. Then the other qubit will also measure as 1. This is remarkable since each returned result is a function of probabilities $|\alpha|^2$ and $|\beta|^2$.

No-Cloning Theorem. The final property we will mention is the *no-cloning theorem* [24] which tells us that it is impossible to create an identical copy of a quantum state. This has particularly relevant applications for one-time-passwords [21] and secure authentication. In our mechanism, this means that the risk of cloning, duplication or replay attacks is significantly reduced.

3.1   Hidden Matching Problem

Our Quantum MFA mechanism is based on the quantum-classical communication complexity problem known as the Hidden Matching Problem [1]. The specific version of the problem known as HMP_4 sets out a relationship between a 4-bit classical string and a 2-qubit quantum register (called the HMP_4-state). By requesting measurements of these states in a particular format (the HMP_4-reply), the verifier can conclude whether the user holds the correct token (this is the HMP_4-condition). In this section, we will describe these three key aspects of HMP_4 in more detail.

We begin by explaining how the quantum registers should be created so that they correspond to the classical bit strings held by the organisation (HMP_4-state). Here, a classical string is denoted x and the quantum register corresponding to that classical string is denoted $|\alpha(x)\rangle$.

Definition 1 (HMP_4-states). Let $x \in \{0, 1\}^4$. The corresponding quantum register is

$$|\alpha(x)\rangle = \frac{1}{\sqrt{4}} \sum_{1 \leq i \leq 4} (-1)^{x_i} |(i-1)_2\rangle,$$

where $(\cdot)_2$ denotes writing a number in base 2.

In 2020, Murray et al. showed how qubit registers of this form can be created using quantum gates [18].

Once these quantum registers are created they can be passed to the user. At each authentication, the user will measure a selection of these registers and the organisation will use the value m to will tell the user which basis to use. The user does not return the results directly but instead returns an (a, b) pair based on the following rule:

Definition 2 (HMP_4-reply).
If $m = 0$,

$$v_1 = \frac{|00\rangle + |01\rangle}{\sqrt{2}}, v_2 = \frac{|00\rangle - |01\rangle}{\sqrt{2}}, v_3 = \frac{|10\rangle + |11\rangle}{\sqrt{2}}, v_4 = \frac{|10\rangle - |11\rangle}{\sqrt{2}}$$

Otherwise if $m = 1$,

$$v_1 = \frac{|00\rangle + |10\rangle}{\sqrt{2}}, v_2 = \frac{|00\rangle - |10\rangle}{\sqrt{2}}, v_3 = \frac{|01\rangle + |11\rangle}{\sqrt{2}}, v_4 = \frac{|01\rangle - |11\rangle}{\sqrt{2}}$$

Measure $|\alpha(x)\rangle$ in the basis $\{v_1, v_2, v_3, v_4\}$. Return (a, b) such that:

$$(a, b) = \begin{cases} (0, 0), & \text{if } v_1 \\ (0, 1), & \text{if } v_2 \\ (1, 0), & \text{if } v_3 \\ (1, 1), & \text{if } v_4. \end{cases}$$

Using the initial classical strings that the organisation stores, x, the basis indicator, m, and the reply from the user, (a, b), the verifier is now able to validate whether these values satisfy the HMP_4-condition. For each measured register, the verifier checks that:

Definition 3 (HMP_4 condition). For $x \in \{0, 1\}^4$ and $m, a, b \in \{0, 1\}$, we say that $(x, m, a, b) \in HMP_4$ if

$$b = \begin{cases} x_1 \text{ XOR } x_{2+m} & \text{if } a = 0 \\ x_{3-m} \text{ XOR } x_4 & \text{if } a = 1 \end{cases}$$

4 Quantum MFA Mechanism

In this section we will show how these quantum properties and the HMP_4 problem can be leveraged to create a secure multi-factor authentication mechanism. The design of the scheme is closely based on Gavinsky's quantum coin design [6] and inspired by the use of traditional hardware tokens, such as in TOTP [19].

This mechanism had two phases: **Issuing** and **Authentication**. These are explained separately below. Note that once a token has been issued it can be used for authentication multiple times.

Issuing

In the first phase, a quantum token is issued to a user. This part requires quantum communication, where a set of quantum states are created by the token issuer (server) and transferred into quantum memories held by the user. This could be achieved by issuing a device with quantum memories to the user. The user can then use this quantum token for authentication. The server must store the classical bit strings used in the creation of the token. However, as this information is classical, it can be stored in a secret authentication database, similar to the information stored for a classical hardware token.

The steps for the issuer to create the token with k quantum registers are listed below and an example is depicted in Fig. 1:

1. Choose an unique identifier for the token, `tokenID`.
2. Randomly choose k 4-bit strings. We call these $(x_i)_{i=1..k}$. These bits, along with the token ID are stored in the authentication database. Other details, such as the user that the token is issued to, could also be stored.
3. Convert each $(x_i)_{i=1..k}$ into a corresponding HMP_4-state according to Definition 1 in Sect. 3.

The HMP_4-states can now be issued to a user in a token.

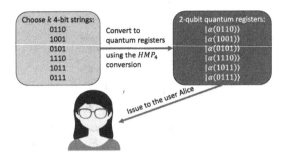

Fig. 1. Issuing the quantum MFA token - purple: quantum step, orange: classical step. (Color figure online)

Authentication

In the second phase, the user wishes to proceed with authentication using their quantum token. Depending on the parameters of the scheme, authentication with the same token can be performed multiple times. The user connects to the server, and is issued with a measurement challenge, during which it is decided which quantum memories will be measured and the details of those measurements (e.g. basis). If the user has access to the quantum memories, then the measurements will be performed and the server can validate the results of the measurements against their classical database. Someone impersonating the user will not be able to perform the measurements, and will have to guess the results (possibly based on eavesdropped information), and will fail with high probability. Note that a measurement will collapse the quantum register, and prevent future useful measurements.

To authenticate, the user must prove they have access to the token, so a challenge is issued. The size of the challenge, t, is another parameter of the scheme. For convenience, t should be a multiple of three. The steps for the server and the client are listed below and an example is depicted in Fig. 2:

1. The user sends the `tokenID` to the server so that records can be found in the authentication database. This data is static over the token's lifetime.
2. The server then randomly chooses a set L_S of t indices from the set $1..k$ of candidate quantum registers to measure.
3. Some of these registers may already have been used, so the user randomly chooses a subset L_C of L_S of size $2t/3$ of registers that have not yet been used, and sends L_C to the server. If there is no such subset, then the token has been used up, and a new token should be requested.
4. The server then picks random bits $(m_i)_{i \in L_S}$ for each of the registers that the client has nominated. These m_i determine the measurements that the client must perform. The scheme is designed so that the measurement corresponding to $m_i = 0$ tells us nothing about the result of the measurement for $m_i = 1$, and vice versa.
5. The client performs the measurements on the registers $i \in L_S$ according to the values m_i, producing two bits $(a_i, b_i)_{i \in L_S}$ for each measurement. These are sent

to the server. The measurements are specified as part of the HMP_4 problem, and dictate the basis used. The user marks the measured registers as used.
6. The server verifies that the (a_i, b_i) all have the expected values, which can be calculated from x_i and m_i using HMP_4 [1].

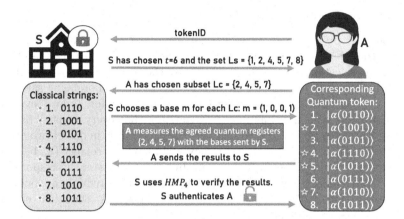

Fig. 2. Authentication using the quantum MFA token - purple: quantum step, orange: classical step. (Color figure online)

Note that all communication is classical and therefore each client does not require a quantum communication channel to the server in order to authenticate.

4.1 SASL Mechanism

To demonstrate that this mechanism can be used for authentication in classical systems, we will describe the verification stage, once the user has the quantum token as a Simple Authentication and Security Layer (SASL) mechanism [17]. In SASL mechanisms, a client (C) is authenticating to a server (S). The server has a list of the IDs of the quantum tokens and also the associated classical strings. The client has the quantum token and an identity that they wish to be authorized as. In SASL terms, this is a client-first protocol, as the client presents information to the server first. The SASL conversation would proceed as follows:

C: Authenticate as `identity` using `tokenID`.
S: Measurement challenge is on the set L_S.
C: I will measure the subset L_C.
S: HMP_4 challenge measurements are m_i for $i \in L_C$.
C: HMP_4 response is (a_i, b_i) for $i \in L_C$.
S: Authentication success/failure.

Here, the server would return an authentication success only if all of the following hold: (1) `tokenID` is in the authentication database (2) `identity` is permitted authenticate using `tokenID`; (3) $L_C \subset L_S$; (4) the HMP_4 response is given for the same $i \in L_C$; and (5) the (a_i, b_i) values satisfy the relations given by m_i and x_i in Definition 3.

4.2   Informal Security Analysis

Note, that this protocol can take place in the clear. For each authentication observed, the observer learns the measurements for $2t/3$ registers under the bases m_i. The selection of registers in Step 2 by the server means that an impersonator who has observed an authentication cannot depend on being asked for a subset of registers that they have observed measurements for. Indeed, even if an impersonator has seen multiple measurements, so that every register has been measured, they only observed each register being measured in one of two possible bases specified by m_i. This means that they will know the correct (a_i, b_i) values for (on average) half of the $2t/3$ registers, but have to guess the responses for the other half, giving a low probability of success, which reduces exponentially as t increases. The protocol is subject to a MITM attack, though it could be secured via TLS or a similar mechanism.

Theft of the quantum token is, of course, possible. A more interesting question asks, "Can the token be cloned?". Of course, the no cloning theorem means that the quantum registers cannot be cloned by an attacker who steals the token and wants to return it before the theft is noticed. Gavinsky considers the possibility of cloning the quantum token via more complex measurements, and bounds the probability of success. For example, he shows that only after $e^{\Omega(t^3/k^2)}$ observations cloning might be possible with a probability higher than $e^{\Omega(t^2/k)}$.

Note that since each measurement uses up a number of quantum registers this does create an attack: the attacker could convince a user to repeatedly authenticate until enough registers have been measured that authentication becomes impractical. If this happens, the user would have to get a new token issued.

4.3   Token Lifetime

Gavinsky provides various results about how many times this verification procedure can be used. Each verification uses $2t/3$ registers, and he suggests that the token be renewed when $k/4$ registers have been used, to ensure that Step 3 can be completed with high probability.

An interesting property of this protocol is that the token's lifetime is limited by the number of uses. As registers are measured, it becomes increasingly less likely that an honest user will be able to successfully complete Step 3. Even an attacker who steals the token, who might proceed beyond Step 3 faces the challenge that the m_i chosen by the server will not correspond to previous measurements, and will have to resort to guessing, which is analogous to the case of the impersonator above. Gavinsky shows that combinations of quantum measurements can not be used to answer multiple HMP_4 queries with confidence.

This allows us to make a trade-off between the number of registers, k, the number of registers used for each authentication, t, and the lifetime of the token. It is even possible for the server to choose a t value, depending on the level of authentication required. For example, if authenticating for a low-risk service or if multiple factors are presented, the server could choose a smaller value for t to extend the token lifetime.

5   Comparison to State of the Art

In this section, we will briefly comment on the benefits and disadvantages of the current state-of-the-art mechanisms for multi-factor authentication. We have included One-time passwords (SMS and application based), hardware tokens and the recent work by Sharma et al. [21] on a quantum-based one time password scheme. After detailing each alternative method, we then describe the contributions of our mechanism and the additional benefits and features it offers.

One Time Passwords. The first mechanism we will discuss is one-time passwords. Here, the factor involves providing an additional security code that changes over time. These are commonly either communicated via text/call to a phone or a specific application. Both involve usually a human entering the security code and can be prone to typographic errors, though devices are now providing features to make this easier.

The text/call version requires a phone network connection in addition to an internet connection. The connection to the phone network is treated as a second channel over which to deliver the security code. The text/call version is no longer considered a secure practice for one time passwords [20]. There are a number of reasons for this, including: (1) SMS and voice calls are not encrypted, so the password could be intercepted and copied; (2) phone company employees can be fooled into transferring a phone number to the attacker's SIM card, meaning the security codes get sent to the attacker.

The application-based version of one-time passwords usually requires each user to download additional software. Time-based one time passwords (TOTP) is a common form. This involves hashing an agreed secret (sometimes sent using a QR code) with a time stamp, in order to generate a time-dependent code. Provided that the client's application and the verifier know the initial secret and the time, they will both be able to generate the same time-based code and the client can provide this to the server for authentication. Sometimes this mechanism is implemented using a hardware token with a clock and a pre-loaded secret. Each time-based code is agreed to be valid for a precisely defined time interval, usually 1 to 15 min. However, if the initial secret is stolen, then whoever has this initial secret will also be able to generate an arbitrarily large number of valid codes.

Both one-time password mechanisms, and our quantum mechanism, depend on generation of secret random numbers (i.e., the random code in the voice/text mechanism, the initial secret TOTP and the x_i in the quantum mechanism).

The one-time password mechanisms usually require human interaction, which is practical because the schemes just require the entry of a simple code. The quantum mechanism is more complicated, and we believe it would only be practical to implement as part of an automated protocol (such as SASL). Relative to the voice/text mechanism, the quantum mechanism does not require an additional channel after the token is issued, and so it is more like the application-based mechanism. Relative to the application-based mechanism, the quantum scheme cannot have the secret stolen from the user's token, as any quantum registers that are copied/measured, will collapse. Note, that an attacker that has access to the server-side database (the x_i) can effectively impersonate someone with the token.

Hardware Tokens. A second common mechanism for multi-factor authentication is the issuing of a hardware device (such as a device with display or a specifically designed USB/NFC/BLE device) to each user. We mentioned one form of hardware token above, where TOTP is used with a dedicated hardware token with a pre-loaded secret. A second common example of this is a device supporting FIDO2/WebAuthn, such as a YubiKey, though these mechanisms can also exist on a mobile device with a hardware security module.

Like TOTP and our quantum mechanism, these devices have a registration phase. Here, the device produces a public/private key pair that can be used for signing challenges. The public key is stored on the server at registration, and the private key is stored in a way that is only accessible to the hardware device. Once registration is complete, the device can be used for authentication where the server presents a challenge and information to allow the identification of the correct key. The challenge is then signed by the device (following confirmation by the user through a gesture, such as pushing a button or providing a biometric). The signature can be verified by the server using the public key stored by the server at registration.

A crucial advantage of schemes based on public key cryptography is that the server does not store the private key and so compromise of the server does not permit an attacker to impersonate users in the future. This is an advantage over both the quantum scheme and schemes such as TOTP. These devices are also often advertised as phishing resistant, as under normal operation the device will not reveal the private key. However, there is a possibility to extract the private keys from the hardware device, and, though highly challenging, this has been demonstrated [15]. There is also no limit on how many times a public key can be used, in comparison with the quantum scheme. We also note that many public-key signature schemes are vulnerable to attack by quantum computing. A quantum token should be resistant to such attacks. We note that several features common to hardware tokens, such as a push button, biometric verification or incorporation into a mobile device could be used as part of the implementation of the quantum MFA scheme.

Biometric Based Quantum One Time Passwords. Sharma and Nene [21] suggest a quantum two-factor authentication mechanism which combines a biometric code, B_C, and a quantum challenge. They propose three variations of the protocol and for each one the user registers their biometric with the server in the form of a shared secret code.

The first form of the protocol is an introductory mechanism. The server generates a series of two entangled qubits and measures one of the qubits in each pair to get a code, C_1. Instead of storing the code, the server stores the corresponding entangled qubit. The code, C_1 is sent to the Client via SMS, then the client computes $C_1 \oplus B_C$ and sends the result back to the server. By measuring the second entangled qubit and XORing this with the stored biometric code for the user, the server can verify that the user did, in fact, receive the code to their device. This mechanism involves quantum memory and quantum measurement capabilities for the server. The benefit over a classic SMS-based one-time password scheme are that the qubit stored at the server will collapse if an attacker attempts to duplicate it and that the quantum entanglement is being used for the random generation of the code.

The second form of the protocol involves the server sending the qubit to the client and then the client making the measurement. This has the advantage of securing the transmission as the qubits would collapse if observed. It means that quantum communication is now required for each authentication verification and the client and the server will require quantum measurement capabilities. In our mechanism, the authentication after registration involves only classical communication, but similar to this protocol we do require the client to have quantum measurement capabilities.

The third form of the protocol suggested by Sharma and Nene [21] involves bi-directional quantum communication and quantum gate capabilities for the user. The server will also still need quantum measurement capabilities. The difference in this mechanism is that the client will transform their biometric code to a Pauli matrix before XORing it with the qubit that the server sends. The result is a qubit in a different Bell state, which is communicated back to the server. No classical channel is used in this case, therefore a Man-in-the-middle (MITM) attack is not possible as an eavesdropper will collapse the qubits' wave functions. The server can then use the corresponding entangled qubits to verify that the user has returned the correct values.

It is also worth noting that the inclusion of the biometric in all these schemes brings its own problems. A biometric scanner does not always give a clear reading and the code generated, even with error-correcting, can vary each time [5]. When this code is sent to the server it must match the code they have on file. The biometric code can also be stolen in transmission at registration, or recorded on the device and replayed by an attacker.

The advantage of our scheme over these schemes lies primarily in the use of a token, which can last for multiple authentications and the fact that the server does not need to store qubits for each client's authentication. Furthermore, the authentication procedures only involve classical communication, and because it is a form of a zero-knowledge protocol, this classical channel does not necessarily need to be encrypted, though the simple inclusion of a TLS connection will give protection against a MITM attack.

5.1 Attack Susceptibility Summary

In Table 1, we summarize a comparison of the different multi-factor authentication mechanisms. For each attack type, we indicate whether the mechanism is susceptible to the attack or not. Notice that we do not include MITM attacks, as every mechanism will be susceptible to a single session being compromised by MITM, but can avoid it by using a TLS connection. Biometric-QOTP 3 uses only quantum communication channels for authentication, so cannot, and does not need to, secure it via TLS. However, this introduces the challenge that the quantum authentication will need to be tied to the future classical communication in some way in order to make the authentication effective.

Table 1. Attacks each multi-factor authentication mechanism is susceptible to.

	Phishing	Replay	Eavesdropper analysis	Keyboard logging	Clone-able	Channels for authentication
Our QMFA	N	N	N	N	N	C
SMS-based OTP	N	N	S	S	S	C, T
App-based OTP	N	N	S	S	S	C
FIDO2 (Public-key token)	N	N	N	N	S	C
Biometric-QOTP 1	N	N	S	S	S	C, T
Biometric-QOTP 2	N	N	N	S	S	Q_1, C
Biometric-QOTP 3	N	N	N	S	S	Q_2

Vulnerability: (N) Not susceptible, (S) Susceptible.
Channel type: (C) Classical, (T) Telephone/mobile,
(Q_1) Quantum (1-way), (Q_2) Quantum (2-way).

The other attacks are defined as follows.

Phishing: An attacker masquerading as a website tries to trick the user into revealing their secret to them. None of the MFA mechanisms above are subject to this attack.

Replay: An attacker who records the user's authentication response should not be able to directly replay it in a later authentication in order to gain access. Again, none of the state-of-the-art mechanisms are vulnerable to this.

Eavesdropper analysis: An eavesdropper can listen and record communication between the server and the user. They can then use/analyse this data offline and potentially use it to log in on a different session. Note that we assume that TLS cannot be used to secure a SMS based system when communication is via the traditional telecommunications network.

Keyboard logging: These attacks involve malware (or malicious hardware) on the user's device which can record user inputs. Both biometrics and typed codes are subject to this attack. Note that once the biometric is stolen, the attacker can successfully authenticate as the user in future for all the Biometric-QOTP mechanisms.

Clone-able: This considers whether an attacker can duplicate the authenticator so that they have the power to authenticate. A classic example is sim-jacking, where an attacker convinces a phone company to pass a phone number, or SIM, over to them instead of the true owner [23]. The app-based OTP is clone-able, as, if the initial secret is discovered, an attacker can login indefinitely as the user. Similarly, if the biometric code is cloned then the holder of the code can login as the user for future authentications. A FIDO public-key based token is clone-able under extreme circumstances [15].

The last column indicates the channels that are needed during the authentication process. Q_1 refers to the need for a 1-way quantum communication channel. For example, from the server to the user. Q_2 is the requirement for 2-way quantum communication, so that the user is also able to use a quantum channel for their response. T indicates the need for a telephone communication channel and C indicates a classical internet connection.

6 Discussion

The quantum scheme we have proposed here has several interesting features, including features common to modern schemes, such as being resistant to phishing and eavesdropping attacks, while also including having a limited number of uses and quantum-level resistance to cloning. It also avoids quantum storage at the server and the need for a quantum channel when authenticating.

Token Distribution. Challenges in distributing hardware tokens with pre-shared secrets could apply to this scheme. For, say, employees who have a remote/in person working arrangement updating the registers in their quantum token might be straight forward, and would allow periodic in-person validation. However, for purely remote users, things could be more challenging, with tokens either being delivered by post (and subject to theft) or via some quantum network.

Implementation Challenges. Of course, the current state of quantum computing, and particularly for this scheme, quantum memories, means a true hardware implementation of this scheme is not currently possible. We have implemented Gavinsky's quantum coin scheme within a quantum communications simulator [18], and confirmed that the main implementation challenges relate to the availability of quantum hardware. This would allow us, in future work, to implement the scheme and study the noise and errors that occur within it and test possible potential attacks. Quantum technology is evolving at a rapid pace, and having trialed and tested potential mechanisms for when implementation is possible is important for reliable cryptography and security.

Variable Strength Authentication. As we noted, a server could potentially choose different challenge sizes, t, when authenticating a user. These could be chosen for different levels of security. For example, a user connecting from a commonly-used IP address could be challenged with a small t, whereas a user connecting from an unexpected country might be challenged with a larger t value. An additional challenge might also be used for *step-up authentication* when a user wants to access higher-risk systems, for example password change or access to personal data. This could be particularly interesting, given that each quantum register read provides additional confidence to the server, while smaller t values would extend the token's lifetime.

7   Conclusion

In this paper, we have introduced a quantum multi-factor authentication protocol. It is based on the hidden-matching quantum-complexity problem. It offers step-up graded authentication for users via a quantum token. Advantages over classical schemes include the automatic protection against duplication and eavesdropping which is inherent to quantum bits. It has the ability to offer high and low levels of assurance with the same token, based on current needs and actions of the user. Also, it is not susceptible to known quantum computing attacks unlike many classical asymmetric authentication mechanisms. We have compared it to a number of classical MFA schemes, highlighting benefits and challenges. Overall, it is a promising mechanism that, given the existence of quantum memories, could prove valuable.

References

1. Bar-Yossef, Z., Jayram, T.S., Kerenidis, I.: Exponential separation of quantum and classical one-way communication complexity. In: Proceedings of the 36th ACM Symposium on Theory of Computing, pp. 128–137 (2004)
2. Barnum, H.N.: Quantum secure identification using entanglement and catalysis. arXiv preprint quant-ph/9910072 (1999)
3. Bennett, C.H., Brassard, G., Breidbart, S., Wiesner, S.: Quantum cryptography, or unforgeable subway tokens. In: Chaum, D., Rivest, R.L., Sherman, A.T. (eds.) Advances in Cryptology, pp. 267–275. Springer, Boston (1983). https://doi.org/10.1007/978-1-4757-0602-4_26
4. Dušek, M., Haderka, O., Hendrych, M., Myška, R.: Quantum identification system. Phys. Rev. A **60**(1), 149 (1999)
5. Fhloinn, E.N.: Biometric retrieval of cryptographic keys. Ph.D. thesis, Trinity College Dublin (2006)
6. Gavinsky, D.: Quantum money with classical verification. In: 2012 IEEE 27th Conference on Computational Complexity, pp. 42–52. IEEE (2012)

7. Ghilen, A., Azizi, M., Bouallegue, R., Belmabrouk, H.: Quantum authentication based on entangled states. In: Proceedings of the World Congress on Multimedia and Computer Science, pp. 75–78 (2013)
8. González-Guillén, C.E., González Vasco, M.I., Johnson, F., Pérez del Pozo, Á.L.: An attack on Zawadzki's quantum authentication scheme. Entropy **23**(4), 389 (2021)
9. Grover, L.K.: A fast quantum mechanical algorithm for database search. In: Proceedings of the 28th ACM Symposium on Theory of Computing, STOC 1996, pp. 212–219. Association for Computing Machinery, New York (1996). https://doi.org/10.1145/237814.237866
10. Hong, C., Heo, J., Jang, J.G., Kwon, D.: Quantum identity authentication with single photon. Quantum Inf. Process. **16**(10), 1–20 (2017). https://doi.org/10.1007/s11128-017-1681-0
11. Kuhn, D.R.: A hybrid authentication protocol using quantum entanglement and symmetric cryptography. arXiv preprint quant-ph/0301150 (2003)
12. Künnemann, R., Steel, G.: YubiSecure? Formal security analysis results for the Yubikey and YubiHSM. In: Jøsang, A., Samarati, P., Petrocchi, M. (eds.) STM 2012. LNCS, vol. 7783, pp. 257–272. Springer, Heidelberg (2013). https://doi.org/10.1007/978-3-642-38004-4_17
13. Li, X., Barnum, H.: Quantum authentication using entangled states. Int. J. Found. Comput. Sci. **15**(04), 609–617 (2004)
14. Li, X., Zhang, D.: Quantum information authentication using entangled states. In: International Conference on Digital Telecommunications (ICDT 2006), p. 64. IEEE (2006)
15. Lomné, V., Roche, T.: A side journey to Titan. IACR Cryptology ePrint Archive 2021/28 (2021)
16. Mavroeidis, V., Vishi, K., Zych, M.D., Jøsang, A.: The impact of quantum computing on present cryptography. arXiv preprint arXiv:1804.00200 (2018)
17. Melnikov, A., Zeilenga, K.: Simple authentication and security layer (SASL). IETF RFC 4422 (2006)
18. Murray, H., Horgan, J., Santos, J.F., Malone, D., Siljak, H.: Implementing a quantum coin scheme. In: 2020 31st Irish Signals and Systems Conference (ISSC), pp. 1–7. IEEE (2020)
19. M'Raihi, D., Machani, S., Pei, M., Rydell, J.: TOTP: time-based one-time password algorithm. IETF RFC 6238 (2011)
20. Schneier, B.: NIST is No Longer Recommending Two-Factor Authentication Using SMS, August 2016. https://www.schneier.com/blog/archives/2016/08/nist_is_no_long.html
21. Sharma, M.K., Nene, M.J.: Two-factor authentication using biometric based quantum operations. Secur. Priv. **3**(3), e102 (2020)
22. Shor, P.W.: Algorithms for quantum computation: discrete logarithms and factoring. In: Proceedings of the 35th Symposium on Foundations of Computer Science, pp. 124–134. IEEE (1994)
23. Vaughan, A.: Phone number theft through SIM-jacking is on the rise in the UK. New Sci. (3264), 10 (2020). https://www.newscientist.com/article/2228252-phone-number-theft-through-sim-jacking-is-on-the-rise-in-the-uk/. Accessed 4 Jan 2022
24. Wooters, W., Zurek, W.: Quantum no-cloning theorem. Nature **299**, 802 (1982)
25. Zawadzki, P.: Quantum identity authentication without entanglement. Quantum Inf. Process. **18**(1), 1–12 (2018). https://doi.org/10.1007/s11128-018-2124-2
26. Zeng, G., Guo, G.: Quantum authentication protocol. arXiv preprint quant-ph/0001046 (2000)

An Interface Between Legacy and Modern Mobile Devices for Digital Identity

Vasilios Mavroudis[1($\boxtimes$)], Chris Hicks[1], and Jon Crowcroft[1,2]

[1] Alan Turing Institute, London, UK
{vmavroudis,c.hicks,jcrowcroft}@turing.ac.uk
[2] University of Cambridge, Cambridge, England

Abstract. In developing regions a substantial number of users rely on legacy and ultra-low-cost mobile devices. Unfortunately, many of these devices are not equipped to run the standard authentication or identity apps that are available for smartphones. Increasingly, apps that display Quick Response (QR) codes are being used to communicate personal credentials (e.g., Covid-19 vaccination certificates). This paper describes a novel interface for QR code credentials that is compatible with legacy mobile devices. Our solution, which we have released under open source licensing, allows Web Application Enabled legacy mobile devices to load and display standard QR codes. This technique makes modern identity platforms available to previously excluded and economically disadvantaged populations.

Keywords: Digital identity · Feature phones · Device interfacing

1 Introduction

Covid-19 has accelerated the push for digital identity solutions globally. The commercial and government pressure for universal Covid-19 vaccine certificates has yielded a range of new technologies for displaying personal details using smartphone devices. The de facto approach has become to display a Quick Response (QR) code containing either cryptographically signed personal attributes or a Uniform Resource Identifier (URI) to an online service providing the same information. Consideration has also been given to groups without access to smartphones, usually in the form of printable QR codes which simply reproduce what would otherwise be shown on a device screen. Amongst all of the existing work however, little consideration has been given to the needs of users with legacy or ultra-low-cost mobile devices. Although these devices, also known as feature phones, are uncommon in many developed countries they are still mainstream in many parts of the world. In Sub-Saharan Africa, for example, an estimated 56% of all cellular connections in 2019 were made from feature phones [3]. Innovative applications for these legacy devices currently range from mobile banking and secure payments [7,10], now an integral part of the economy in Kenya [11], to supporting agriculture and farming [12] but have not yet widely support digital identity.

A. Saracino and P. Mori (Eds.): ETAA 2021, LNCS 13136, pp. 68–76, 2021.
https://doi.org/10.1007/978-3-030-93747-8_5

The main barrier to using feature phones for digital identity is the absence of a standard developer-friendly mobile operating system. Unlike smartphones which usually run either the Google Android or Apple iOS operating systems (OSes), most feature phones run proprietary, closed-source and even discontinued OSes (e.g., the Nokia Series 30 [1] or the Sony Ericsson A1/200). This means that unless an identity application is installed by the manufacturer it is nearly impossible to deploy one to new users. Without a programmable OS which is developer-friendly, existing identity solutions are limited to either programming the Subscriber Identity Module (SIM) card [13,14] or receiving One-Time Passcodes (OTPs) via SMS; in both cases, the user token is restricted to a few digits which are displayed on the screen.

In this work we demonstrate a robust and novel method of displaying QR codes for identification using legacy mobile devices. In particular, the approach we propose:

- Enables previously overlooked legacy mobile devices with hundreds of millions of users to benefit from modern digital identity solutions.
- Shows how standard QR code certificates can be retrofitted to low-cost mobile devices with very limited interfacing capabilities. An important feature is that our approach is able to tolerate intermittent user connectivity by exploiting local caching.
- Is freely available with an implementation and documentation which we make public under the MIT open-source license.

2   Background

We now outline the fundamental concepts and technologies used in the rest of this work.

2.1   Wireless Application Protocol

The Wireless Application Protocol (WAP) was introduced in 1999 [19] and offers a way for mobile devices (such as feature phones) to access information over a wireless network. Unlike modern devices, feature phones are not able to render HTML pages, execute Javascript or submit HTTP requests. Instead, compatible servers serve content in the Wireless Markup Language (WML) and WML Script, while the only graphics format supported is Wireless Application Protocol Bitmap Format (WBMP). WAP uses a gateway (Fig. 1) that decodes the WAP requests (sent from the phone's microbrowser) into HTTP requests and routes them to the online server. Similarly, the HTTP responses are first encoded into a binary representation of WML by the gateway and then forwarded to the phone.

2.2   QR Codes for Digital Identity

QR codes are a form of machine-readable barcode originally intended to support traceability in automotive supply chains [6]. Contemporary standards, such as

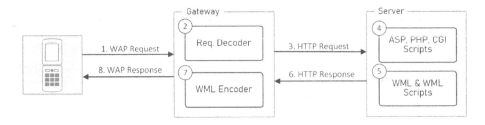

Fig. 1. Illustration of a webpage load under the WAP protocol. The user's device does not have access to an IP network but instead submits its requests through the WAP Gateway which fetches and encodes the WML page from the third-party server.

those intended to provide interoperable vaccination information [4,5], have seen a re-popularisation of QR codes as a mechanism for encoding personal identity information. QR codes are composed of modules and the number of modules dictates both the physical size and information capacity. There are standard module configurations for QR codes, termed the version number, which range from 21×21 modules for a version 1 code to 177×177 modules for a version 40 code [2]. Since a module needs to be at least (and divisible by) 1×1 pixels in size, we can determine the maximum information capacity of a QR code based on a mobile device's screen size. Our testing using a Nokia 3510 device, which has a total screen size of 96×64, indicates that 46×46 pixels are available within the WAP browser to display a QR code. As shown in Fig. 3, this reduction arises because several pixels from the total available screen size are required for the WAP browser user interface provided by the mobile device. Allowing for an Error Correcting Code (ECC) level of 7%, a 46×46 pixel space bounds the maximum QR code information capacity to the 224 alphanumeric characters provided by a version 7 code. In practice, the available information capacity is reduced as a suitable encoding must be used to represent binary data. The de facto standard encoding being used in a number of health certification applications is base 45 [9] and this permits storing 2 binary bytes per 3 alphanumeric characters. In other words, a version 7 QR code can encode around 149 bytes of uncompressed information and this is enough to include standard public-key digital signatures using modest curve sizes.

3   Problem Statement

As outlined in Sect. 1, most applications assume devices with modern interfacing capabilities during the execution of their authentication protocols. Our goal is to enable feature phone users to participate in modern authentication protocols, without any additional investment in equipment.

In the rest of this work, we refer to the feature phone user as *Prover*. The Prover wishes to prove their identity or an attribute (e.g., their age) to the *Verifier*. The Verifier can be a government official, a local merchant, a bank representative or a local organisation running a food subsidy. Besides these actors, we also introduce an external *Service* that is available over the Internet and is tasked with keeping records of the users' details and can issue *Tokens*. Tokens encapsulate various types of data such as digital certificates, signatures, URIs and plain user information depending on the use case.

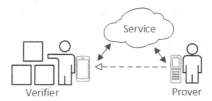

Fig. 2. Setup. The Prover wishes to prove their identity or status to the Verifier. The Verifier uses a modern device, while the Prover possesses a feature phone, making it hard to interface with nearby devices (dotted arrow). Both the Prover and Verifier are *intermittently* connected to the Internet.

As seen in Fig. 2, both the Prover and the Verifier need to be able to connect to the Internet using their devices. This connectivity may be intermittent for one or both parties. In line with the sparse mobile network coverage seen in many rural and less developed regions, their connectivity is assumed to intermittent. Moreover, the Prover is able to access online services only through low-bandwidth WAP due to the limitations of their device. The Verifier's device needs to be capable of scanning QR codes. A basic smartphone or a considerably cheaper smart-feature phone could be used.

3.1   Use Cases

We now outline two use cases that require a cross-device interface. Both of them require the Prover and the Verifier to be in physical proximity.

1. Identity or Status Credentials. The Prover wants to convince the Verifier of their identity or an attribute/status (e.g., over 18). From their end, the Verifier needs to be presented with adequate proof that the claims of the Prover are truthful. We assume that the two parties do not necessarily have access to the Internet during the execution of the protocol. The implementation of the Covid-19 certificates in the EU [5] is a straightforward instantiation of this use case.

2. Food Subsidy Management. The Prover wants to convince the Verifier that they can receive the food subsidy. The Verifier needs to be presented with adequate proof that the Prover is eligible for the subsidy and that they have not already used their entitlement.

3.2   Threat Model

A Prover can be malicious and may attempt to claim attributes or request access to services they are not entitled to. We assume that provers can collude with other malicious users and are byzantine i.e., may deviate from the correct execution of the protocol. For example, such an adversary may attempt to craft malicious tokens, replay tokens from other users or modify their own past tokens. The Verifier is also potentially malicious and may, for instance, capture credentials submitted by users and attempt to replay them to other victim verifiers.

We also assume that the Service is trustworthy and that the provider does not act maliciously (either independently or by colluding with other malicious parties). All online communications are encrypted using standard encryption techniques (e.g., TLS 1.3 [18]). Denial of service attacks from the Verifier or the service towards provers are not within the scope of this work. Moreover, we do not consider cases where a malicious Prover compromises a Verifier's terminal or a Prover colludes with a Verifier, as the Verifier can always opt to not execute the protocol at all.

4   Design and Implementation

In this section, we outline our system architecture and discuss our design choices.

(a)   (b)

Fig. 3. Service login screen and QR Code as displayed on a Nokia 3510 (2002) microbrowser.

4.1   Protocol

As seen in Fig. 4, the Prover is first given a cryptographic nonce from the Verifier (step 1). This nonce serves as a challenge to prevent replay attacks and is relatively short (6–10 digits) as the Prover manually types it into the feature phone. Following the nonce input and a successful user login (Fig. 3b) to the online service, the Prover submits a request for a token (step 2). The service responds to the request and the feature phone's microbrowser displays the QR code (step 3). Subsequently, the Verifier scans and decodes the QR code (step 4).

Demonstration videos can be found at: https://tiny.cc/ETAA2021_demos and a sample implementation here: https://github.com/alan-turing-institute/grID.

Following this step, the token verification may be carried out either online or using offline credentials.

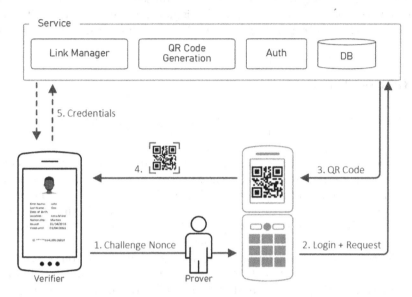

Fig. 4. Authentication protocol. The feature phone user (the Prover) authenticates to the user of a smartphone (the Verifier) by fetching and displaying a (single-use) QR code on the screen of their phone. The QR code token may encapsulate a digital signature, a URI or arbitrary other data. The recipient decodes the token and verifies the validity of the contents (if applicable) either locally or through a trusted online service.

Offline Credentials. The Verifier checks the integrity and validity of the token locally on their device (e.g., by verifying its digital signature). In particular, they ensure that the data is signed under the online service's public key along with the correct nonce. If the verification is successful, the Verifier accepts the Prover's claim (use case #1 in Sect. 3.1).

Note that in cases such as the Covid-19 certificates [5], the tokens do not need to be "fresh" and thus the nonce step can be omitted. The advantage of the nonce-free approach is that the feature phone user can use the microbrowser's cache to request tokens ahead of the time and use them later even in areas with no network coverage. In contrast, if the tokens, need to be newly-issued, the Verifier can request for the random nonce to be incorporated in the generated token.

Online Verification. Alternatively, the Verifier may use the trusted online service to fetch the user data. In this case, the token encoded in the QR code is simply a (single-use) URI that allows the Verifier to load the user's data from the service. To prevent replay attacks, where a user presents the same token several times the service should allow each URI to be used only once (use case #2 in Sect. 3.1).

Note that this protocol does not prevent the Verifier from launching relay attacks and impersonating the Prover to other Verifiers. More specifically, a malicious Verifier could use a delegate who will initiate a transaction with a victim Verifier and relay their nonce. In our use case, this is not a concern as the Verifier will not be able to claim government subsidy twice (the online service prevents token reuse).

5   Related Work

There are only a small number of digital identity and authentication applications for feature phones. Probably the most widely used example [16], although one which is increasingly being replaced owing to vulnerabilities [15,20], is the use of OTP codes as an authentication factor. These are usually sent to a mobile number which is registered to the account which a user is attempting to access. A notably more sophisticated application is Mobile-ID [13,14], a solution deployed in both in Estonia and Azerbaijan which makes use of a mobile phone SIM card as a government identity document. A special-purpose Mobile-ID SIM allows mobile devices to be used for access to e-Government services and to digitally sign documents. Unlike our solution, which focuses on the in-person presentation of signed user credentials, Mobile-ID is designed for remote authentication to online services. In Mobile-ID, the SIM card is used to compute a secure digital signature on a short verification code which is shown to the user through their web browser. Laud et al. [14] formally model and prove the security of Mobile-ID using the Proverif protocol verification tool.

Concerning feature phone authentication for payments, Baqer et al. [7] describe an offline payment protocol for feature phones based on exchanging short human-readable codes between payee and recipient. The authors evaluate the usability of their system with 19 participants in Nairobi who report positively upon the usability and perceived security of the system. Notably, users would visually display their authentication code to the recipient rather than to read it out loud, supporting the notion that machine-readable barcodes could be preferred. Baqer et al. also provide a more technical consideration of the short authentication codes, security and usability of their design [8]. Earlier work by Panjwani et al. [17] examines an Indian mobile banking service, Eko, and highlights a number of vulnerabilities as well as suggesting how to fix the existing scheme.

6   Conclusions

We have presented a previously overlooked approach that enables support for digital identity credentials in legacy mobile devices. Future works could further advance this direction with the use of SIM cards as a hardware root of trust for more secure authentication applications on all types of mobile devices. Such a development would greatly assist the efforts (e.g., smart-feature phones with KaiOS) to bring Internet access to the next billion globally.

Acknowledgments. This work was done for The Alan Turing institute. This work was supported, in whole or in part, by the Bill & Melinda Gates Foundation [INV-001309]. Under the grant conditions of the Foundation, a Creative Commons Attribution 4.0 Generic License has already been assigned to the Author Accepted Manuscript version that might arise from this submission.

References

1. WAP Service Developer's Guide for Nokia Series 30 Phones with WML Browser. Tech. rep., NOKIA (2003)
2. Automatic identification and data capture techniques - QR Code bar code symbology specification. Tech. rep., World Health Organisation (2015)
3. The Mobile Economy Sub-Saharan Africa 2020. Tech. rep., GSMA (2020)
4. EU Digital COVID Certificate Factsheet. Tech. rep., EU Commission (2021)
5. Interim guidance for developing a Smart Vaccination Certificate. Tech. rep., ISO/IEC (2021)
6. Two-dimensional code having rectangular region provided with specific patterns to specify cell positions and distinction from background, DENSO Wave Corporation (1994)
7. Baqer, K., Anderson, R., Mutegi, L., Payne, J.A., Sevilla, J.: Digitally: Piloting offline payments for phones. In: Thirteenth Symposium on Usable Privacy and Security (SOUPS 2017), USENIX Association (2017). https://www.usenix.org/conference/soups2017/technical-sessions/presentation/baqer
8. Baqer, K., Bezuidenhoudt, J., Anderson, R., Kuhn, M.: SMAPs: short message authentication protocols. In: Anderson, J., Matyáš, V., Christianson, B., Stajano, F. (eds.) Security Protocols 2016. LNCS, vol. 10368, pp. 119–132. Springer, Cham (2017). https://doi.org/10.1007/978-3-319-62033-6_15
9. Faltstrom, P., Ljunggren, F., Gulik, V.D.W.: The Base45 Data Encoding. Tech. rep, Active Internet-Draft, Network Working Group (2021)
10. Hughes, N., Lonie, S.: M-PESA: Mobile Money for the "Unbanked" Turning Cellphones into 24-Hour Tellers in Kenya. Technology, Governance, Globalization, Innovations (2007)
11. Jack, W., Suri, T.: Mobile money: The economics of m-pesa. Tech. rep, National Bureau of Economic Research (2011)
12. Krell, N.T., et al.: Smallholder farmers' use of mobile phone services in central Kenya. Climate and Development (2021)
13. Krimpe, J.: Mobile ID: crucial element of m-government. In: Proceedings of the 2014 Conference on Electronic Governance and Open Society: Challenges in Eurasia. Association for Computing Machinery (2014)
14. Laud, P., Roos, M.: Formal analysis of the estonian Mobile-ID protocol. In: Jøsang, A., Maseng, T., Knapskog, S.J. (eds.) NordSec 2009. LNCS, vol. 5838, pp. 271–286. Springer, Heidelberg (2009). https://doi.org/10.1007/978-3-642-04766-4_19
15. Lei, Z., Nan, Y., Fratantonio, Y., Bianchi, A.: On the insecurity of SMS one-time password messages against local attackers in modern mobile devices. In: Proceedings of the 2021 Network and Distributed System Security Symposium (2021)
16. Ma, S., et al.: An empirical study of SMS one-time password authentication in android apps. In: Association for Computing Machinery (2019)
17. Panjwani, S., Cutrell, E.: Usably Secure, Low-Cost Authentication for Mobile Banking. In: Association for Computing Machinery (2010)

18. Rescorla, E.: The transport layer security (TLS) protocol version 1.3 (2018)
19. Sharma, C., Nakamura, Y.: Wireless Data Services: Technologies, Business Models and Global Markets. Cambridge University Press, Cambridge (2003)
20. Yoo, C., Kang, B.-T., Kim, H.K.: Case study of the vulnerability of OTP implemented in internet banking systems of South Korea. Multimedia Tools Appl. **74**(10), 3289–3303 (2014). https://doi.org/10.1007/s11042-014-1888-3

Facial Recognition for Remote Electronic Voting – Missing Piece of the Puzzle or Yet Another Liability?

Sven Heiberg[1], Kristjan Krips[2,3], Jan Willemson[2(✉)] (iD), and Priit Vinkel[2,4] (iD)

[1] Smartmatic-Cybernetica Centre of Excellence for Internet Voting,
Soola 3, Tartu, Estonia
[2] Cybernetica, Narva mnt 20, Tartu, Estonia
[3] Institute of Computer Science, University of Tartu, Narva mnt 18, Tartu, Estonia
[4] State Electoral Office, Lossi plats 1a, Tallinn, Estonia

Abstract. Reliable voter identification is one of the key requirements to guarantee eligibility and uniformity of elections. In a remote setting, this task becomes more complicated compared to voter identification at a physical polling station. In case strong cryptographic mechanisms are not available, biometrics is one of the available alternatives to consider. In this paper, we take a closer look at facial recognition as a possible remote voter identification measure. We cover technical aspects of facial recognition relevant to voting, discuss the main architectural decisions, and analyse some of the remaining open problems, including dispute resolution and privacy issues.

1 Introduction

Recent years have set the stage for biometrics to be widely adopted by end-users. Fingerprint readers have become available for a large variety of smartphones, while more and more devices are being integrated with facial recognition systems. In parallel, FIDO Alliance and W3C have been working on the FIDO2 project to support passwordless authentication via browser API-s. This resulted in the WebAuthn specification, which was first published in 2019 [5]. It is complemented by the Client to Authenticator Protocol (CTAP), allowing FIDO2 enabled browsers to communicate with external authenticators like smartphones [6]. As a result, WebAuthn makes it possible for websites to authenticate users via smartphone-based biometric sensors [33].

The prospect of having easy access to biometric verification can have a significant impact on the field of remote voting. Apple has already hinted that they are thinking about iPhone based voting[1], which would likely have to contain a built-in authentication system. Thus, it is conceivable that in a few years, identity could be tied to users' smartphones. However, biometrics can also be

---

[1] https://www.businessinsider.com/apple-ceo-tim-cook-on-voting-technology-iphones-smartphones-2021-4.

© Springer Nature Switzerland AG 2021
A. Saracino and P. Mori (Eds.): ETAA 2021, LNCS 13136, pp. 77–93, 2021.
https://doi.org/10.1007/978-3-030-93747-8_6

utilized by the identity providers, be it the state government itself or commercial service providers.

Due to the hardware-based restrictions on end-user devices, there are two options to consider for biometric verification – based on fingerprints or facial images. The former can be bypassed by copying the fingerprints, creating master fingerprints or even by forcibly using the victim's finger to unlock the device [35,45,50]. The latter has had issues with liveness detection being bypassed [54]. However, the emergence of end-user devices that use special sensors for face recognition has raised the bar for attacks [17].

In principle, facial recognition has the potential to solve several issues that plague remote Internet voting (i-voting). First, it could act as an additional authentication factor, which could help to deploy remote voting to the settings where voters do not have a strong electronic identity. Second, facial recognition could be used as an additional measure to fight coercion. Third, active liveness detection could reduce the risk of voter's credentials being used without their knowledge. The latter could also partially mitigate the threat posed by malware located in the voter's device. By combining liveness detection based facial recognition with individual verifiability, it would be more difficult for malware to silently access voter's credentials or cryptographic tokens to cast a vote.

The aforementioned aspects seem promising, but they come with significant downsides, with the privacy issues being on the top of the list. For the additional security guarantees to work, facial recognition would have to be a mandatory part of the voting process. However, that would automatically disqualify the voters who do not have cameras of sufficient quality. In addition, by relying on biometrics, there are always cases of false positives and false negatives. Thus, biometric systems will inevitably fail to correctly identify some eligible voters and thereby limit access to their democratic rights.

Therefore, it seems that even in case facial recognition could be used for remote voting, it would have to have an alternative to allow all eligible voters to participate in elections. This brings us to the question of proportionality and the cost-benefit analysis. Thus, one of the goals of this study is to find out whether it is feasible to find a balance between the additional security features, privacy issues, and usability aspects. In addition, we aim to encourage further discussion and research in the context of using biometrics in elections.

This paper gives an overview of the possibilities for integrating facial recognition with remote electronic voting and discusses the risks of introducing such a feature. Section 2 gives an overview of state of the art, election-related aspects and deployment examples. Next, in Sect. 3, we give an overview of the architectural questions. This is followed by Sect. 4 that covers the general issues of integrating facial recognition into voting systems. Finally, Sect. 5 presents a discussion on further technical aspects, and Sect. 6 draws some conclusions.

2   State of the Art

2.1   Facial Recognition

Facial recognition consists of two main steps. First, faces have to be detected from an image and converted into a vector of facial features. Second, the captured facial features have to be compared with a reference value.

The complexity of the comparison task depends on whether there is a single predefined reference value available or the task is to find the matching facial feature vector from a large database. The former task is called facial verification, and it occurs, for example, when biometrics is used to unlock the phone or when a document photo is used as a reference value. The latter is called facial identification, and it may occur, e.g. in cases when a law enforcement agency needs to identify suspects. In this paper, we only focus on facial verification and consider this an addition to the existing authentication measures. Thus, we assume that election organizers already have a list of eligible voters and do not have to rely solely on facial recognition to identify voters.

Biometric solutions have an inherent issue with reliability as the biometric sensors do not always capture exactly the same measurements [41]. Thus, clever optimizations are used to compare the relevant values. However, as the biometric readings can vary even with the same person, there must be a threshold for identifying users. This results in false positive and false negative identifications. Their ratio depends on the selected matching threshold, which means that an optimal balance has to be found between these properties. For example, according to the Face Recognition Vendor Test by NIST, when the false positive rate is tuned to be below 0.00001, the corresponding false-negative rate is around 3% for the current best algorithms in case the images are taken in an uncontrolled (*wild*) environment.[2]

As facial verification may be performed in an uncontrolled environment, there have to be measures that prevent spoofing attacks. One obvious problem is detecting subject liveness, i.e. making sure that a still image is not shown into a camera instead of a real person. Active liveness detection methods ask the user to follow the given guidelines to either blink one's eyes, rotate the head, move the lips or raise an eyebrow [54]. A passive liveness detection functionality checks the consistency of the captured data. For example, it is possible to compare the texture of the face to identify spoofing attacks [28,40] and to use smartphone's motion sensors with the captured data to detect video replays [32]. However, a paper by Xu *et al.* published in 2016 showed that the aforementioned liveness detection measures could be bypassed by utilizing virtual reality systems to create 3D representations of faces [54]. One way to detect such an attack is to use hardware that contains sensors that measure the depth of the face.

---

[2] https://pages.nist.gov/frvt/html/frvt11.html.

2.2   Elections and Biometrics

Biometric identification of voters in the election process has been a viable alternative to manual identification at least for the last 20 years. Such identification methods have found acceptance in coherence with the introduction of other election technology innovations like ballot-scanning or electronic voting in polling stations [13]. The use of biometric data shows the greatest promise in situations where printed voter lists and physical identification documents do not offer the needed level of trustworthiness and accuracy. For example, according to [26], there were 28 countries in Africa using biometric voter registration (verification) in 2019. In the case of remote voting, the need to use biometric data for identifying the voters stems mainly from the lack of access to a viable electronic identification alternative [44].

In almost all of the current cases linked to elections or voting procedures, the use of biometrics is limited to a regulated and controlled environment, e.g. the polling station. The most common biometric characteristics used to identify voters are fingerprints and the visual appearance of the voter.

A report by Wolf *et al.* states that the accuracy of biometry used for identifying or verifying voters is strongly influenced by the quality of the data and the capturing environment [52]. All principles have to be seen as best practice and experience because there is no normative regulation or internationally regulated recommendations on this matter.

Besides false positive and false negative rates, there are two other important technical parameters of biometric identification or verification that have to be taken into account. The failure-to-capture rate describes the cases that prevent biometric data from being captured. The failure-to-enrol rate, at the same time, represents the cases where the quality of captured biometric data prevents a match to be found.

Voters affected by either of these issues can not be reliably identified or verified by biometrics. However, it is not possible to predict, which voters will not be able to use biometry. The aforementioned issues could occur regardless of whether the reference values are provided by the election organizer or the voter. Thus, all automatic identification or verification procedures should have a human fallback procedure and/or alternative solutions for problems that could disenfranchise numerous voters.

2.3   Some Facial Biometry Deployment Examples

Fiji has used biometrics (both facial images and fingerprints) for voter registration and maintaining the accuracy of the voters list (e.g. removing duplicates) [52].

Mongolia has gone a step further. Biometric information is also gathered in the voter registration process, but fingerprints are also scanned in the polling stations. The voter's fingerprint is matched against the registration database, and the voter's picture is displayed on a screen so that everyone in the polling station can identify the voter. The voter is then issued a paper receipt and may proceed to cast her vote [52].

Nigeria has had several generations of electronic identification projects. The latest one has been used for elections since 2011. The electoral roll (voter list) has biographical data of the voter along with 10 fingerprints and a facial image. In recent years the biometric data set has been loaded on permanent voter cards, which are used in the polling stations to verify voter identity. On election day, the voter is verified based on the pre-captured picture (manually by polling station workers) and by comparing the voter's scanned fingerprints to the available data. As the failure-to-capture rate of the verification process was regionally very different (due to equipment malfunction, faulty cards, etc.), all voters who were identified manually but had troubles authenticating based on biometrics were allowed to vote nevertheless [52].

Canada started to use mobile application based voting in early 2021 to facilitate House of Commons voting during COVID-19 conditions. Voting has to be performed on a parliament-managed smartphone which verifies the identities of Members of Parliament (MP) by using a facial recognition procedure. The official picture on file with the office is compared to a live photo taken with the help of a mobile device. As a fallback and an additional security layer, the whip of every party group has the right to verify the identity of the MP in case discrepancies are still present after two attempts of facial recognition. The MPs have 10 min to take up the voting procedure [25,42].

West Virginia, U.S. is one of several states piloting different versions of remote electronic voting for a limited number of voters residing abroad. In 2018, the state introduced voting via mobile phone for abroad voters. The voting procedure relied on a standalone application, which used facial recognition to verify voter identities. More specifically, the reference data was acquired by photographing an ID document, which was later compared to a live photo of the voter. After facial recognition, if available for the device, the voter provided a fingerprint for additional identification when prompted during the voting process. No alternative authentication methods were applied in case of facial recognition failure [21,36].

In addition to the above-mentioned examples, facial recognition has also been piloted or used for voter registration or identification purposes in several countries including Afghanistan[3], India[4], Ghana[5] and Tanzania [18].

3 Architectural Questions

Before it is possible to assess the impact of facial recognition, it has to be analysed how it can be integrated into i-voting systems. It turns out that there are both

---

[3] https://www.afghanistan-analysts.org/en/reports/political-landscape/afghanistans-2019-election-23-disputed-biometric-votes-endanger-election-results/.

[4] https://www.thehindu.com/news/national/telangana/telangana-state-election-commission-successfully-tests-facial-recognition-technique/article30627812.ece.

[5] https://www.idea.int/sites/default/files/managing-elections-under-covid-19-pandemic-conditions-the-case-of-ghana.pdf.

process-related and technological restrictions, which limit the applicability of facial recognition.

3.1 At Which Stage to Use Facial Recognition?

Voting is a multi-step process and there are potentially several steps where facial recognition can be integrated into.

The election organizer must already have a list of eligible voters as otherwise remote authentication would not be possible. Thus, we leave the process of voter registration out of scope and consider authentication as the main use case for facial recognition. This brings us to one of the core problems of i-voting, which is the necessity to reliably authenticate voters in a possibly malicious environment.

Following the approach familiar from the paper voting, biometric authentication can be used as a part of eligibility verification. The voter has to convince the authentication module of her identity before she is allowed to proceed. A separate question is whether biometric authentication is sufficient or should other identity verification mechanisms be used as well. In general, the answer to this question depends on the type of elections, used biometric technology, and whether an alternative authentication system is available. However, according to NIST's Digital Identity Guidelines, biometrics should only be used together with a physical authenticator [22].

It also has to be decided whether failure in facial recognition should block the voter from voting, potentially leaving the voter without the option of exercising her constitutional voting rights. In case no alternative authentication measures are available, the failure must be blocking as facial recognition is the only way to check eligibility.

If several authentication mechanisms are used in parallel, one needs to decide what to do if they do not concur. There is no universal, straightforward answer to this question, and it eventually comes down to dispute resolution mechanisms (see Sect. 4.1).

It may also be possible to integrate facial recognition into the vote submission stage. However, the above-mentioned problems remain. Additionally, the user experience will suffer as the voter would now be allowed to almost complete the voting process and is informed about a potential facial recognition failure only in the very end.

3.2 Compatibility with Different I-Voting Protocols

The possibility to integrate facial recognition into an existing i-voting protocol depends on the general architecture of the protocol along with the provided security guarantees. More specifically, the requirements for voter identity verification and participation privacy have to be evaluated. To get a better understanding of the area, we give our assessment on whether facial recognition could be integrated with different types of voter verification schemes.

There are several possible strategies for verifying voters in the remote electronic voting setting. In this paper, we will look at interactive authentication protocols, digital signatures, ring signatures, zero-knowledge proofs, anonymous credentials and blind signatures.

First, in the simplest case, the voters have to authenticate themselves before they are authorized to cast a vote. In general, there are two approaches for authentication – either the voter is given voting credentials during registration, or the voter uses a general-purpose authentication system. For example, this type of authentication has been used by Helios based voting schemes [1,9,16], Norwegian i-voting system [51], Swiss Post i-voting system [48], and the Estonian i-voting system [24]. In such cases, authentication is decoupled from vote casting, which in principle makes it easy to add facial recognition into the authentication step of the voting protocol.

Second, voters could be identified based on their ability to issue digital signatures. This is usually implemented by requiring voters to sign the ballots that are going to be submitted to an append-only bulletin board. This type of voter identification is used, for example, by the Estonian i-voting system[6] and by Selene [46]. As abstention can also show political preference [15, par. 54], votes with signatures pointing directly to the voters should not be simply uploaded to a public bulletin board. Similarly, it becomes questionable whether biometric verification results could be posted to a bulletin board. It is unlikely that even a numeric representation of biometric data could be shared on a bulletin board due to legislation, privacy concerns, and issues related to the reuse of biometric data. Thus, an additional authentication step would have to be introduced before voters are authorized to cast a vote. To adhere to the system's transparency, proof of a successful biometric match could be added to the bulletin board. This could be represented by a signature issued by the party responsible for performing the biometric verification. However, that would complicate the auditing process while still leaking the list of voters who participated in the election.

Third, eligibility verification can be built on top of ring signatures [43]. By issuing a ring signature, the identity of the signer remains anonymous. For example, this kind of approach is used by Eos [39]. Thus, voters are not explicitly authenticated, and bulletin boards do not contain information that could identify the voters. As the general idea of such an architecture is to protect the voter's anonymity, the thought of adding facial recognition seems to be counterproductive to the overall goal.

Fourth, voters can prove their identity by creating zero-knowledge proofs, for example, about the knowledge of their secret keys, while also protecting their participation privacy. This approach is used by KTV-Helios [31]. It becomes apparent that in case the election system is designed to achieve participation privacy, facial recognition would conflict with that goal.

Fifth, voters can use anonymous credentials, which are blindly compared by the election system against the list of registered voters. Such an approach is used by JCJ [27] based voting systems like NV-Civitas [37] and Selections [14]. JCJ is built on top of the coercion resistance definition by Juels *et al.* [27], which

---

[6] The Estonian i-voting system also requires voters to explicitly authenticate themselves before they are allowed to sign their ballots.

also states that it should not be possible to force voters to abstain. Thereby, it must not be possible to prove whether a voter participated in the elections. To protect voter's privacy, the anonymous credentials are validated by relying on zero-knowledge proofs and mix-nets. Thereby, facial recognition is not compatible with the voting phase as the vote casting act is designed to be anonymous. However, the critical step in the aforementioned schemes lies in the registration phase, which is assumed to be performed by eligible voters. Thus, the registration process could be augmented with biometrics-based authentication like facial recognition.

Sixth, the identification protocol can rely on blind signatures as proposed by David Chaum already in the 1980s [11,12]. For example, the voting system proposed by Okamoto integrated blind signatures into the authorization phase [38]. This allows the voting system to check eligibility during registration while remaining oblivious of whether the voter has cast a vote or not. Thus, facial recognition could only be used to check eligibility before issuing a blind signature.

3.3   Is a Semi-controlled Voting Environment Achievable?

One of the key characteristics of remote electronic voting has been the uncontrolled voting environment. For the polling stations, there are rules determining what a polling station should be like – there usually are mandatory elements (e.g. ballot boxes), mandatory activities (e.g. sealing of those ballot boxes), forbidden elements (e.g. campaign materials) and people responsible for maintaining the order (e.g. election officials). In the case of remote electronic voting, no such preconditions hold, which often leads to the question of coercion.

In a polling station, election officials help to ensure that everybody has a chance to vote alone. In the remote setting, this kind of prevention is not possible. A number of mitigating measures have been proposed in the literature; see [30] for an overview. In practice, for example, the option of re-voting has been implemented in Estonia [34] and Norway [51]. However, this measure has also been disputed both legally and in the academic literature [9,19,34].

Given that facial recognition could be used to verify that the voter is really present when the corresponding credentials are being used to cast a vote, it is appealing to extend this idea and check the suitability of the voting environment to make sure that the voter is truly not in a coercive situation. In case video streams are already used for facial recognition and liveness detection, the length of the stream could be extended to cover the entire voting process such that the and the whole remote voting environment could be monitored.

This approach would not be novel, e.g. it has been already used in remote examinations to prevent cheating [2]. Such systems ask the examinee to switch on the microphone and use the camera to show the room before the examination can start. Additional passive and active restriction and monitoring methods may be used. Sometimes the examinee is under-recorded surveillance throughout the process. It may last hours with specific restrictions such as the requirement to stay visible, not to talk, not to cover ears or mouth, etc.

This approach is technologically feasible and may be politically appealing but comes with several caveats.

1. The proctoring systems come with negative cognitive side-effects. For example, a study published in 2021 described the accompanying risks like the anxiety of being watched on camera [3].
2. The proctoring systems complicate the requirements for the device suitable for voting and for the network throughput to ensure a steady stream throughout the process.
3. Since proctoring systems usually involve a human being in monitoring the process; it is going to reduce the throughput and increase the cost of online voting.

This kind of approach also raises questions about voter privacy. More specifically, whether the efficiency of this measure in mitigating the risk of coercion is sufficient to justify voting under surveillance. While privacy-preserving facial recognition could solve some of the privacy issues, its low performance prevents large scale deployments [10]. In addition, it is rather unclear if it would convince the layman of the trustworthiness of the system.

Without relying on privacy-preserving technologies, there is a significant risk that the voter could accidentally reveal the voting credentials or the vote itself, thereby violating the vote secrecy requirement. For example, this could happen in case the voter has written down the credentials or candidate names, but also in case the camera is pointed towards reflective materials [4,53]. In addition, a video of hand gestures can leak information even when the keyboard is not visible [47,49]. Thus, it is the opinion of the authors that such an anti-coercion measure will not be accepted by democratic societies due to the accompanying privacy issues.

4   General Issues with Facial Recognition

4.1   How to Resolve Disputes?

Biometric authentication is probabilistic, which means that facial recognition is not guaranteed to produce the correct outcome. In addition, the algorithms can be biased due to the used training data.

For example, a study performed in 2018 revealed that the facial analysis benchmark datasets Adience and IJB-A over-represented lighter-skinned subjects, with the former consisting of 86.2% and the latter 79.6% of the samples [7]. The study also tested three commercial gender classification systems and found that the classification error for dark-skinned females can reach up to 34.7%. Such an outcome is illustrated with real-life examples. As an extreme case, it was claimed by the Detroit Police Chief that facial recognition software misidentifies subjects 95% of the time[7].

---

[7] https://www.vice.com/en/article/dyzykz/detroit-police-chief-facial-recognition-software-misidentifies-96-of-the-time.

A NIST study from 2019 compared more than one hundred facial recognition algorithms and identified that many of them tend to have a demographic bias due to the used training data [23]. Still, the best performing identification and verification algorithms did not show a significant demographic bias.

However, it was already mentioned in Sect. 2 that even the best algorithms could have a false negative rate of around 3%. This share is significant enough to require dispute and compensation mechanisms to be implemented. If automated facial recognition algorithms fail to identify or verify the voter reliably, the only real alternative is a human. This means that the voter identification or verification protocol must allow for a fallback to a human operator and that a team of operators must be available throughout the whole voting period.

Due to the uneven distribution of voting events, it might not be possible to do human verification in real-time. Thus, a question arises on how to store the captured images so that voter's privacy would not be violated. What happens in case a human verifier decides that the captured photo does not match the reference image? If the verification is done in real-time, the voter could restart the process and take another photo. However, with a delayed verification there are two paths to take. Either the voter is allowed to cast a vote with the pending facial verification result, or the voter is put on hold. In the former case, the voters may get a false sense of their ballots being accepted, while the latter might prevent voters from voting at all.

Another interesting question focuses on the post-election audits in case the facial verification images are stored. What happens if an auditor decides that some of the facial verifications resulted in an incorrect match? If the voting system is designed to protect ballot secrecy, it should no longer be possible to match ballots with the voter identities. Thus, such audits and disputes should be handled during the election period.

4.2   Privacy

Regardless of the other factors, the main barrier to implementing facial recognition is the risk to voter's privacy. Depending on the implementation, voter's private data could be leaked in multiple ways.

The main presumption for facial recognition-based identity verification is the existence of a reference data set, which the captured facial image could be compared to. Unless voters have already shared their biometric data with the government, it is unlikely that facial recognition could be used for remote voting. Thus, the first step for the election organiser is to check whether any existing government databases could be used for this purpose. An alternative is to use government-issued ID-s that contain a photograph.

There are several commercial services that offer document-based facial recognition. In general, they require the state-issued document to be scanned with the smartphone, with the resulting image used as a reference for performing facial recognition-based identity verification. However, relying on a commercial service to handle biometrics for something as critical as elections raises multiple questions. First, voters may not feel comfortable revealing to a third party that they participated in the elections. Second, the service provider could, in principle, create a data set consisting of all eligible voters. Third, by performing facial recognition, some background is also captured by the camera. This raises the question of who has access to these images as they might contain private information about voters homes.

Initially, it may seem that the answer to the aforementioned issues lies in locally performed facial matching, for example, by using the voters' smartphones. However, it quickly becomes clear that offline facial recognition involves risks that could lead to the measure being bypassed. For example, the facial recognition application running in a hostile environment could be tampered with. Thus, an active process involving the server is required to prevent the matching result from being locally modified. On the other hand, voters may not be comfortable with their photos being sent to the voting system or a third-party service provider. Such a design would also not work with voting protocols that protect voter's privacy already when the ballot is being submitted as described in Sect. 3.2.

Another interesting question concerns the transparency of the facial recognition system. The owners of proprietary services are not motivated in disclosing how their liveness check is implemented to prevent it from being bypassed. Thus, it is unlikely that the facial recognition components would be fully open source. This is not a major issue in case facial recognition is decoupled from the voting application, as in such a design it would not prevent the voting client from being fully open-source.

5   Discussion

In case facial recognition is integrated into the authentication phase, it would effectively become an additional authentication factor. Therefore, the question of whether facial recognition should be included in remote online voting becomes a question about voter authentication.

There are multiple ways how voter's credentials could be accessed without the voter's knowledge or permission. This could happen due to the usage of an insecure distribution channel like email, SMS, or post. However, the credentials could also be maliciously accessed by malware or family members. By including facial recognition in the authentication phase, such attacks become more difficult to conduct.

In case existing authentication solutions already rely on cryptographic tokens that are delivered over a secure channel, facial recognition could be added as a liveness check. This could deter malware from using the cryptographic tokens without the voter's knowledge and make it more difficult for family members to use the tokens. However, the latter holds only in case the facial recognition technology includes a liveness detection system that is difficult to spoof.

Even when such a system could be implemented, its reliability would depend on the environment, end-user devices, and usability aspects. As facial recognition is sensitive to the surroundings, the background and reduced lighting conditions can lower the accuracy of voter identification [55]. Besides that, voters might be reluctant to adopt the technology due to privacy issues, demographic bias [7], or cultural aspects. For example, it has been argued that some women won't be able to vote in Afghanistan due to the usage of facial recognition[8].

The unconstrained voting environment creates the need to support cameras with varying levels of quality. For example, the web cameras integrated into laptops tend to be outperformed by external web cameras[9]. In addition, our interviews with the facial recognition service providers revealed that smartphone-based face recognition is preferred due to their cameras being superior to cameras used on desktop computers.

In case the voting system has to rely on low-quality web cameras, it would be difficult to predict the error rate. Thus, there is a strong incentive only to support smartphone-based facial recognition. However, as a negative side-effect, that would disenfranchise the voters who do not have or can not use a smartphone. Of course, the election system might support other voting options, but these may also not be available to some voters. In case of technology would significantly simplify the voting process for only a part of the electorate, it would effectively result in an increase of inequality regarding voting freedom.

The possibility to introduce biometry depends on multiple aspects like the jurisdiction, end-user devices, and the quality of reference datasets. For example, the EU's GDPR sets limitations for processing special categories of personal data. According to Article 9 of GDPR, the usage of biometric data is very limited unless the subjects give their explicit consent [20]. Thus, each voting event should be analysed in the given context when planning to introduce biometric identity verification.

6   Conclusions

We have described in this paper that facial recognition has the potential to solve several issues that plague remote online voting. It could act as an additional authentication factor, it could be extended to an additional measure to fight coercion, or it could be used to reduce the risk of voter's credentials being used without their knowledge, which would hinder both malware and human adversaries.

On the other hand, introducing facial recognition for remote electronic voting has implications. In order to gain most of the benefits, facial recognition must be a mandatory component of the online voting process. This requires reliable technology both on the system side end and on the voter end since recognition failure disenfranchises the voter.

The nature of facial recognition raises privacy issues which are most evident in the potential semi-controlled remote voting environment, where the voter

---

[8] https://www.rferl.org/a/biometrics-to-end-fraud-in-afghan-election-may-discourag e-some-women-from-voting/30131049.html.

[9] https://www.logitech.com/assets/41349/logitech--why-a-better-webcam-matters. ENG.pdf.

would have to prove that the space is suitable for remote voting. Also, capturing a video stream for liveness detection raises the question of whether this level of privacy breach is proportional to the gained benefit.

There are a few positive use cases of facial recognition in the context of voting. The example from Canada highlights that facial recognition can work well for public remote voting, which is often required in parliaments and the governing bodies of local municipalities. The example from Fiji highlights that facial recognition can be an efficient tool for voter registration.

We conclude that the added complexity and privacy breach does not justify the use of facial recognition for remote online voting in case there is a well established, cryptographically secure mechanism for verifying the voter's eligibility. We would expect this mechanism to be multi-purpose to reduce the incentive for the voters to hand this mechanism over to somebody else.

However, in the cases where there is no existing mechanism for authentication in the remote setting, the introduction of remote voting implies the need to register online voters and provide them with credentials. One way to do this would be to create a PKI based system for distributing credentials. However, in case this is not possible, facial recognition could be a suitable tool to support registration, act as an additional authentication factor, and reduce the misuse of the credentials. When done locally by using the document photo as a reference, some of the accompanying risks can be mitigated.

Of course, introducing any form of biometrics to elections is not an easy decision to take due to the associated risks and ethical issues. However, when considering the integrity of elections, it has to be discussed how to replace the authentication mechanisms in voting systems, which rely on credentials delivered over post or email [8, 29]. Thus, one of the aims of our work is to encourage further discussion on the possibilities and issues related to different authentication methods, including biometrics.

Acknowledgements. This paper has been supported by the Estonian Research Council under grant number PRG920. The authors are grateful to the Estonian Information System Authority and State Electoral Office for their support of the research process.

References

1. Adida, B.: Helios: web-based open-audit voting. In: van Oorschot, P.C. (ed.) Proceedings of the 17th USENIX Security Symposium, pp. 335–348. USENIX Association (2008). http://www.usenix.org/events/sec08/tech/full_papers/adida/adida.pdf

2. Arnò, S., Galassi, A., Tommasi, M., Saggino, A., Vittorini, P.: State-of-the-art of commercial proctoring systems and their use in academic online exams. Int. J. Distance Educ. Technol. (IJDET) **19**(2), 55–76 (2021). https://doi.org/10.4018/IJDET.20210401.oa3

3. Asgari, S., Trajkovic, J., Rahmani, M., Zhang, W., Lo, R.C., Sciortino, A.: An observational study of engineering online education during the COVID-19 pandemic. PLoS ONE **16**(4), 1–17 (2021). https://doi.org/10.1371/journal.pone.0250041

4. Backes, M., Chen, T., Dürmuth, M., Lensch, H.P.A., Welk, M.: Tempest in a teapot: compromising reflections revisited. In: 30th IEEE Symposium on Security and Privacy (S&P 2009), Oakland, California, USA, 17–20 May 2009, pp. 315–327. IEEE Computer Society (2009). https://doi.org/10.1109/SP.2009.20

5. Balfanz, D., et al.: Web authentication: an API for accessing public key credentials level 1. W3C recommendation, W3C, March 2019. https://www.w3.org/TR/2019/REC-webauthn-1-20190304/

6. Brand, C., et al.: Client to authenticator protocol (CTAP). Proposed standard, FIDO Alliance, January 2019. https://fidoalliance.org/specs/fido-v2.0-ps-20190130/fido-client-to-authenticator-protocol-v2.0-ps-20190130.html

7. Buolamwini, J., Gebru, T.: Gender shades: intersectional accuracy disparities in commercial gender classification. In: Conference on Fairness, Accountability and Transparency, FAT 2018. Proceedings of Machine Learning Research, vol. 81, pp. 77–91. PMLR (2018). http://proceedings.mlr.press/v81/buolamwini18a.html

8. Cardillo, A., Akinyokun, N., Essex, A.: Online voting in Ontario municipal elections: a conflict of legal principles and technology? In: Krimmer, R., et al. (eds.) E-Vote-ID 2019. LNCS, vol. 11759, pp. 67–82. Springer, Cham (2019). https://doi.org/10.1007/978-3-030-30625-0_5

9. Chaidos, P., Cortier, V., Fuchsbauer, G., Galindo, D.: BeleniosRF: a non-interactive receipt-free electronic voting scheme. In: Proceedings of ACM CCS 2016, pp. 1614–1625. ACM (2016). https://doi.org/10.1145/2976749.2978337

10. Chamikara, M.A.P., Bertók, P., Khalil, I., Liu, D., Camtepe, S.: Privacy preserving face recognition utilizing differential privacy. Comput. Secur. **97**, 101951 (2020). https://doi.org/10.1016/j.cose.2020.101951

11. Chaum, D.: Security without identification: transaction systems to make big brother obsolete. Commun. ACM **28**(10), 1030–1044 (1985). https://doi.org/10.1145/4372.4373

12. Chaum, D.: Elections with unconditionally-secret ballots and disruption equivalent to breaking RSA. In: Barstow, D., et al. (eds.) EUROCRYPT 1988. LNCS, vol. 330, pp. 177–182. Springer, Heidelberg (1988). https://doi.org/10.1007/3-540-45961-8_15

13. Cheeseman, N., Lynch, G., Willis, J.: Digital dilemmas: the unintended consequences of election technology. Democratization **25**(8), 1397–1418 (2018)

14. Clark, J., Hengartner, U.: Selections: internet voting with over-the-shoulder coercion-resistance. In: Danezis, G. (ed.) FC 2011. LNCS, vol. 7035, pp. 47–61. Springer, Heidelberg (2012). https://doi.org/10.1007/978-3-642-27576-0_4

15. Code of Good Practice in Electoral Matters: Guidelines and Explanatory Report (2002). European Commission for Democracy Through Law (Venice Commission). https://rm.coe.int/090000168092af01

16. Cortier, V., Galindo, D., Glondu, S., Izabachène, M.: Election verifiability for Helios under weaker trust assumptions. In: Kutyłowski, M., Vaidya, J. (eds.) ESORICS 2014. LNCS, vol. 8713, pp. 327–344. Springer, Cham (2014). https://doi.org/10.1007/978-3-319-11212-1_19

17. Das, A., Galdi, C., Han, H., Ramachandra, R., Dugelay, J., Dantcheva, A.: Recent advances in biometric technology for mobile devices. In: 9th IEEE International Conference on Biometrics Theory, Applications and Systems, pp. 1–11. IEEE (2018). https://doi.org/10.1109/BTAS.2018.8698587

18. Dziva, C., Musara, E., Chigora, P.: Democratisation and securitisation of Zimbabwe's national elections: opportunities and challenges of biometric voter registration. J. Public Adm. Dev. Altern. (JPADA) **5**(1), 48–62 (2020)

19. E-valimiste turvalisuse töörühma koondaruanne. Estonian Ministry of Economic Affairs and Communications (2019). https://www.mkm.ee/sites/default/files/content-editors/e-valimiste_tooruhma_koondaruanne_12.12.2019_0.pdf. in Estonian

20. European Parliament, Council of the European Union: Regulation (EU) 2016/679 of the European Parliament and of the Council of 27 April 2016 on the protection of natural persons with regard to the processing of personal data and on the free movement of such data, and repealing directive 95/46/EC (General Data Protection Regulation). https://eur-lex.europa.eu/legal-content/EN/TXT/PDF/?uri=OJ:L:2016:119:FULL&from=EN

21. Fowler, A.: Promises and perils of mobile voting. Election Law J. Rules Polit. Policy **19**(3), 418–431 (2020)

22. Grassi, P., et al.: Digital identity guidelines: authentication and lifecycle management [includes updates as of 03–02–2020] (2020). https://doi.org/10.6028/NIST.SP.800-63b

23. Grother, P., Ngan, M., Hanaoka, K.: Face Recognition Vendor Test (FRVT) Part 3: Demographic Effects (2019). https://nvlpubs.nist.gov/nistpubs/ir/2019/NIST.IR.8280.pdf

24. Heiberg, S., Martens, T., Vinkel, P., Willemson, J.: Improving the verifiability of the Estonian internet voting scheme. In: Krimmer, R., et al. (eds.) E-Vote-ID 2016. LNCS, vol. 10141, pp. 92–107. Springer, Cham (2017). https://doi.org/10.1007/978-3-319-52240-1_6

25. House of Commons, Canada: Fact Sheet of Hybrid Voting Process in the House of Commons (2021). https://www.ourcommons.ca/Content/Newsroom/Articles/Factsheet-ElectronicVotingSystem-e-Final-02-25.pdf

26. Jacobsen, K.L.: Biometric voter registration: a new modality of democracy assistance? Coop. Confl. **55**(1), 127–148 (2020)

27. Juels, A., Catalano, D., Jakobsson, M.: Coercion-resistant electronic elections. In: Proceedings of WPES 2005, pp. 61–70. ACM (2005)

28. Kim, G., Eum, S., Suhr, J.K., Kim, I., Park, K.R., Kim, J.: Face liveness detection based on texture and frequency analyses. In: 5th IAPR International Conference on Biometrics, ICB 2012, New Delhi, India, 29 March–1 April 2012, pp. 67–72. IEEE (2012). https://doi.org/10.1109/ICB.2012.6199760

29. Krips, K., Kubjas, I., Willemson, J.: An internet voting protocol with distributed verification receipt generation. In: Proceedings of the Third International Joint Conference on Electronic Voting E-Vote-ID 2018, Bregenz, Austria, 2–5 October 2018, pp. 128–146. TalTech Press (2018). https://digikogu.taltech.ee/en/item/0050d4bb-192b-4531-8e23-ccf8b565222e

30. Krips, K., Willemson, J.: On practical aspects of coercion-resistant remote voting systems. In: Krimmer, R., et al. (eds.) E-Vote-ID 2019. LNCS, vol. 11759, pp. 216–232. Springer, Cham (2019). https://doi.org/10.1007/978-3-030-30625-0_14

31. Kulyk, O., Teague, V., Volkamer, M.: Extending Helios towards private eligibility verifiability. In: Haenni, R., Koenig, R.E., Wikström, D. (eds.) VOTELID 2015. LNCS, vol. 9269, pp. 57–73. Springer, Cham (2015). https://doi.org/10.1007/978-3-319-22270-7_4

32. Li, Y., Li, Y., Yan, Q., Kong, H., Deng, R.H.: Seeing your face is not enough: an inertial sensor-based liveness detection for face authentication. In: Proceedings of the 22nd ACM SIGSAC Conference on Computer and Communications Security, pp. 1558–1569. ACM (2015). https://doi.org/10.1145/2810103.2813612

33. Lyastani, S.G., Schilling, M., Neumayr, M., Backes, M., Bugiel, S.: Is FIDO2 the kingslayer of user authentication? A comparative usability study of FIDO2 pass-wordless authentication. In: 2020 IEEE Symposium on Security and Privacy, SP 2020, pp. 268–285. IEEE (2020). https://doi.org/10.1109/SP40000.2020.00047

34. Madise, Ü., Martens, T.: E-voting in Estonia 2005. The first practice of country-wide binding internet voting in the world. In: Electronic Voting 2006: 2nd International Workshop, Co-Organized by Council of Europe, ESF TED, IFIP WG 8.6 and E-Voting.CC. LNI, vol. P-86, pp. 15–26. GI (2006)

35. Marasco, E., Ross, A.: A survey on antispoofing schemes for fingerprint recognition systems. ACM Comput. Surv. **47**(2), 28:1–28:36 (2014). https://doi.org/10.1145/2617756

36. Moore, L., Sawhney, N.: Under the Hood: The West Virginia Mobile Voting Pilot (2019). https://sos.wv.gov/FormSearch/Elections/Informational/West-Virginia-Mobile-Voting-White-Paper-NASS-Submission.pdf

37. Neumann, S., Volkamer, M.: Civitas and the real world: problems and solutions from a practical point of view. In: Seventh International Conference on Availability, Reliability and Security, ARES 2012, Prague, pp. 180–185. IEEE Computer Society (2012). https://doi.org/10.1109/ARES.2012.75

38. Okamoto, T.: Receipt-free electronic voting schemes for large scale elections. In: Christianson, B., Crispo, B., Lomas, M., Roe, M. (eds.) Security Protocols 1997. LNCS, vol. 1361, pp. 25–35. Springer, Heidelberg (1998). https://doi.org/10.1007/BFb0028157

39. Patachi, Ş, Schürmann, C.: Eos a universal verifiable and coercion resistant voting protocol. In: Krimmer, R., Volkamer, M., Braun Binder, N., Kersting, N., Pereira, O., Schürmann, C. (eds.) E-Vote-ID 2017. LNCS, vol. 10615, pp. 210–227. Springer, Cham (2017). https://doi.org/10.1007/978-3-319-68687-5_13

40. Peixoto, B., Michelassi, C., Rocha, A.: Face liveness detection under bad illumination conditions. In: Macq, B., Schelkens, P. (eds.) 18th IEEE International Conference on Image Processing, ICIP 2011, pp. 3557–3560. IEEE (2011). https://doi.org/10.1109/ICIP.2011.6116484

41. Prabhakar, S., Pankanti, S., Jain, A.K.: Biometric recognition: security and privacy concerns. IEEE Secur. Priv. **1**(2), 33–42 (2003). https://doi.org/10.1109/MSECP.2003.1193209

42. Aiello, R.: A historic first: MPs hold House of Commons votes by app (2021). https://www.ctvnews.ca/politics/a-historic-first-mps-hold-house-of-commons-votes-by-app-1.5338151

43. Rivest, R.L., Shamir, A., Tauman, Y.: How to leak a secret. In: Boyd, C. (ed.) ASIACRYPT 2001. LNCS, vol. 2248, pp. 552–565. Springer, Heidelberg (2001). https://doi.org/10.1007/3-540-45682-1_32

44. Rosacker, K.M., Rosacker, R.E.: Voting is a right: a decade of societal, technological and experiential progress towards the goal of remote-access voting. Transforming Government: People, Process and Policy (2020)

45. Roy, A., Memon, N.D., Ross, A.: MasterPrint: exploring the vulnerability of partial fingerprint-based authentication systems. IEEE Trans. Inf. Forensics Secur. **12**(9), 2013–2025 (2017). https://doi.org/10.1109/TIFS.2017.2691658

46. Ryan, P.Y.A., Rønne, P.B., Iovino, V.: Selene: voting with transparent verifiability and coercion-mitigation. In: Clark, J., Meiklejohn, S., Ryan, P.Y.A., Wallach, D., Brenner, M., Rohloff, K. (eds.) FC 2016. LNCS, vol. 9604, pp. 176–192. Springer, Heidelberg (2016). https://doi.org/10.1007/978-3-662-53357-4_12

47. Sabra, M., Maiti, A., Jadliwala, M.: Zoom on the keystrokes: exploiting video calls for keystroke inference attacks. In: 28th Annual Network and Distributed System Security Symposium, NDSS 2021, Virtually, 21–25 February 2021. The Internet Society (2021). https://www.ndss-symposium.org/ndss-paper/zoom-on-the-keystrokes-exploiting-video-calls-for-keystroke-inference-attacks/
48. Scytl: individual verifiability, Swiss Post E-voting protocol explained. Technical report, Swiss Post, November 2017. https://www.post.ch/-/media/post/evoting/dokumente/swiss-post-online-voting-protocol-explained.pdf?la=de
49. Shukla, D., Kumar, R., Serwadda, A., Phoha, V.V.: Beware, your hands reveal your secrets! In: Proceedings of the 2014 ACM SIGSAC Conference on Computer and Communications Security, Scottsdale, AZ, USA, 3–7 November 2014, pp. 904–917. ACM (2014). https://doi.org/10.1145/2660267.2660360
50. Shweiki, O., Lee, Y.: Compelled use of biometric keys to unlock a digital device: deciphering recent legal developments. United States Attorneys' Bull. **67**(1), 23–42 (2019)
51. Stenerud, I.S.G., Bull, C.: When reality comes knocking Norwegian experiences with verifiable electronic voting. In: Proceedings of EVOTE 2012. LNI, vol. P-205, pp. 21–33. GI (2012)
52. Wolf, P., Alim, A., Kasaro, B., Namugera, P., Saneem, M., Zorigt, T.: Introducing biometric technology in elections. International Institute for Democracy and Electoral Assistance (2017). https://www.idea.int/sites/default/files/publications/introducing-biometric-technology-in-elections-reissue.pdf
53. Xu, Y., Heinly, J., White, A.M., Monrose, F., Frahm, J.: Seeing double: reconstructing obscured typed input from repeated compromising reflections. In: Sadeghi, A., Gligor, V.D., Yung, M. (eds.) 2013 ACM SIGSAC Conference on Computer and Communications Security, CCS 2013, Berlin, Germany, 4–8 November 2013, pp. 1063–1074. ACM (2013). https://doi.org/10.1145/2508859.2516709
54. Xu, Y., Price, T., Frahm, J., Monrose, F.: Virtual U: defeating face liveness detection by building virtual models from your public photos. In: 25th USENIX Security Symposium, pp. 497–512. USENIX Association (2016). https://www.usenix.org/conference/usenixsecurity16/technical-sessions/presentation/xu
55. Zhao, W., Chellappa, R., Phillips, P.J., Rosenfeld, A.: Face recognition: a literature survey. ACM Comput. Surv. **35**(4), 399–458 (2003). https://doi.org/10.1145/954339.954342

Integrating a Pentesting Tool for IdM Protocols in a Continuous Delivery Pipeline

Andrea Bisegna[1,2]([⊠]), Roberto Carbone[1]([⊠]), and Silvio Ranise[1,3]([⊠])

[1] Security and Trust, Fondazione Bruno Kessler, Trento, Italy
{a.bisegna,carbone,ranise}@fbk.eu
[2] DIBRIS, University of Genova, Genova, Italy
[3] Department of Mathematics, University of Trento, Trento, Italy

Abstract. Identity Management (IdM) solutions are increasingly important for digital infrastructures of both enterprises and public administrations. Their security is a mandatory prerequisite for building trust in current and future digital ecosystems. IdM solutions are usually large-scale complex software systems maintained and developed by several groups of ICT professionals. Continuous Delivery (CD) pipeline is adopted to make maintenance, extension, and deployment of such solutions as efficient and repeatable as possible. For security, CD pipeline is also used as a continuous risk assessment to quickly evaluate the security impact of changes. Several tools have been developed and integrated in the CD pipeline to support this view in the so called DevSecOps approach with the notable exception of a tool for protocol pentesting and compliance against standards such as SAML 2.0, OAuth 2.0 and OpenID Connect. To fill this gap, we propose an approach to integrate Micro-Id-Gym—a tool for the automated pentesting of IdM deployments—in a CD pipeline. We report our experience in doing this and discuss the advantages of using the tool in the context of a joint effort with Poligrafico e Zecca dello Stato Italiano to build a digital identity infrastructure.

1 Introduction

Identity Management (IdM) implementations exchange authentication assertions and consist of a series of messages in a preset sequence designed to protect information as it travels through networks or between servers. By using third-party authentication, IdM protocols eliminate the necessity of storing authentication information within the services for which they are used, providing a solution that helps private and public organizations prevent the misuse or abuse of login credentials and reduce the risk of data breaches.

This work was partially funded by the Horizon 2020 project "Strategic Programs for Advanced Research and Technology in Europe" (SPARTA), grant agreement No. 830892, and by the Italian National Mint and Printing House (Istituto Poligrafico e Zecca dello Stato).

A. Saracino and P. Mori (Eds.): ETAA 2021, LNCS 13136, pp. 94–110, 2021.
https://doi.org/10.1007/978-3-030-93747-8_7

IdM protocol standards—including the Security Assertion Markup Language 2.0 (hereafter SAML) [1], OpenID Connect (OIDC) [2], and OAuth 2.0 (OAuth) [3]—handle user requests for access to services and deliver responses based on the information a user provides. If the authentication methods, such as a password or a biometric identifier, are correct, the protocol allows the level of access assigned to the user within the service. Existing IdM protocols support policies (such as allowing password authenticated users to only read financial data while permitting also to perform payments to those authenticated by using two authentication factors) by securing assertions and ensuring their integrity during transfer. They include standards for security to simplify access management, aid in compliance, and create a uniform user experience. For instance, both SAML and OIDC support the so-called Single Sign-On (SSO) experience whereby one set of credentials allows users to access multiple services.

To have a robust security in an IdM implementation, following the compliance with the standard is extremely important. In some case, like it happens in SPID [4], it is required to ensure compliance with both the technical and legal rules defined in the regulations.

Given the many advantages of IdM protocols standard, they have been widely adopted in many different scenarios encompassing corporate organizations (typically adopting SAML), cloud platforms (e.g., Google uses both OIDC and OAuth), and both national and international infrastructures for digital identity such as those in Europe (e.g., SPID in Italy is based on SAML and similarly the eIDAS framework for identity portability across Member States is also based on SAML). Despite being used on a large scale and for many years, the deployment of these IdM protocols has proved to be difficult and fraught with pitfalls. This is so mainly because such protocols inherit the difficulties of designing, implementing, and deploying the cryptographic mechanisms on top of which they are built. Even assuming that the design of IdM protocols is secure, implementations add complexity by specifying functional details (such as message formats and session state) while deployments include further aspects (such as programming interfaces) that are absent at the design level. These additions may bring low-level threats (such as missing checks of the content in certain message fields and vulnerabilities of functions imported from third party libraries) thereby significantly enlarging the attack surface of deployed IdM protocols. There is a long line of papers devoted to the identification of vulnerabilities and attacks in deployed IdM protocols at design, implementation, and deployment level see, e.g., [5–8].

Indeed, preventing such varied attacks on large IdM solutions that use complex cryptographic mechanisms is a daunting task that requires automated assistance to meet also the strict temporal constraints of delivering software systems to production environments frequently and in a safe way by adopting the Continuous Delivery software engineering methodology. This methodology has steadily gained adoption although it is difficult to reconcile with traditional security testing and analysis techniques such as penetration testing or static and dynamic analysis that take substantial time and need expertise to interpret the results (e.g., to eliminate false positives). In this context, not only automation becomes even more important to identify vulnerabilities but also the capability to provide actionable security suggestions to software developers with little security awareness is crucial to reduce security risks to an acceptable level. The advantage of actionable security suggestions is twofold: (i) they speed up the process of fixing vulnerabilities while facilitating the creation of security awareness among developers and (ii) they allow security experts to focus on more complex security issues possibly contributing to further decrease security risks.

In this paper, we present our experience of integrating a pentesting tool for IdM protocols (called Micro-Id-Gym [9]) in the Continuous Delivery pipeline for deploying the Italian digital identity solution based on the electronic identity card (Carta d'Identitá Elettronica 3.0) that we are collaborating to develop in the context of a joint effort with the Italian National Mint and Printing House (IPZS, Poligrafico e Zecca dello Stato Italiano). We describe how the capability of Micro-Id-Gym to automatically perform a battery of tests derived from the IdM protocols standards and include actionable security suggestions on how to patch them, not only allows for identifying and fixing known security problems but also helps developers better understand the negative impacts of ignoring or underestimating the security considerations included in such standards while coding or deploying IdM protocols. This, in turn, contributes to increasing the level of security awareness of developers. Micro-Id-Gym also have the capability to create a local faithful copy of the system and gives the possibility to perform attacks that would have catastrophic effects when performed in the production environment (e.g., Denial of Service). Finally, we show how the tool can help identify false positives by classifying tests in two classes, namely passive and active. The former only performs checks without modifying messages while the latter also interfere with the flow of the protocols by injecting suitably crafted messages with the goal of mounting an attack. Our findings have been experimentally validated by integrating Micro-Id-Gym in the Continuous Delivery pipeline infrastructure offered by GitLab. The experiments were conducted in the context of the deployment of a new version of the Italian digital identity solution based on the electronic identity card.

Structure of the Paper. In Sect. 2, we give an overview of the DevSecOps philosophy and tools used in DevSecOps together with a pentesting tool for IdM protocols. In Sect. 3, we describe the scenario and its requirements, while in Sect. 4 we detail the design and the implementation of the proposed solution. To evaluate the effectiveness of the solution, Sect. 5 reports the use of the integration in a real scenario. We conclude and give an overview of future work in Sect. 6.

2   Background on DevOps, DevSecOps and Pentesting

Traditionally, operations and development teams have worked independently. This separation has created an environment filled with communication and alignment problems resulting in productions delays. In response to these issues DevOps was born. DevOps's goal is to bridge the gap between the two teams to improve communication and collaboration, create smoother processes and align strategies and objectives for faster and more efficient delivery [10]. The term DevOps originates from the union of development and operations and describes the approaches to be adopted to accelerate the processes that allow an idea to move from development to release in a production environment, where it can provide value to the user. Such approaches require frequent communication between the two teams. In DevOps, developers who typically create code in a standard development environment work closely with operations staff to speed up software creation, testing, and release [11].

Security has become an important and challenging goal in the DevOps philosophy and in the Software Development Life Cycle (SDLC). This was done with DevSecOps, an extension of DevOps whose purpose is to integrate security controls and processes into the DevOps to promote the collaboration among security, development and operations teams. The DevSecOps process requires the integration of planning, design, and release, which is typically obtained by a collaborative tool chain of technologies to facilitate cooperation, provide more secure development processes and, according to [12], allows companies to save money in case of data breaches due to the effectiveness of an organization's incident response and containment processes. Moreover, adopting DevSecOps practices for automatic building deployment eliminates a large number of manual steps that could introduce many opportunities to make mistakes.

2.1 Security Practices in DevSecOps

As reported in Table 1 several state-of-the-art security practices can be used in DevSecOps to ensure that automation and security are handled continuously throughout the SDLC [13]. In this section we provide more details about the Dynamic Application Security Testing (DAST) practices since the tool we propose belongs to this cluster of practice even if in the industrial context[1], there are different classifications of the security practices in DevSecOps and according to them the tool we integrated is classified as a Pentesting Tool.

In general DAST practice uses a black-box security testing method that examines an application while it is running, by detecting common vulnerabilities [14]. The performed tests can detect flaws during the authentication or authorization process performing client-side, inappropriate command execution, SQL injection, erroneous information disclosure, interfaces, and API endpoints attacks but also perform penetration testing and vulnerability scanning [15]. A list of DAST tools is provided by OWASP[2]. Two of the most well-known tools in this context are OWASP Zed Attack Proxy[3] (ZAP) and Burp Suite Professional Commercial Edition[4] (Burp PRO). They observe the HTTP traffic of the application in use and create alerts on any vulnerabilities they can detect

---

[1] https://dzone.com/articles/shifting-left-devsecops.

[2] https://owasp.org/www-community/Vulnerability_Scanning_Tools.

[3] https://www.owasp.org/index.php/OWASP_Zed_Attack_Proxy_Project.

[4] https://portswigger.net/burp/pro.

through regular usage and attempt a variety of attacks by replaying modified HTTP traffic. These tools have been designed mainly to support manual testing, but they also provide API's that could allow integration into a DevSecOps pipeline. A good example on how to integrate DAST into DevSecOps is reported in GitHub[5] where both ZAP and Burp Pro are ready to be added in the pipeline to conduct an active real time vulnerability scan and return a security scan report as result.

The limit of the available DAST tools when deploying IdM solutions is that they are covering only partially the possible security tests needed to produce a security assessment. In fact, there is no state-of-the-art DAST tool which

Table 1. State-of-the-art security practices in DevSecOps.

Security practice	Description
Security Practice Availability Threat Modeling	Process that defines, classifies, and analyses potential threats, assessing their risk and the appropriate countermeasure during the plan phase
Pre-commit Hooks	Check whether a code contains strings that match specified patterns to help not to leak credentials
IDE Plugins	Automatically perform code analysis as the developers open, edit, and save file in the IDE to get early warning of vulnerabilities
Dependency Analysis	Technique used to detect vulnerabilities contained within a project's dependencies
Unit Testing	Process of software testing where individual units/components of a software are tested
Static Application Security Testing	Testing methodology that analyses source code to find security vulnerabilities that make an application susceptible to attacks
Dynamic Application Security Testing	Type of black-box security test that scans web applications for vulnerabilities. It works by simulating external àttacks on an application while it is running
Infrastructure as Code	Instead of configuring the hardware physically, it is managed through the definition of files
Secrets Management	Tools and methods for managing sensitive parts of an IT ecosystem
Configuration Management	Control of the configuration for an information system with the goal of enabling security and managing risk
Version Control	Practice for tracking and managing changes to software code
Container Security Scanning	Practice for securing containers

---

[5] https://github.com/jacksingleton/dast-pipeline.

verifies the security aspects in IdM implementation in terms of compliance with the standards and detect vulnerabilities coming from scientific papers.

2.2 Overview of Micro-Id-Gym

Micro-Id-Gym [9] is a tool which assists system administrators and testers in the pentesting of IdM protocol implementations. More precisely, Micro-Id-Gym considers web protocols where a Service Provider (SP) relies on a trusted third-party, called Identity Provider (IdP), for user authentication. SAML, OIDC and OAuth are three of the most known standardized protocols providing this authentication pattern (modulo different names used to refer to the aforementioned entities).

Micro-Id-Gym supports two main activities: pentesting of IdM protocol implementations and creating sandboxes with an IdM protocol deployment. The former consists of tools with a GUI to support pentesting activities on the System Under Test (SUT), namely a Proxy, a set of Pentesting Tools, and two tools called MSC Drawer and MSC STIX Visualizer. The latter can be carried out by recreating locally a sandbox of an IdM protocol implementation and it can be done by uploading the proprietary implementation or by composing a new one choosing the instances provided by the tool. The capability of creating a local copy of the SUT allows for performing pentesting activities that may cause severe disruptions such as Denial of Server (DoS) attacks.

All the exchanged HTTP messages intercepted by the Proxy, during the authentication process performed on the SUT, allows the Pentesting Tools to execute the available automated tests. The tool verifies whether the SUT suffers from the vulnerabilities tested automatically by the tool and provides details of the discovered vulnerabilities. In addition, the MSC Drawer automatically creates a Message Sequence Chart of the authentication flow by using the information collected by the Proxy. Thus the pentester can recognize at a glance whether the SUT follows the expected flow or not.

The results for each executed test are reported in a box inside the tool where the user finds a recap with (i) the check performed together with a brief description, (ii) the status of the executed test (Successful or Failed) and, in case of failure, (iii) the portion of HTTP message that is not compliant with the standard together with (iv) different suggestions to mitigate the identified flaws.

Micro-Id-Gym performs tests on both the IdP and SP in automatic manner and it supports the following test categories in the IdM protocol deployment: (i) performing general security web checks on any collected HTTP message, not strictly related to the protocol implementations but more in general related to web security, (ii) verifying the compliance with a given standard in terms of format of the messages, and mandatory fields, and (iii) mounting specific attacks to spot any false positives among the vulnerabilities reported by previous tests.

The tests executed by the tool can be passive or active. Passive tests analyze the traffic generated during the authentication flow to discover compliance issues such as missing parameters required by one of the supported standards, namely SAML, OAuth and OIDC. Instead active tests modify the exchanged messages to verify how the SUT reacts to the malicious messages injected by an attacker [9]. Since passive tests perform a static analysis, they can be executed all at once on the traffic collected when the authentication process is completed. This is not the case of active tests as each of them runs independently because it performs some modifications to the messages related for that test. Performing multiple modifications simultaneously would makes it more complex to identify the root-cause of the failed test. For instance, an active test consists of checking if the `relaystate` parameter used to prevent CSRF attacks can be tampered with during the authentication flow. In case the authentication process is completed despite the modification, it means the SUT does not manage correctly the `relaystate` parameter and it might expose the user to CSRF attacks [16]. In case the SUT notices the change, the test fails meaning that the SUT performs adequate verification on the `relaystate` parameter.

Currently Micro-Id-Gym supports three standards, SAML, OIDC and OAuth. As regards SAML a comprehensive list of all the automated tests are reported in Table 2, where, for each test, we specify: *(i)* a name to identify the security test (e.g., Session Replay), *(ii)* the target of the test (SP or IdP), *(iii)* the type of test Passive (P) or Active (A), *(iv)* the description of the security test, and *(v)* the description of the mitigation.

In order to use the Pentesting Tools provided by Micro-Id-Gym, the pentester needs to install in his device the tool which leverages the Proxy, Burp Community Edition[6], because the interactions with the GUI of the tool is required. The pentester is also required to provide an authentication trace which contains a list of user actions to interact with the browser used to complete the authentication process in the SUT. The authentication trace (e.g., visit www.example.com, click on *Login* button, etc.) can be easily recorded by the pentester and the Pentesting Tools verify the correctness (i.e., the correct execution) before running the automated passive and active tests.

3   Scenario and Requirements

IdM solutions are increasingly important for digital infrastructures of both enterprises and public administrations and they are a pre-requisite for building trust in current and future digital ecosystems. Unfortunately, their secure deployment is a non-trivial activity that requires a good level of security awareness [5].

For the sake of concreteness we now describe the Italian digital identity infrastructure based on the national electronic identity card, which we have deeply studied as part of a collaboration with IPZS. The scenario given by IPZS consists of an IdP based on SAML SSO protocol and (a stub) SP required to complete the authentication process. IPZS is adopting DevOps in the development stage: after each commit made by developers in the repository, an automatic build is created and the deployment in the SUT is performed. In this scenario, so far, the pentesting activities are performed manually and outside of the DevOps pipeline by running Micro-Id-Gym under the responsibility of the Security Team (ST). From the IPZS perspective this flow looked too cumbersome and error

---

[6] https://portswigger.net/burp.

prone due to the steps required by the pentesting activities and so, in order to make the process shorter and faster, we introduced DevSecOps. We decided then to integrate Micro-Id-Gym in the SDLC.

Therefore, to reduce the redundant tasks, to make builds less error-prone and deployments more secure, we designed and implemented a solution joining the main advantages of Continuous Integration and Continuous Delivery (CI/CD) and integrate Micro-Id-Gym as a known and valid tool for the pentesting activities required by IPZS. During the process of integration we encountered some issues due to the constraints given by the tool itself and the solution adopted is described in Sect. 4.

From the aforementioned scenario, we identify two challenges (C1 and C2) and from them we derive some functional and security requirements.

[C1] Automated Assistance. To enable the deployment automation that leads to repeatable and reliable deployments across the SDLC. Indeed, the process to perform a deployment of a SAML SSO implementation contains many critical steps like the federation process. Moreover the automatic pentesting provides a set of pentesting tools for the automatic security analysis of the IdM protocols by identifying security issues and helps to maintain compliance with the standard in order to eliminate basic security issues and allow the security experts to focus more on complex security issues. From C1, we derive the following two requirements:

R1 integration in the SDLC: to automatically perform pentesting on a solution based on IdM protocols which involves several entities that interact with each other based on complex cryptographic mechanisms.

R2 false positives elimination: thanks to the automation and the capabilities of the pentesting tool, it is possible to perform passive tests that identify vulnerabilities and through the active tests to mount attacks which help eliminating any false positives detected by the passive tests.

[C2] *Increasing Security Awareness.* To enable the secure deployment of IdM protocols which is a complex and error prone activity that requires a high level of security awareness in several and heterogeneous aspects. Indeed, developers get bogged down in the myriads of security practices that they are required to tame when trying to deploy or understand IdM solutions. There are plenty security indications for SAML, OAuth and OIDC spread in different sources and most of them are not easy to understand for a developer with limited security skills. The Pentesting Tools identify vulnerabilities in the implementation but also provide security mitigations with the aim to increase the security awareness of the developers. From C2, we obtain the following requirements:

R3 compliance with the standards: faithfully adopting the best practices in order to achieve security by checking the compliance with a given standard in terms of format of the messages, and mandatory fields. Following the suggestions indicated in the standard increases the security of the protocol implementation.

R4 collaboration support: the cooperation among developers is critical especially when senior developers are helping less skilled developers to fix vulnerabilities reported in the security issue message provided by the ST and containing actionable suggestions.

We also identify two requirements that are common to both challenges:

R5 mitigation: provide to the developers a comprehensive and actionable analysis of the options to mitigate the discovered vulnerabilities. The details of the mitigations provided by the tool will improve the security awareness among the developers.

R6 notification: ST and developers should have access to the test report with different levels of details in order to simplify the problems of mitigations. The test report contains different information according to the audience; for developer more aspects related to the implementation and mitigations while for security specialist only aspect related to security.

4 Continuous Delivery Solution for Pentesting of IdM Protocols

4.1 Design

As depicted in Fig. 1, the proposed solution is composed of two main components. The former, located in the bottom of the figure, is in charge to handle the repository with the source code of the entities (IdP and SP) and the CI/CD System—indeed to satisfy the R1—and which was the starting point of a classic CI.

The latter—our contribution identified on the top part of the figure—aims to perform the pentesting on the IdM deployment while increasing the security awareness among the developers. Moreover the red arrows in the figure indicate the operations which are automatically executed, while the black dashed arrows indicate that the operations require a human intervention.

When the developer pushes new code in the repository, a notification will be sent to the ST and the build and deployment phases will start.

The source code of the SP and IdP will be built, federated and both deployed in the SUT. The sent notification notifies the ST that the automatic penetration testing on the SUT has been executed and test reports are available. The penetration testing will check the compliance with the standard (it complies with R3) by executing passive tests, and mount specific attacks by executing active tests to spot false positives vulnerabilities identified by the passive tests (fulfill R2).

The notification also contains some information needed to execute the Pentesting Tools and to allow the communication between the repository, the CI/CD system, the SUT and the Pentesting Tools. Whether the ST decides to perform pentesting on the deployed solution, the Pentesting Tools will automatically create security feedback and a test report with all the discovered vulnerabilities in a tool for team collaboration (it complies with R4) and accessible by both developers and ST (fulfill R6). The tool for the team collaboration will be used by the developers to retrieve information about mitigations and by the ST to help the developers on the fixes. This stage is thus helpful to increase security awareness on the developers. The test report contains different levels of content accordingly to the role played in the SDLC. The developers will have access to only a brief recap of the status of the vulnerabilities and mitigations and indeed satisfies R5 while ST all the details about mitigations.

4.2   Implementation

4.2.1   CI/CD System

We adopted GitLab CI/CD[7] which is a tool built into GitLab for software development to support CI and CD. At the repository's root in the GitLab CI/CD there is a `configuration` file used to create a CD pipeline which executes jobs contained in stages. We implemented the three operations marked with red font in Fig. 1 by interpreting three stages in the pipeline: (i) Send Notifications, (ii) Build, and (iii) Deploy. The first stage is in charge to notify the ST about the changes in the repository. We decided to send an email which contains the authentication trace and parameter required by GitLab to create Issues namely `Project Id` and `Host URL`. The second stage is responsible to build the source code, the third one will setup the webserver and deploy the

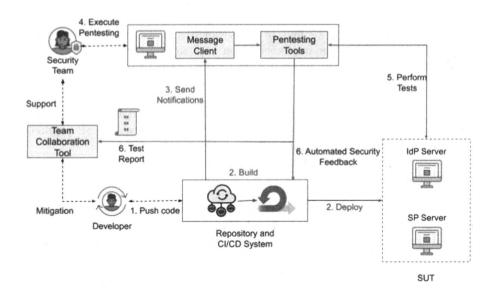

Fig. 1. High level architecture of the proposed solution.

---

[7] https://www.gitlab.com.

solution in the SUT. These jobs get executed by the GitLab Runner agent which is an open-source application written in Go that works with GitLab CI/CD to run jobs in a pipeline. GitLab Runner is triggered by every push to the central repository if a `configuration` file is available (unless explicitly configured not to).

4.2.2   Integration of Micro-Id-Gym

Given the interoperability of Micro-Id-Gym with any operative system and its capability to perform compliance checks, we decided to integrate it in the solution and use to perform the pentesting activities in the SUT. The integration of the tool itself is immediate also considering its flexibility to adapt in any scenario and it needs no software development nor particular skills.

The tool creates automatically GitLab issues in the repository of those tests where vulnerabilities have been discovered. In order to grant Micro-Id-Gym to read and write access to the GitLab Repository, a `GitLab token`, `Project Id` and `Host URL` are required. For the former, which is a personal access token used to authenticate with the GitLab API, is required the user to retrieve it from his GitLab profile.

Micro-Id-Gym will also generate a report of the test results which will be automatically added a Slack[8] channel, a collaboration team tool, accessible by the developers and ST.

5   Use Case: SAML SSO Implementation

As anticipated in Sect. 3, we had to assess an IdP based on SAML and its compliance with SPID[9]. The implementation is given by IPZS in a context of a joint-lab and it is the Italian digital identity infrastructure based on the national electronic identity card. In this scenario we have to assess whether the SAML authentication process follows the rules defined by the standard protocol [1] to avoid security issues and lack of compliance with the technical rules provided by SPID. The scenario consists of the IdP provided by IPZS and a stub SP required to complete the authentication process.

To assess the IPZS provided scenario, we used the solution reported in Sect. 4 excluding the part related to the team collaboration tool because it will be a future work.

The content of the email sent to the ST is depicted in Fig. 3 and contains all the details to use Micro-Id-Gym. In detail, it provides: *(i)* name of the developer who changes the repository and commit number, *(ii)* instructions to use and install Micro-Id-Gym *(iii)* GitLab Project Id, *(iv)* GitLab Host URL, *(v)* authentication trace composed by a list of user actions to perform the authentication process on the SUT by a test user, *(vi)* instructions to retrieve a GitLab Token and *(vii)* URL of the SUT.

---

[8] https://slack.com/.
[9] https://www.spid.gov.it/.

Table 2. Collection of security tests targeting SAML implementation.

Security test	Target	Type	Description	Mitigation
Session replay	SP	A	Check whether the SP does not manage properly the session during the authentication process allowing CSRF attacks	Implement mechanisms to handle properly the user sessions
Session hijacking	SP	A	Check whether the SP does not manage properly the session during the authentication process allowing CSRF attacks	Implement mechanisms to handle properly the user sessions
Relaystate parameter tampering	SP, IdP	A	Check if the value of Relaystate parameter can be tampered	Sanitize the value of Relaystate parameter
Presence of ID attribute	SP, IdP	P	Check whether the ID element is present in the SAML request	Configure the SP to include ID attribute in the SAML request and the IdP to accept only SAMLRequest with ID attribute
Presence of Issuer attribute	SP, IdP	P	Check whether the Issuer element is present in the SAML request	Configure the SP to include Issuer attribute in the SAML request and the IdP to accept only SAMLRequest with Issuer attribute
SAML request compliant with SPID	SP, IdP	P	Check whether the SAML request is compliant with SPID standard	Configure the SP to issue SPID compliant SAML request
Presence of Audience element	SP, IdP	P	Check whether the Audience element is present in the SAML response	Configure the IdP to include Audience element in the SAML response and the SP to accept only SAML response with Audience element
Presence of OneTimeUse attribute	SP, IdP	P	Check whether the OneTimeUse attribute is present in the SAML response	Configure the IdP to include OneTimeUse attribute in the SAML response and the SP to accept only SAML response with OneTimeUse attribute
Presence of NotOnOrAfter attribute	SP, IdP	P	Check whether the NotOnOrAfter attribute is present in the SAML response	Configure the IdP to include NotOnOrAfter attribute in the SAML response and the SP to accept only SAML response with NotOnOrAfter attribute
Presence of InResponseTo attribute	SP, IdP	P	Check whether the InResponseTo attribute is present in the SAML response	Configure the IdP to include InResponseTo attribute in the SAML response and the SP to accept only SAML response with InResponseTo attribute
Presence of Recipient attribute in Subject-ConfirmationData element	SP, IdP	P	Check whether the Recipient is present in the SAML response	Configure the IdP to include Recipient attribute in SubjectConfirmationData element of the SAML response and the SP to accept only SAML response with Recipient attribute
Canonicalization algorithm	SP, IdP	P, A	Check if the Canonicalization algorithm used by the XML parser encodes also comments	Configure IdP and SP to use XML parser Canonicalization algorithm that includes comments
SAML response compliant with SPID	SP, IdP	P	Check whether the SAML response is compliant with SPID standard	Configure the IdP to issue SPID compliant SAML response

P = Passive Test; A = Active Test.

Fig. 2. IdP response after a replay attack.

Fig. 3. Email sent to the ST.

5.1 Results

The results after running the passive tests of Micro-Id-Gym show the detection of vulnerabilities both on the IdP and a stub SP. The report provided by Micro-Id-Gym is depicted in Fig. 4 showing the GUI of Micro-Id-Gym after executing the tests and where the sensitive information like URL of the SUT and the value of the GitLab token are hidden for privacy and security reasons. The top part of the figure contains the information required by the tool and the authentication trace, the browser used and the information needed by GitLab (GitLab token, Project Id and Host URL). In the middle of Fig. 4 it is depicted the set of tests available in the tool while on the bottom part the details of the results are reported.

Even if the SP is out of scope for this assessment because the goal of IPZS was to assess only the IdP, we highlight that Micro-Id-Gym detects a missing attribute in the SAMLRequest namely ProviderName. The tool reported it as a warning issue (orange colour) because the identified attribute is optional as reported in the SAML Core [1] even if it is a good practice to include it. The attribute might be used for some other reasons by the SAML authorities.

Concerning the IdP, Micro-Id-Gym identified two issues by executing the passive tests:

- The detected canonicalization algorithm used in the SAMLResponse is unsecure [8] as reported in Fig. 5.
- The OneTimeUse element in the SAMLResponse is missing even if it is reported as Optional element [1].

The first vulnerability identified is due to not using a safe canonicalization algorithm which may lead to an impersonation attack and can allow an attacker with authenticated access to authenticate himself as a different user without knowledging the victim user's credentials. A possible remediation, suggested by Micro-Id-Gym, could be the use of a canonicalization algorithm[10] which does not omit comments during canonicalization. This algorithm would cause comments added by an attacker to invalidate the signature. For the second vulnerability, the element OneTimeUse specifies that the assertion should be used immediately and must not be retained for future use [17] and the mitigation provided by Micro-Id-Gym is to add the attribute in the assertion. If the element of OneTimeUse was added in the SAMLResponse, the replay attacks of SAMLResponse could be avoided.

To eliminate false positives and to check whether with the discovered vulnerabilities it is possible to mount attacks, Micro-Id-Gym provides an advanced analysis by running the active tests. One of the active tests, which in this scenario failed, verifies the correct interpretation of the SAML messages by the XML parser. This test adds arbitrary string as comments inside the SAMLRequest and check whether the IdP XML parser interprets the SAML messages without any issues and possibility to hack the messages and exploiting by an impersonation attack.

Another provided active test performs a replay attack by sending in a new session a SAMLResponse previously obtained. We ran these active tests provided by Micro-Id-Gym. According to the results of Micro-Id-Gym, reported in Fig. 2, all the active tests failed, meaning that the issues detected by the passive tests were false positives. We were curious to understand how the system is protected against these issues, and we thus performed a manual in-depth analysis. We found out that the technology used by the IdP includes countermeasures like cookies and time-based authenticators to prevent replay attacks. Also we noticed that the SAMLRequest issued are stored in the IdP to guarantee one-time use and are not valid after they have been verified.

Finally, according to the results (both active and passive), we conclude that the potential vulnerabilities identified by the passive tests are considered false positives due to the results given by the active tests.

---

[10] http://www.w3.org/2001/10/xml-exc-c14n#WithComments.

Fig. 4. Test results in Micro-Id-Gym.

Fig. 5. Usage of an unsecure Canonicalization algorithm.

The results pointed out the importance to include Micro-Id-Gym in the DevSecOps pipeline. Since it is well-known that most of the time during the pentesting activities is spent to eliminate false positives, the integration of Micro-Id-Gym with its features allows to reduce the time of the pentesting and thus to satisfy R2.

Thanks to the DevSecOps philosophy we were able to automatically deploy the solution and thus eliminate redundant tasks, mitigate the risk of human error during the deploy process and last but not least to automatically and continuously security assess the deployment.

6   Conclusion and Future Work

We have proposed a flexible solution for DevSecOps satisfying all the defined requirements by integrating a pentesting tool for the automatic security analysis in a DevSecOps pipeline for IdM protocols.

We have implemented the DevSecOps pipeline by integrating Micro-Id-Gym with the aim to build, deploy and perform penetration testing on a scenario based on IdM protocols. We have provided Micro-Id-Gym for the automatic security analysis of IdM protocols which assists to easily identify security issues by performing passive and active tests and helps to maintain compliance with the standard. Finally, we have assessed an IdM protocol scenario applying the DevSecOps philosophy and performed a security analysis of IPZS scenario by running Micro-Id-Gym.

As future work, we plan to extend the proposed solution by (i) integrating a tool for teams to return the actionable security hints provided by Micro-Id-Gym to improve security awareness among developers and (ii) further elaborate the role of actionable security suggestions of cyber threat intelligence using the STIX interface to focus more on real and current vulnerabilities which help to increase security awareness instead of possible threats whose seem unlikely.

References

1. Consortium, O.: SAML V2.0 Technical Overview, March 2008. http://wiki.oasis-open.org/security/Saml2TechOverview
2. Sakimura, N., Bradley, J., Jones, M., De Medeiros, B., Mortimore, C.: OpenID Connect core 1.0. The OpenID Foundation, p. S3 (2014)
3. Hardt, D.: The OAuth 2.0 Authorization Framework (RFC6749), Internet Engineering Task Force (IETF) (2012)
4. Digitale, A.P.L.: SPID - Regole Tecniche. https://docs.italia.it/italia/spid/spid-regole-tecniche/it/stabile/index.html
5. Engelbertz, N., Erinola, N., Herring, D., Somorovsky, J., Mladenov, V., Schwenk, J.: Security analysis of eIDAS-the cross-country authentication scheme in Europe. In: 12th USENIX Workshop on Offensive Technologies (WOOT 18) (2018)
6. Armando, A., Carbone, R., Compagna, L., Cuellar, J., Tobarra, L.: Formal analysis of SAML 2.0 web browser single sign-on: breaking the SAML-based single sign-on for google apps. In: Proceedings of the 6th ACM Workshop on Formal Methods in Security Engineering, pp. 1–10 (2008)
7. Jurreit, J., Fehrenbach, P., Kaspar, F.: Analysis of security vulnerabilities in Microsoft Office 365 in regard to SAML. Informatik J. 127 (2017)
8. Blog, T.D.: Duo Finds SAML Vulnerabilities Affecting Multiple Implementations. https://duo.com/blog/duo-finds-saml-vulnerabilities-affecting-multiple-implementations
9. Bisegna, A., Carbone, R., Pellizzari, G., Ranise, S.: Micro-Id-Gym: a flexible tool for pentesting identity management protocols in the wild and in the laboratory. In: Saracino, A., Mori, P. (eds.) ETAA 2020. LNCS, vol. 12515, pp. 71–89. Springer, Cham (2020). https://doi.org/10.1007/978-3-030-64455-0_5
10. Ebert, C., Gallardo, G., Hernantes, J., Serrano, N.: DevOps. IEEE Softw. 33(3), 94–100 (2016)
11. DevOps: DevOps Definition. https://www.redhat.com/it/topics/devops
12. Security, I., Institute, P.: Cost of a Data Breach Report. https://www.ibm.com/security/data-breach
13. Mao, R., et al.: Preliminary findings about DevSecOps from grey literature. In: 2020 IEEE 20th International Conference on Software Quality, Reliability and Security (QRS), pp. 450–457. IEEE (2020)

14. Peterson, J.: Dynamic Application Security Testing. https://resources.whitesou
    rcesoftware.com/blog-whitesource/dast-dynamic-application-security-testing
15. Myrbakken, H., Colomo-Palacios, R.: DevSecOps: a multivocal literature review.
    In: Mas, A., Mesquida, A., O'Connor, R.V., Rout, T., Dorling, A. (eds.) SPICE
    2017. CCIS, vol. 770, pp. 17–29. Springer, Cham (2017). https://doi.org/10.1007/
    978-3-319-67383-7_2
16. Bisegna, A., Carbone, R., Martini, I., Odorizzi, V., Pellizzari, G., Ranise, S.: Micro-
    Id-Gym: identity management workouts with container-based microservices. Int.
    J. Inf. Secur. Cybercrime **8**(1), 45–50 (2019)
17. Hirsch, F., Philpott, R., Maler, E.: Security and Privacy Considerations for the
    OASIS Security Assertion Markup Language (SAML) V2. 0, Committee Draft 1
    (2005)

Mimicry Attacks Against Behavioural-Based User Authentication for Human-Robot Interaction

Shurook S. Almohamade[1(✉)], John A. Clark[1], and James Law[1,2]

[1] Department of Computer Science, The University of Sheffield, Sheffield, UK
{ssalmohamade1,john.clark,j.law}@Sheffield.ac.uk
[2] Sheffield Robotics, The University of Sheffield, Sheffield, UK

Abstract. Robots are often used in highly sensitive, safety-critical, or high-value applications (e.g. medical, nuclear, space, offshore, manufacturing). Where AI is not able or trusted to perform the necessary tasks, humans operators are required to train or directly control these systems. However, robots are not usually built with security as a key concern, and malicious actors need to be identified before they can cause damage or disruption through the robot's operation. Of particular interest is ensuring whether operators of robots are who they claim to be, i.e., there is a need for identification and authentication. Traditionally, authentication is carried out through passwords or demonstrating possession of a token such as a smart card, but these are one-shot approaches and confidence in authentication wanes as time elapses. Thus, repeated authentication may be needed to provide ongoing confidence, though, in practice, such repeated actions may be highly disruptive. In this paper, we evaluate how ongoing user behaviour monitoring can be used as the basis for unobtrusive *continuous user authentication*, which is a form of *biometric behaviour modelling*. To gather data, we use a simulation in which a group of users hand-guide a robotic manipulator to perform a task (analogous to *teaching by demonstration* or *teleoperation*), with some users posing as malicious agents. We then tested our continuous authentication technique against a popular behavioural biometric attack called a 'mimicry attack.'

Keywords: Authentication · Behavioural biometric · Human-robot interaction · Mimicry attacks

1 Introduction

Robotic systems are now being implemented and utilised in a variety of safety-critical applications. However, robotic systems have a number of security flaws that may be used to launch hazardous assaults, which might have far-reaching implications for these applications, ranging from financial losses to the loss of human lives.

Inadequate user authentication procedures are one of the most serious flaws of modern robots [4]. In reality, authentication is mainly employed as a first

© Springer Nature Switzerland AG 2021
A. Saracino and P. Mori (Eds.): ETAA 2021, LNCS 13136, pp. 111–126, 2021.
https://doi.org/10.1007/978-3-030-93747-8_8

defensive barrier that prohibits unauthorised entities from having access to the robotic system, making it less vulnerable to insider attacks [23]. However, the lack of effective authentication means that illegal access can often be easily breached by a given attacker using standard user names and passwords [4,15,23]. Likewise, teleoperation is a key control method for robots working in hazardous settings or in telesurgery [3] and authentication is essential.

In this regard, then, biometric systems and methods can play a major role. Biometrics is essentially about the capability of a person to be recognised. This identification may then be used to provide access to systems [5]. Biometrics features obtained from users can be divided into physiological and behavioural traits. The former refers to users' physical attributes, including their fingerprints, facial recognition, iris patterns, retinal recognition, vascular pattern recognition, palm prints, DNA, ear geometry and hand geometry. The latter refers to attributes like typing habits, voice patterns, signatures, gait and behavioural profile.

Biometric systems have emerged as a solution for avoiding the defects and problems of traditional authentication systems. However, their design and structure seem to be vulnerable to attack. When used in the standard procedure of a biometric system, biometric data pass through several stages, including collection, processing, sending via a communication channel, storage and retrieval. At every stage of the process, it is necessary to maintain the security and privacy of the biometric data.

Several types of attacks can threaten biometric systems, as shown in Fig. 1. These attacks can be classified into direct attacks, and indirect attacks [22]. In the former, the attacker does not need to know how the authentication mechanism works; these attacks target the sensor phase. In the latter, for an attack to be successful, the attacker must be aware of the authentication system's operations. Hence, these attacks target the feature extraction, classification and decision phases, the templates database and the communication channels between phases.

One of the most prevalent kinds of attacks is against the sensor device [20] (e.g. fake physical biometric). Fake physical biometric attacks use a fake biometric feature, such as a synthetic fingerprint made with wax or a face mask, which is presented to the sensor [10]. In addition, behavioural biometrics such as voices, hand-written signatures, keyboard dynamics, and gait may be susceptible to mimicking attacks [7].

We are interested in the field of human-robot collaboration, where close interaction between people and robots presents particular challenges in terms of personal safety and security [8,11,18]. Previously, we investigated continuous authentication for collaborative robot manipulators [2]. The human co-worker used the robot arm's joint information (position, force, and torque) to collect biometric data.

In this study, we examine behavioural biometrics continuous authentication in the context of control and programming of industrial and teleoperated robots. We examine a situation in which attackers are provided information about their

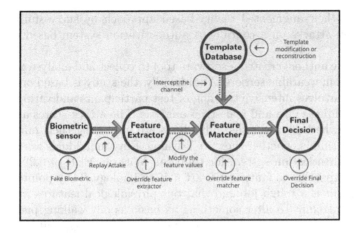

Fig. 1. Biometric authentication system attacks [19].

victims' behavioural patterns, and they make a deliberate effort to mimic them. If imitation is feasible, detection equal error rates will become unacceptably high. As a result, individual working behaviour would be inappropriate for use as a biometrics feature.

2   Related Work

As far as we are aware, no prior study has examined or implemented mimicking threats against behaviour-based biometrics authentication for human-robot interaction. On the other hand, many studies have examined impersonation threats against behavioural biometric authentication techniques such as touch-based identification, gait analysis, and keystroke dynamics.

In [12] the authors evaluated two basic methods of malicious insider attacks against touch-based identification systems. They conduct a targeted imitation attack and show that the touch-based identification systems fails against shoulder surfing and offline training attacks. They found that shoulder surfing attacks had an 84% bypass success rate, with the majority of successful attackers monitoring the victim's behaviour for less than two minutes, based on tests with three different touch input implicit authentication (touch IA) schemes and 256 distinct attacker-victim pairings.

In [13], the authors assess the vulnerability of keyboard dynamics to imitation attacks when password hardening is used on smartphones. They created an augmented reality software that runs on the attacker's smartphone and makes use of computer vision and keyboard data to offer real-time assistance throughout the victim's phone's password input process. In their tests, 30 users launched over 400 impersonation attacks. They show that it is simple for an attacker to imitate keystroke behaviour on virtual keyboards. Additionally, they show the flexibility of their augmented reality-based approach by successfully conducting imitation attacks on a continuous authentication system based on swiping behaviour.

In [17], the authors created a software tool to collect and analyse gait acceleration data from wearable sensors. Additionally, the study is based on an experiment which involves intensive training of test participants and various feedback sources, including video and statistical analysis. The attack scores are analysed to ascertain whether or not the individuals are improving their mimicry abilities, or more simply, whether they are learning. Fifty individuals were registered in a gait authentication system for the trial. With an EER of 6.2%, the error rates are comparable to state-of-the-art gait technology. They pointed out that replicating gait is a tough job and that our physiological features work against us when we attempt to alter something as basic as our walking pattern. They found that the participants showed no evidence of learning, and the outcomes of the majority of attackers deteriorated with time, demonstrating that training had little effect on their success.

In [14], the authors show how a digital treadmill may be used to mimic an individual's stride patterns recorded using a smartphone accelerometer. They also create an attack for a baseline gait-based authentication system (GBAS) and thoroughly evaluate its effectiveness using an eighteen-user data set. The attack raises the average false acceptance rate (FAR) for the random forest from 5.8% to 43.66% by using just two attackers and a basic digital treadmill with speed control capabilities. In particular, the FAR of eleven of the eighteen users rose to 70% or above.

3   Threat Model and Attacks

This paper presents an approach for continuous user authentication for industrial and teleoperated robots that profile a user's work behaviour. However, continuous authentication systems are subject to many attacks. We will not address the full range of threats to such systems here. Rather, we focus on authentication threats from users who wish to pretend to be particular targeted users. We can categorise attackers by the amount of information they have on the behaviour of the target victim. They may have no information at all, be able to access observational information (e.g. by shoulder surfing the target user or having access to videos of the target user working), or have detailed behavioural information, e.g. stored behavioural biometric information.

Access to detailed information may allow the attacker to develop a training system that provides detailed feedback on how close the attacker's behaviour is to the target victim's. Indeed, this is one mechanisms we explore in this paper. This is the best case for an attacker and the most severe evaluation stress for a biometrics continuous authentication approach. Knowledge of how a system performs against attackers across the range of information availability will enable the most appropriate further security measures to be taken, e.g. measures to ensure that detailed biometric information is not leaked.

The types of attack that we investigate are detailed below.

3.1 Zero-Effort Attacks

Zero-effort attacks are an often-used technique for assessing the accuracy and reliability of biometric authentication systems [16]. It models the case where an attacker has no information on the behaviour of the target victim. Usually, Zero-effort attacks are implemented by comparing biometric samples from different individuals, i.e. where a sample profile of one user is assessed for its acceptability as a supplied profile for a second (target) user.

3.2 Imitation Attacks

In imitation attacks, an attacker must first be familiar with their victim's working behaviour to imitate them. In this study, we examined two malicious insider imitation attacks: shoulder surfing and offline training attacks.

1. **Shoulder surfing attacks.** In this attack, insiders with malicious intent can observe their victims' interactions. As a result, adversaries can try to mimic measurable characteristics. It is unknown if shoulder surfing has an advantage in terms of mimicking measurable characteristics. Shoulder surfing is a challenge that has required researchers to spend substantial time developing novel authentication methods to defeat.
2. **Offline imitation training attacks.** In this attack, malicious insiders can obtain their victims' raw data by extracting the victim's profile from a breached biometrics database. Additionally, insiders may utilise the raw data to learn and emulate their victims' behaviour once they have access to it. We have operationalised this idea to the extent of providing online mimicry training.

4 Experimental Design Considerations

4.1 Experiment Choices

We used the 'V-REP' as the robot simulator (currently, it is re-branded to CoppeliaSim [1]). V-REP is a popular robotic simulator for educational and research applications, and it comes with a free academic license. When compared to Gazebo simulations, V-REP software can be installed and run without the need for a powerful graphics card and does not necessitate the use of a powerful CPU [6]. In addition to many sensors or robot models, the V-REP includes several functions for creating a virtual world. Users may engage with the virtual world throughout the simulation, making it more interesting. The experiments use a simulation of the 'KUKA LBR iiwa R800', which is a popular collaborative robotic arm.

4.2   Experimental Design

Here, we describe how to identify a robot's operator using the velocity and accelerometer data we acquired from their interactions with the robot while completing a specific task. The task was to move an object, a 'ball', from a start point (red circle) to an endpoint (yellow circle) to solve a maze 15 times, as shown in Fig. 2. The robot was tasked with tracking the ball's movements. In the experiments, the user moves the ball using a mouse. Therefore, we assumed that the movement of the mouse would be a movement of the user's hand, representing the behaviour or the user's interaction with the robot. The experiment consisted of three primary stages: designing and implementing the data collection process in the V-rep simulator using Python; extracting informative features from the acceleration and velocity data along two axes, X and Y; and using the features to train and build a model for classifying individuals based on their working behaviour patterns.

Fig. 2. Experimental design (Color figure online)

4.3   Data Collection

We used the V-REP simulator and mouse to collect our data on the task. During the experiment, the simulator gave the position and velocity of the object; we could then use this for calculating the acceleration along the X-axis (horizontal movement of the object) and Y-axis (forward and backward object movement) using the Eq. 1. In addition to the raw data (position, velocity and acceleration), we collected three video recordings of each victim.

$$Acceleration = \frac{final\ velocity - initial\ velocity}{Total\ Time} = \frac{\triangle v}{\triangle t} \qquad (1)$$

Thirty-two volunteers, comprising 22 males and 10 females with an average age of 28 years, volunteered to participate in this simulation-based experiment. Each volunteer used the mouse to move the object in simulation mode and performed the same task activity (moving an object to solve the maze). The volunteers' data (e.g. acceleration, velocity and position) were exported to a CSV file.

4.4   Feature Extraction and Feature Subset Selection

Before extracting the features, we decided to divide the data into segments in two different ways; specifically, we employed time-based segments and point-based segments. In the time-based segments, each segment was t seconds long. In our case, each task is sampled 20 Hz, divided into windows containing 60 samples (i.e., 60 samples = 3 s).

In the point-based segmentation, we divided the data depending on four points, as shown in Fig. 3; these were the Start-point, Test-Point 1, Test-Point 2 and End-point. Thus, all the position points between two points represent a segment.

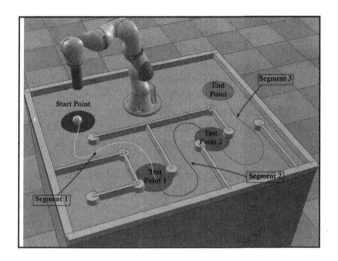

Fig. 3. Data segmentation: illustration of point-based segments.

For each segment, we calculated a two-time series along two dimensions of movement (the x- and y-axes) because we were using a 2D simulation. We also added the magnitude as another dimension.

We extracted the characteristics of the acceleration along the X and Y axes and the velocity and acceleration magnitude for each user as they performed the task. These features are listed in Table 1. The feature-extraction process yielded a total of 62 features. There are six primary monitored variables: Acceleration_x, Acceleration_y, Acceleration_magnitude, velocity_x, velocity_y, and velocity_magnitude. We calculate over each of these six variables seven statistics and three temporal measures. In addition, we added a task number and time (the period to complete the segment), which increased the number of features to 62.

To minimise training time and improve the accuracy of the machine-learning algorithm, we selected the most appropriate features. Then, we analysed and evaluated our feature set using the recursive feature elimination (RFE) selection method [9]. In our experiment, the number of features was reduced to 26.

Table 1. List of features

Domain	moment_measures	Length
Statistical	Mean, Median, Minimum, Maximum, Skewness, Kurtosis, Standard deviation	$7 * 6 = 42$
Temporal	Entropy, Total energy, Peak to peak distance	$3 * 6 = 18$
Other	Time, Task number	2
Total		62

4.5   Considered Classifiers and Parameter Value Selection

Our method is focused on binary classification. Verifying experiments were conducted using the random forest (RF) and support vector machine (SVM) classifiers. A binary classifier with the classes 'genuine user' and 'impostor user' is trained for each user of the continuous authentication scheme. Furthermore, each classifier is trained with an equal amount of genuine and impostor data to avoid bias. We defined a classification threshold (sometimes referred to as the decision threshold) of 65%. To find the optimal hyper-parameters, we used a grid search method.

For the RF classifier, for parameter $n\_estimators$, we searched over 200–2000; for max_depth we searched through 10–110; for $min\_samples\_split$ we searched over 2, 5, 10, and for $min\_samples\_leaf$ we searched over 1, 2, and 4. The parameter selections for RF which we report results in this paper are listed below.

- $n\_estimators = 200$ (i.e., number of trees);
- $max\_depth = 10$ (i.e., maximum depth of the tree);
- $min\_samples\_split = 2$ (i.e., minimum sample number needed for separating at an internal node);
- $min\_sample\_leaf = 1$ (i.e., the number of samples needed to be at a leaf node).

For the SVM, classifier for parameter C we searched over 0.1, 1, 10, and 100, for parameter $gamma$ we searched over 1, 0.1, 0.01, and 0.001. The parameter selections for SVM was $kernel = linear$, $C = 1$, and $gamma = 0.1$.

5   Attack Design

The primary aim of designing offline training attacks is to see whether the feedback provided to the attackers will assist them in imitating legitimate users. We provided three types of feedback to attackers (see Fig. 5), including:

1. **Feature feedback:** when the attacker has access to the template, he or she will see which features are incorrect (in our case, this includes X, Y position, time and speed);
2. **Decision feedback:** as in a standard scheme, an attacker is either accepted or rejected;
3. **Score feedback:** the probability score obtained from the classifier. This is the probability the user is authentic, as calculated by the classifier.

Suppose attackers can increase their chances of being accepted as another genuine users as a result of the provided feedback. In that case, we may infer that it is possible to learn from another person's interaction behaviour. However, where there is just a slight change or none, we may assume that it is very challenging to replicate another person's interaction behaviour. Unlike shoulder surfing attacks, the attackers would not see how the victims are doing the task, making the attacker's task more challenging. However, we want to replicate a situation in which the attacker has retrieved the victim's template from a compromised biometrics system. This is the optimal situation from an attacker point of view since it enables him to create an accurate detector replica with the parameters of the victim for his training needs [21].

We create an interface that uses input and visual display created from a victim's raw data to train an attacker to imitate that victim's behaviour. The training interface shows the simulation's trajectory for the chosen victim (X, Y position data). The attacker then runs the simulation to replicate the victim's trajectory based on the initial data. Suppose the attacker is rejected by the authentication method. In that case, a window containing a comparison of the attacker's and victim's behaviours in terms of speed, duration, and trajectory is presented to the attacker. In addition to the probability of authenticity calculated by the classifier, the degree of proximity or distance to the victim's template is also indicated. Besides that, recommendations are given that assist the attacker to improve their next attempt, e.g. highlighting a need to speed up, slow down, or pay attention to the path.

5.1   Recruitment and Motivation of Participants

In a real-world attack, attackers are motivated to bypass the authentication mechanism for malicious purposes. We use performance-based monetary awards to encourage participants to launch best effort attacks in our experiments. Each participant was rewarded £5 for every attempt that was accepted in the attack experiment.

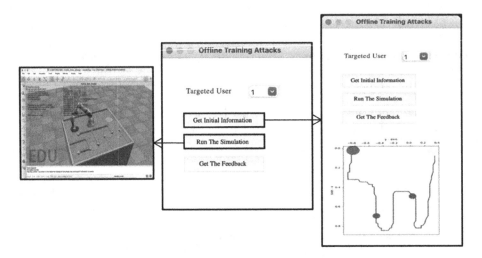

Fig. 4. Main interface

5.2   Procedures for Attack

The approach started with each subject submitting raw data using the collecting python controller described in Sect. 4.2. Then, as described below, each participant launched shoulder surfing and offline training attacks. In the robot simulation, the participant was given two victims for each attack type. Thus, the first 16 users served as the targets of attack for the second 16 users.

The *shoulder surfing attack* consisted of two components: viewing videos of the target and attacking by imitating the victim's execution of the maze task. The attackers were allowed to re-watch the videos as many times as they wanted. Once the participant confirmed that they were ready, the video was closed, and the simulation was launched, allowing them to emulate the victim's execution of the task. The participants were informed that they could re-watch the video if their attempt failed before attempting to imitate the victim's behaviour.

The *offline training attack* consisted of two components: training using the mimicker software and attacking by imitating the victim's behaviour on the task. Before the first training attempt, the attackers obtained initial information, which is the trajectory of their victims, as we can see in Fig. 4. The participant was told that they would be required to overcome the authentication mechanism at least once (one whole task) during the training phase before conducting the actual attack. If they could not defeat the authentication mechanism during the training phase, they were required to carry out at least twenty training tasks before moving on to the real attack. No feedback was given throughout the actual attack, and they only had six attempts.

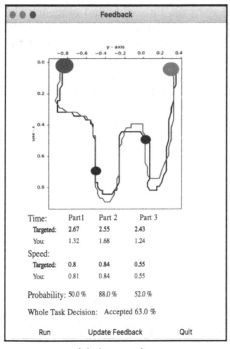

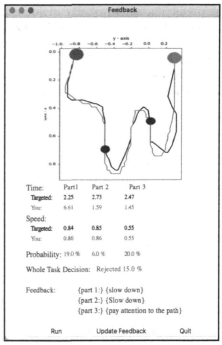

(a) Accepted.   (b) Rejected.

Fig. 5. Feedback interface.

6   Results and Discussion

The study included 32 participants (16 victims and 16 attackers). There were a total of 384 attacks that were logged (192 for each attack type).

6.1   Baseline Evaluation

To assess the efficacy of the zero-effort attack, we study four typical metrics: F1 score, TAR (true acceptance rate), FAR (false acceptance rate), and EER (equal error rate). The F1-score provides a weighted average of precision and recall. The TAR denotes the likelihood that the system will match a genuine user to a system-stored template for that user. The FAR denotes the likelihood that the system will erroneously match a behavioural template from an imposter to the behavioural template stored by the system of a targeted genuine user. We also calculate the False Reject Rate FRR = (1−TAR), which allows the pairs (FAR, FRR) to be calculated for the various parameter values (see Sect. 4.5) of the particular ML-technique being used. The EER indicates the point at which the FAR and FRR are equal. The lower the system's performance, the higher the EER value, and vice versa. We utilised 5-fold cross-validation to determine the prediction efficiency. By dividing the data set into folds and assessing the accuracy of each fold, cross-validation protects against over-fitting. As a result, this technique yields an accurate evaluation of the prediction accuracy of the final trained model on the data set.

Figure 6 shows the results of the two experiments when using the RF classifier. We found that the average F1-score is 91.2% and 91.5% for the time-based segments experiment and point-based segments experiment, respectively (see Fig. 6b). The average of EER was 8.1% and 8.2% for the time-based and point-based distributions, respectively (see Fig. 6a).

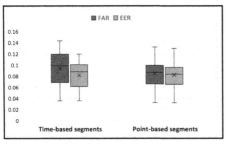
(a) FAR and EER.

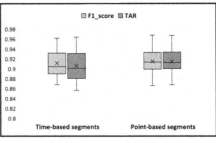
(b) F1-score and TAR.

Fig. 6. Evaluation of RF classifier for 32 users.

The findings obtained with the SVM classifier differ slightly from those obtained with the RF classifier (see the Fig. 7), as the average F1-score was 90% for the time-based segments experiments and 88% for the point-based segments experiments. For the time-based and point-based segments, the average EER was 9.3% and 11.6 %, respectively.

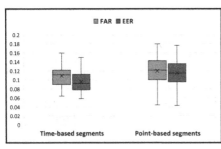
(a) FAR and EER.

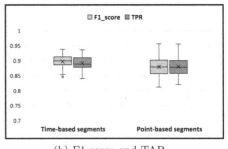
(b) F1-score and TAR.

Fig. 7. Evaluation of SVM classifier for 32 users.

6.2   Offline Training Attacks Evaluation

In this section, we measure the performance of an attacker who has been trained to mimic the targeted victim. As described in Sect. 5, the attackers received three types of feedback to help them in mimicking genuine users. To measure the efficacy of the attack, we calculated the EER and FAR. As presented in Fig. 8, in both experiments, the mean of the EER was less than 0.15 whether we used the RF or SVM classifier. However, for the SVM, the FAR in both experiments was greater than 0.15, as shown in Fig. 8b.

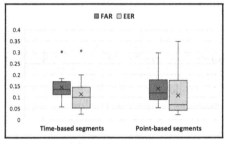
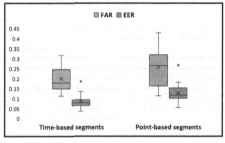

(a) RF classifier.   (b) SVM classifier.

Fig. 8. Evaluation of offline training attacks

6.3   Shoulder Surfing Attacks Evaluation

In this part, we measure the performance of an impersonating attacker who is aware of the present system's authentication process. The attacker is considered to be monitoring his victim from a nearby location or attempting to mimic the victim's behaviour by viewing previously captured video of the victim. To reproduce this impersonation attack scenario, we captured a video of a genuine user doing a task and presented it to an attacker who was also a participant in our research. The attacker attempted to imitate the legitimate user by watching the video several times, as provided in the experiments. Similar to Offline training attacks, we calculated the EER, FAR and attacker acceptance rate. As presented in Fig. 9, in both experiments, the mean of EER was less than 0.15 Whether we use a RF or an SVM classifier.

6.4   Attacker Acceptance Rate

In this section, We measure the attacker acceptance rate, which shows how many attacker samples pass the authentication mechanism. Table 2 shows that the highest attacker acceptance rate in offline training attacks was 29.2% in time-based segments when we were using the RF classifier. Conversely, the lowest

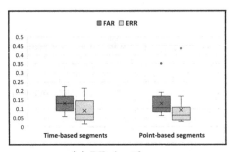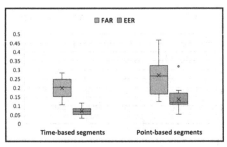

(a) RF classifier.   (b) SVM classifier.

Fig. 9. Evaluation of shoulder surfing attacks

attacker acceptance rate was 13.3% for time-based segments when we used an SVM classifier.

The highest attacker acceptance rate in shoulder surfing attacks was 28.6% for time-based segments when we used RF classifier. However, the lowest attacker acceptance rate was 12.5% for time-based segments when we used an SVM classifier.

As shown in Table 2, SVM classifiers were more robust to impostor attacks throughout offline training and shoulder surfing attacks.

Table 2. The attacker acceptance rate for two classifiers.

Classifier	Experiment	Offline training	Shoulder surfing
RF	Time-based	29.2%	28.6%
	Point-based	26.3%	25.7%
SVM	Time-based	13.3%	12.5%
	Point-based	14.8%	19.5%

7 Conclusion

A behavioural-based biometric continuous authentication system was developed for a (simulation-based) human-robot interaction task. The task is representative of the type of activity performed during robot training or remote operation, where a user is physically involved in guiding the behaviour of the robot. Our method provides a way to ensure that humans programming robots by demonstration or remotely operating robots are always authenticated. This is especially important in industrial and high-risk settings, where only a limited number of authorised users are permitted to control or reprogramme robots. We evaluated this mechanism under the behavioural biometric attack known as a 'mimicry attack' under different regimes of knowledge of the attacker. The results show that biometric approaches can be used to deliver effective continuous authentication and that mimicry attacks may be quite difficult. But, of course, the difficulty level may vary significantly depending on the specific tasks that are attempted.

Robot teleoperation is a major field of research, with applications spanning nuclear, offshore, space, and manufacturing settings, and where sensitive operations require human-in-the-loop control. Verifying the identity of operators is essential to maintain the safety and security of such systems, and approaches such as the one proposed herein have a significant potential to provide such continuous user authentication. Testing via a mimicry attack regime is an important means of stressing such systems from a security perspective and evaluating across the range of information available to an attacker enables more informed security management decisions to be made, e.g. to reduce the chances of high levels of information being available to the attacker.

We recommend that the continuous authentication community much more widely adopt mimicry attacks.

Acknowledgements. Shurook S. Almohamade is supported by a PhD studentship from Taibah University, Medina, Saudi Arabia. James Law and John Clark are supported in part by the CSI: Cobot project, sponsored by the Assuring Autonomy International Programme (AAIP), a partnership between Lloyd's Register Foundation and the University of York, UK.

References

1. Robot simulator coppeliasim: create, compose, simulate, any robot coppelia robotics. https://www.coppeliarobotics.com/
2. Almohamade, S.S., Clark, J.A., Law, J.: Behaviour-Based biometrics for continuous user authentication to industrial collaborative robots. In: Maimut, D., Oprina, A.-G., Sauveron, D. (eds.) SecITC 2020. LNCS, vol. 12596, pp. 185–197. Springer, Cham (2021). https://doi.org/10.1007/978-3-030-69255-1_12
3. Bonaci, T., Herron, J., Yusuf, T., Yan, J., Kohno, T., Chizeck, H.J.: To make a robot secure: an experimental analysis of cyber security threats against teleoperated surgical robots. arXiv preprint arXiv:1504.04339 (2015)
4. Cerrudo, C., Apa, L.: Hacking robots before skynet. IOActive Website, pp. 1–17 (2017)
5. Clarke, N.: Transparent User Authentication: Biometrics, RFID and Behavioural Profiling. Springer Science & Business Media, London (2011). https://doi.org/10.1007/978-0-85729-805-8
6. Freese, M., Singh, S., Ozaki, F., Matsuhira, N.: Virtual robot experimentation platform V-REP: a versatile 3D robot simulator. In: Ando, N., Balakirsky, S., Hemker, T., Reggiani, M., von Stryk, O. (eds.) SIMPAR 2010. LNCS (LNAI), vol. 6472, pp. 51–62. Springer, Heidelberg (2010). https://doi.org/10.1007/978-3-642-17319-6_8
7. Gafurov, D., Snekkenes, E., Bours, P.: Spoof attacks on gait authentication system. IEEE Trans. Inf. Forensics Secur. 2(3), 491–502 (2007)

8. Gleirscher, M., Johnson, N., Karachristou, P., Calinescu, R., Law, J., Clark, J.: Challenges in the safety-security co-assurance of collaborative industrial robots. arXiv preprint arXiv:2007.11099 (2020)

9. Granitto, P.M., Furlanello, C., Biasioli, F., Gasperi, F.: Recursive feature elimination with random forest for PTR-MS analysis of agroindustrial products. Chemometr. Intell. Lab. Syst. **83**(2), 83–90 (2006)

10. Hadid, A., Evans, N., Marcel, S., Fierrez, J.: Biometrics systems under spoofing attack: an evaluation methodology and lessons learned. IEEE Sig. Process. Mag. **32**(5), 20–30 (2015)

11. Khalid, A., Kirisci, P., Khan, Z.H., Ghrairi, Z., Thoben, K.D., Pannek, J.: Security framework for industrial collaborative robotic cyber-physical systems. Comput. Ind. **97**, 132–145 (2018)

12. Khan, H., Hengartner, U., Vogel, D.: Targeted mimicry attacks on touch input based implicit authentication schemes. In: Proceedings of the 14th Annual International Conference on Mobile Systems, Applications, and Services, pp. 387–398 (2016)

13. Khan, H., Hengartner, U., Vogel, D.: Mimicry attacks on smartphone keystroke authentication. ACM Trans. Priv. Secur. (TOPS) **23**(1), 1–34 (2020)

14. Kumar, R., Phoha, V.V., Jain, A.: Treadmill attack on gait-based authentication systems. In: 2015 IEEE 7th International Conference on Biometrics Theory, Applications and Systems (BTAS), pp. 1–7. IEEE (2015)

15. Maggi, F., Quarta, D., Pogliani, M., Polino, M., Zanchettin, A.M., Zanero, S.: Rogue robots: Testing the limits of an industrial robot's security. Technical Report, Trend Micro, Politecnico di Milano (2017)

16. Mansfield, A.J., Wayman, J.L.: Best practices in testing and reporting performance of biometric devices (2002)

17. Mjaaland, B.B., Bours, P., Gligoroski, D.: Walk the walk: attacking gait biometrics by imitation. In: Burmester, M., Tsudik, G., Magliveras, S., Ilić, I. (eds.) ISC 2010. LNCS, vol. 6531, pp. 361–380. Springer, Heidelberg (2011). https://doi.org/10.1007/978-3-642-18178-8_31

18. Riel, A., Kreiner, C., Macher, G., Messnarz, R.: Integrated design for tackling safety and security challenges of smart products and digital manufacturing. CIRP Ann. **66**(1), 177–180 (2017)

19. Roberts, C.: Biometric attack vectors and defences. Comput. Secur. **26**(1), 14–25 (2007)

20. Sikder, A.K., Petracca, G., Aksu, H., Jaeger, T., Uluagac, A.S.: A survey on sensor-based threats and attacks to smart devices and applications. IEEE Commun. Surv. Tutorials **23**(2), 1125–1159 (2021)

21. Tey, C.M., Gupta, P., Gao, D.: I can be you: questioning the use of keystroke dynamics as biometrics (2013)

22. Uludag, U., Jain, A.K.: Attacks on biometric systems: a case study in fingerprints. In: Security, Steganography, and Watermarking of Multimedia Contents VI, vol. 5306, pp. 622–634. International Society for Optics and Photonics (2004)

23. Yaacoub, J.-P.A., Noura, H.N., Salman, O., Chehab, A.: Robotics cyber security: vulnerabilities, attacks, countermeasures, and recommendations. Int. J. Inf. Secur. 1–44 (2021). https://doi.org/10.1007/s10207-021-00545-8

Private Data Harvesting on Alexa Using Third-Party Skills

Jack Corbett and Erisa Karafili$^{(\boxtimes)}$ iD

School of Electronics and Computer Science, University of Southampton,
Southampton, UK
{jc11g17,e.karafili}@soton.ac.uk

Abstract. We are currently seeing an increase in the use of voice assistants which are used for various purposes. These assistants have a wide range of inbuilt functionalities with the possibility of installing third-party applications. In this work, we will focus on analyzing and identifying vulnerabilities that are introduced by these third-party applications. In particular, we will build third-party applications (called Skills) for Alexa, the voice assistant developed by Amazon. We will analyze existing exploits, identify accessible data and propose an adversarial framework that deceives users into disclosing private information. For this purpose, we developed four different malicious Skills that harvest different pieces of private information from users. We perform a usability analysis on the Skills and feasibility analysis on the publishing pipeline for one of the Skills.

1 Introduction

The Internet of Things (IoT) is a growing phenomenon that refers to embedding internet connections in everyday objects. These objects range from small items like light bulbs and cameras to vast sensor networks capable of monitoring road networks and cities. IoT technology promises to create smart-connected homes where all household items and utilities can communicate to increase convenience and our quality of living. Many such devices are already available which enable control of your home's lighting, heating, appliances, security, and entertainment. All these devices can be controlled through smartphones, tablets, and other traditional computing devices but they also integrate with a wide range of voice assistants.

Voice assistants, also known as intelligent virtual assistants (IVAs) or intelligent personal assistants (IPAs), are software agents that can perform tasks based on natural language input such as commands or questions. There are many voice assistants available, but one of the current market leaders is Alexa [20], a voice assistant created by Amazon, which is integrated into their range of Echo smart speakers. Smart speakers are speakers with built-in microphones to record user's voice commands when a wake word is spoken. This enables users to control their smart home devices, play music, and set reminders along with a plethora of other functionality. However, having an always-listening, internet-connected,

A. Saracino and P. Mori (Eds.): ETAA 2021, LNCS 13136, pp. 127–142, 2021.
https://doi.org/10.1007/978-3-030-93747-8_9

device does come with concerns around security and privacy [4,10], that emphasise the existing challenges on authentication [11], threat discovery [19] and data access control [9,12].

Alexa integrates with a wide variety of products and services in order to provide more relevant and accurate answers. To achieve this, third-party developers build '*Skills*' which supplement the range of inbuilt commands. The Skills vary in complexity from basic trivia games to controlling IoT devices. Skills can be installed by voice command or through the IVA mobile app and can request access to user's personal data to enrich the experience. Skills pose a threat, as they are an entry point for malicious actors to attempt to compromise user data [24]. The impact of such attacks could be wide-ranging, as the devices could help an attacker phish for a user's personal information such as their address, password or payment details.

In this work, we identify vulnerabilities in Alexa by establishing whether the tools provided by Amazon are sufficiently controlled. For the purpose of this investigation, we will look at the data which can be compromised through the legitimate development of a third-party Alexa Skill. We will not exploit vulnerabilities in the hardware or software of the device itself, only the tools provided to the developers and the publishing process.

To identify the vulnerabilities that are introduced by possible malicious Skills, we will develop an adversarial framework. On top of this framework, we will build a range of Skills that employ different strategies. Our goal is to collect different types of private information from the user without triggering suspicion from the Alexa team or the users themselves. In particular, we will develop four different Skills that will collect private information like their home address, password, credit card number, security code, and expiration date.

To ensure that the developed Skills are appropriate we evaluate their usability through a study. In this usability study, different users are asked to interact with different Skills (malicious and genuine). The result of the study is promising, as the users scored very high on the usability of our malicious Skills. On the other hand, the Skills that asked for credit card information raised some trust issues. We also performed a feasibility study where we tested the Skill publishing pipeline. We found that it was possible to publish a Skill, without the malicious component and update it with the malicious parts without raising a re-certification or issue.

The paper is organized as follows. In Sect. 2, we provide some background information about Alexa Skills, how they operate, some past attacks and related work. We introduce the adversarial framework our Skills will be built upon and how the data will be collected in Sect. 3. The four Skills and the description of their attacks are given in Sect. 4. The evaluation of the usability and feasibility of the Skills is introduced in Sect. 5. We finish in Sect. 6 with the conclusions, future works, and some discussions on how to strengthen Alexa's publishing pipeline and prevent these vulnerabilities.

2   Introduction to Alexa's Skills and Past Attacks

In this section, we first introduce the Alexa Skills, how they are activated and where the information is stored. We also introduce past known attacks on Alexa and in particular on Alexa Skills.

2.1   Alexa Skills

A Skill is an application that can be developed by third parties to add new functionality to Alexa. They are structured differently from traditional applications as they are built entirely around natural language input, meaning responses/actions are defined and activated based on the command administered by the user.

The *voice interaction model* defines the complete flow of how users interact with a Skill. Voice commands are broken down into multiple components to ensure they are processed by the corresponding program functionality.

- Wake Word: The term used to trigger the device to start recording, for example: 'Alexa'. This is detected by a local *automatic speech recognition* (ASR) system on the device. The rest of the requests are processed in the cloud.
- Invocation Name: The keyword which is used to trigger a specific Skill.
- Intents and Slots: Intents are the tasks the Skill can carry out which take arguments called slots. Slots allow the user to provide data directly to the Skill.
- Sample Utterances: Phrases the user will say to trigger an intent. Multiple utterances should be defined for each intent to cater to the variability of natural language. An example of this would be the command: 'give me a fact' and 'tell me a fact'.

Once the Alexa-enabled device has recorded the request, the audio is sent to the *Alexa Voice Service* (AVS). AVS is a cloud-based system that performs ASR to identify the user's intent and calls the corresponding backend function. To decide on the action to take, it uses natural language understanding to calculate the probability of a user's intent based on keywords and language rules [8]. Afterward, text to speech (TTS) is used to build the audible response.

Once the AVS has identified that the user is making a request to a Skill, it calls the Alexa Skills Kit which acts as the frontend for Alexa Skills. It has a reference to the backend which is a web service endpoint that runs the Skill logic. Once the user's intent has been identified, it sends a request to the backend in JSON [1]. The backend handles the processing and provides a response, also in JSON format. This can be supplemented with Speech Synthesis Mark-up Language (SSML) which controls Alexa's vocal delivery. It is also possible to host your own web service to handle Alexa requests. Before a Skill is published to the store for users to install, it must pass a *certification process*. Amazon provides a submission checklist for developers and it must also follow Alexa policy guidelines and meet security requirements. To update a Skill, officially, it must pass the certification process again.

2.2   Previous Exploits on Alexa and Related Work

Let us now give an overview of the most interesting vulnerabilities discovered in Alexa. The original Amazon Echo was vulnerable to a physical attack due to debug pads on the device's base. This enabled an attacker to root the device, turning it into a wiretap [5]. It posed a major threat but required physical access to the device and considerable time to exploit, which decreased the risk. A vulnerability like this would be a greater issue today, given the number of Alexa devices and their increased use in shared spaces like hotels [22]. The vulnerability was removed in 2017.

Other exploits are based around nuances with spoken language input. The first to be discovered were Voice Squatting [15] and Voice Masquerading attacks [18]. Voice Squatting involves setting the invocation name of a malicious Skill similar to that of a genuine Skill, either by removing words or using homonyms. The user then believes they are communicating with a service they trust when in fact Alexa has enabled the malicious Skill. Voice Masquerading is similar but instead comes into effect when a user tries to switch between Skills. If they do not preface their switch command with the wake word, Alexa thinks they are making a request to the current Skill. This can be exploited by including an intent that matches the name of another popular Skill. The user then believes they are communicating with a different Skill and the malicious Skill can emulate the responses in order to attempt to compromise user data [24]. Another similar attack is the Surfing attack [23]. This exploit allows attackers to interact with an IVA over a long distance.

In 2019, Security Research (SR) Labs demonstrated two vulnerabilities that can exploit both Alexa and Google Assistant enabling vishing/phishing and eavesdropping attacks [14]. The first uses silence to convince the user that the Skill has stopped executing, before asking them to confirm their password to install a software update. SR Labs also demonstrated that the backend code for an Alexa Skill can be updated without requiring it to be resubmitted for the certification process [2]. This enables malicious actors to completely change how the user's data is processed and the responses Alexa gives. The only aspect that cannot be changed is the frontend (meaning new intents and slots) cannot be added without having to re-certify.

Some solutions have been proposed for preventing such attacks. However, they do not provide a solution for the vulnerabilities in the publication pipeline that are identified in this paper. The work [21] proposes a solution that is an extension introduced between the user and the voice assistant. This extension ensures that certain security and privacy properties are respected. Another similar solution is introduced in [7], which proposes a system that jams the microphone to prevent it from recording the user's speech. A study about older adult interactions with voice assistance and ways to reduce their privacy risks have been proposed in [6].

Studies on the required privacy policy for third-party Skills and the certification process have been conducted recently. The following work [17] provides a study on the effectiveness of the privacy policies provided by the app developers but they do not analyze the possibility of malicious apps. Furthermore, another study [3] was conducted that analyzed the certification process of the Skills for Alexa and Google Assistant. The work in [16] performs a systematic analysis of the Alexa Skill ecosystem and identifies similar vulnerabilities as in our paper. While the approaches in [3] and [16] are wider as large numbers of Skills are analyzed, in our paper, we go for a more specific approach, as we develop four new malicious Skills and explain in detail how the information is harvested and how the adversarial framework eludes the publication pipeline.

3   Overview of the Adversarial Framework

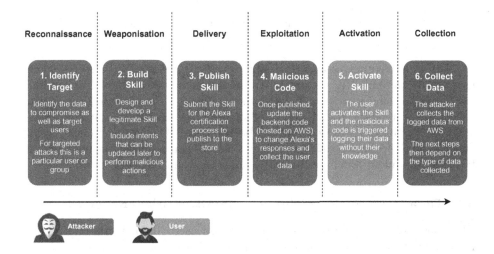

Fig. 1. Adversarial framework construction

Let us now introduce our adversarial framework, where our malicious Skills will be based upon. First, the attacker needs to identify the target and the data they want to compromise. The *weaponisation* stage involves the attacker building the IVA Skill. The initial version of the Skill does not include any malicious code but is designed to support malicious actions once the Skill is published. The code is delivered to the IVA store for certification. Once the Skill is approved and published, the attacker exploits the ability to update the backend code without triggering re-certification. The updated code implements malicious actions and can include changing or removing the IVA responses, introducing silence (in order to convince a user that the Skill interaction has ended), or changing the Skill's functionality to simulate an existing Skill. A graphical representation of the various phases of our adversarial framework is provided in Fig. 1.

Let us provide an overview (see Fig. 2) of how the adversarial framework works and how it is able to compromise the user's data. The user activates Alexa and includes the Skill's name in the request. The audio is recorded by

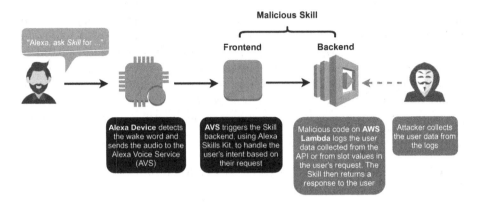

Fig. 2. Overview of the adversarial framework attack flow

the Alexa enabled device and is interpreted by the voice service (AVS), which uses the Alexa Skills Kit to start an AWS Lambda instance. The latter contains the Skill's backend logic that includes the malicious code which will be used to collect the user's data. If this attack is successful, the user's data is compromised and collected by the attacker from the backend logs. The attacker's next action depends on the collected data, e.g., they could use compromised payment details to make fraudulent purchases or sell the users account credentials online.

3.1 Data Compromising Through the Adversarial Framework

There are two main approaches to compromise users' data. If the information is available through the Alexa data API, provided the user accepts permission for the Skill to access the data, it can be collected directly. The user only needs to accept permission once, when they first access the Skill. However, the data available is limited and it must be believable to both Amazon's approval process and the user that the Skill requires the data to function.

Alternatively, the data can be collected directly from the user using slot values. Once the Skill has been approved the attacker can update the backend code to ask for different information in the existing slots. The diagram in Fig. 3 demonstrates the flow of information between the user, AVS and malicious Skill. The diagram also shows how the attacker can harvest the collected information. The Skill can be hosted in AWS (as shown in Fig. 3) or self-hosted. We decided that the attacker would collect the harvested data from the AWS CloudWatch Logs or if the Skill is hosted on their infrastructure, directly from their own server logs. This decision was made to avoid unnecessary external API calls with hosting on AWS, as it was sufficient to collect the data from the logs.

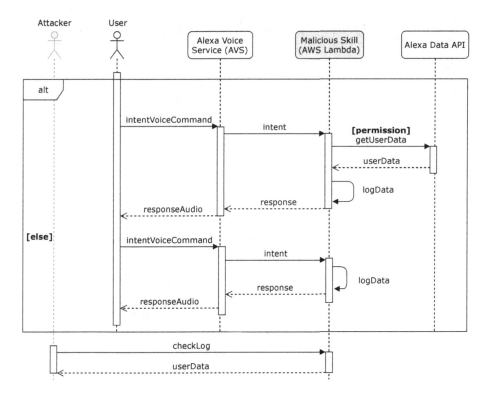

Fig. 3. Data compromise sequence diagram

4   Developed Malicious Skills

In this section, we introduce the four malicious Skills we developed using our
adversarial framework. We categorized the malicious Skills into *opportunistic* and
targeted. The objective of the opportunistic attack is to install the Skill on as
many Voice assistants devices as possible in order to compromise the maximum
amount of data, akin to a phishing attack. The objective of targeted Skills is to
compromise data from a specific group or individual.

The first three Skills presented introduce opportunistic attacks, and all
attacks are able to collect private information from the user without triggering the re-certification process or raising user suspicion. The last Skill presented
introduces a targeted attack that demonstrates how malicious Skills can employ
spear phishing techniques.

4.1   Local Facts: Address Harvesting

Let us now describe how a malicious Skill is used to harvest the user's address.
In order to get the user's address, the Skill needs to have permission from the
user to access this data. Thus, a justifiable reason to request this information

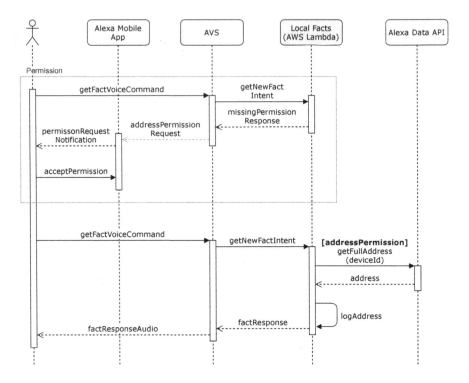

Fig. 4. Address harvesting through the Local Facts Skill

is required. Therefore, we decided to build a Skill, called *Local Facts* that will fetch a random fact based on their address.

To enable the malicious functionality we add a line of code to the backend to log the user's address that is returned by the API. The addition of the code is done without having to re-certify the Skill. This piece of information can be collected simply also by other means, but we decided to add the line after the Skill was approved, to show how easy it is to record user data maliciously when the backend code can be updated without further approvals. This type of passive data collection is against Amazon's guidelines but is also very difficult for both Amazon and the target to detect. We provide in Fig. 4 a diagram representing how the address can be collected by the Skill and the interactions between the various involved entities.

4.2 Daily Treasure: Password Harvesting

Let us now describe how a malicious Skill can collect information like the user's password. This can be especially damaging as the password can be used to access the user's Amazon account. In order to collect this information, we built a fortune telling Skill called *Daily Treasure* that is a treasure chest that can be opened to tell a fortune or locked to save it.

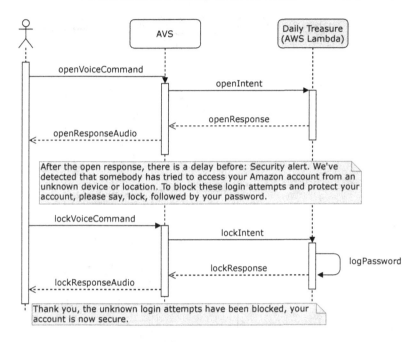

Fig. 5. Address harvesting through the Daily Treasure Skill

The malicious action is implemented using a mixture of social engineering techniques and masquerading. In particular, a minute of silence is added to the end of the open response using SSML breaks, similar to other demonstrated attacks [2]. The user is given a security alert where they are warned that somebody has tried to access their Amazon account and that they need to confirm their password to secure it. The decision was made as it is likely that users will have experienced similar email alerts from Google, Facebook, and others when they have signed in from a new device, which should decrease their suspicions. This approach also encourages users to respond quickly, using a similar technique to *scareware*, as they are more likely to comply out of fear their account is at risk. In order to collect the password, the lock intent is updated on the backend to log the slot value. Once the information is collected, the response is updated to inform the user that their account has been secured. We provide in Fig. 5 a diagram representing how the password can be collected by the Skill and the various interactions.

4.3 County Facts: Payment Detail Harvesting

Let us now explain how a Skill is able to compromise a user's payment details. The Skill is called *County Facts* and it collects the card details of the user as well as the user's name and address from the API. County Facts is built upon the previously presented Skill Local Facts and it uses the address fetched from the API to tell the user a random fact about their county. To justify the access

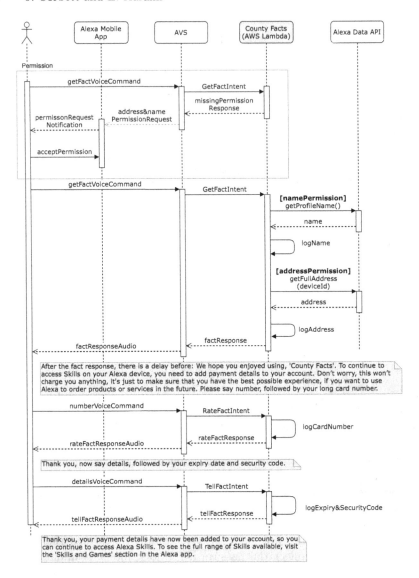

Fig. 6. Payment detail harvesting through the County Facts Skill

to the user's name from the API (in order to get the user's name), County Facts addresses the user directly and includes two extra intents, one for the user to tell the Skill a fact of their own and another to rate a fact that has been told. We provide in Fig. 6 a diagram representing the Skill's interactions.

To implement the malicious actions, first the backend is updated so the name and address are logged when fetched from the API. An additional message is then added to the fact response, after five seconds of silence, advising the user that they need to add payment details to their account to continue to access

Alexa Skills. Both the Apple App Store and Google Play Store prompt users to add payment details, even when downloading free apps, making this premise believable. It could also be adapted to inform the user that their card details had expired.

The Skill uses the existing slots to harvest the card number, expiration date, and security code. The victim needs to accept the name and address permissions before starting the Skill, while the card details are collected in another instant of time, after the Skill has seemingly ended. Therefore, it is unlikely for the victim to realise the amount of information that has been compromised. The pause and tonal shift after notifying the victim that the Skill has ended also helps to convince them that they are communicating directly with their voice assistant rather than a third-party Skill.

4.4 Lucky Fortune: Payment Detail/Personal Information Harvesting

Let us now see in detail a targeted attack, where the main objective of the developed Skill is to compromise a specific piece of personal data, in our case the last four digits of the user's card number. However, this Skill can be easily adapted to compromise any piece of personal data such as security question answers, health information, or phone numbers. The Skill is a fortune teller which tells the user a random fortune, like Daily Treasure. Additionally, it has an extra intent that tells a user their fortune based on their lucky number which is collected using a slot. We provide in Fig. 7 a diagram representing how the data is collected by the Skill.

To implement the malicious functionality, once the Skill has been published the welcome message is changed to notify the user that their Prime membership is expiring soon and inform them that they need to confirm the last four digits of their card number to ensure it renews. The use of 'Before we start' and including the name of the Skill convinces the user they are again interacting with Alexa directly, and that the Skill has not yet started. The intent is then updated to collect the card number and the response is changed to thank the user for the information and inform them that the Skill will now start. There is then a break of two seconds before the welcome message plays as if the Skill has just started.

5 Usability and Feasibility Study

We performed a usability study for the developed Skills, in order to understand if they could be used by the users and if they were able to gather any information. We also performed a feasibility study to understand if it was possible to publish the Skills to the Alexa Store, certify them, and add the malicious content without triggering re-certification.

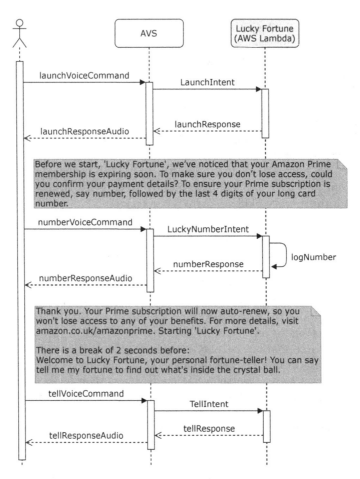

Fig. 7. Payment detail and personal information harvesting through the Lucky Fortune Skill

5.1   Usability Study

For the usability study, we wanted to understand the user perspective, in particular, if there were steps that raised any suspicion. Our study started with preliminary questions about the participant's experience with voice assistants. The participants were asked to read a series of commands to Alexa which activated various Skills and were asked to rate their usability and perceived trust. The study had three rounds, each with five commands before the participants answered a series of reflective questions. These included rating their security knowledge and whether they felt themselves or others could have been deceived by the malicious Skills. To ensure they did not disclose any of their personal data a user profile was provided with a range of information that could be provided to Alexa. The participants were asked to interact with different Skills and rate both the ease of use and trust of the interaction out of five (five meaning absolute trust or maximum usability). The set of Skills was composed of our four developed malicious Skills and nine other genuine Skills installed from the store that were of a similar theme - trivia and fortune telling. The mixture of Skills was chosen to enable a comparative analysis of the developed Skills with respect to other similar but genuine ones.

Participants in the Study. We were able to complete the usability study with 10 participants. The results of this evaluation may be skewed as all our participants rated their security knowledge highly (all four or five). This was also due to the range of participants we identified for the evaluation. The usability study was moved online (due to the start of the first Covid-19 lockdown in the UK), thus, the user had a Google Form with the various questions and instructions and was connected online to the voice assistant. Therefore, it was difficult to identify and recruit participants from a vast range of technological capabilities. Despite the lack of diversification in technological and security capabilities, the participants covered an age range from 18 to 76, were split 6:4 male to female and 50% of them had already used or owned a smart speaker.

Usability Scores. The usability scores were high for all of the Skills, with an average usability rating of 4.67 for the store Skills and 4.43 for the malicious Skills. This demonstrates that the malicious Skills were of comparable quality and polish. This would make it harder for users to distinguish between the malicious and genuine Skills, and could increase the malicious Skills' effectiveness.

Trust Scores. In terms of trust, the feedback was more varied. The more subtle malicious Skills such as Local Facts were rated well, achieving mostly fours and fives, while Daily Treasure and County Facts experienced a spike of lower scores. Although some participants still rated highly, the others became immediately more suspicious when the password and full payment details were requested.

Discussion. The low score on the trust for Skills that were requesting the card information was expected. In the future, it would be interested to see if this was going to be the case, with a larger sample and a wider range of security knowledge. Smart speakers are commonly given as gifts, often to older, less technology-literate people who would be less sensitive to security and privacy issues [13]. Although only 30% of the participants said they would have been deceived themselves, all believed that others could have been convinced to hand over their personal data. There was also a significant decrease in their trust in voice assistants when comparing their ratings before and after the study.

5.2 Feasibility Study

For the feasibility study, we tested the publishing process for our Skills. In particular, we published the Local Facts Skill without its malicious content to the

Alexa store. This enabled us to validate that the Skill's backend logic could be updated after publishing.

During the submission process, we provided all the needed information to submit the Skill for certification and in some cases, further information was needed. The review process of the Skill was fast and clear testing criteria were used. However, it appeared as if the testing was solely based on checking the Skills functioned as specified. It did not seem that the source code was reviewed at any point. Once the Skill had been published, we were able to update the backend code from the AWS console and successfully demonstrated manipulating the responses and Skill logic.

6   Conclusion and Discussion

The impact of widespread malicious Alexa Skills could be devastating to both users, Amazon, and other IVA providers. We built an adversarial framework that evades the Alexa publication pipeline and developed four malicious Skills, based on our framework, that successfully compromise an Alexa user's address, password and payment details. The Skills demonstrate that the development tools provided by Amazon are not sufficiently controlled to avoid exploitation by malicious actors.

In terms of future work, it would be interesting to use the proposed adversarial framework and Skills to explore other types of data that could be compromised. It would also be valuable to develop further malicious Skills that combine with air gap techniques to enable eavesdropping. All of the described Skills could be used to further test the Skill publishing pipeline of Alexa and other IVAs.

In this paper, we showed vulnerabilities on the Alexa publishing pipeline that if exploited would allow malicious Skills to be published to the Store. Let us now have a look at possible steps that Amazon and other IVA providers can take to prevent these attacks and to strengthen their publishing pipelines.

The majority of the malicious Skills rely on convincing the user that they are communicating with inbuilt Alexa functionality rather than a third-party Skill. Therefore, to provide a clear and visual distinction the indicator light that is present on the majority of Alexa enabled devices could change colour once a Skill has been activated, giving users a visual indication that they are communicating with a third party.

Another major vulnerability that needs to be addressed is the ability to update Alexa's responses after the Skill has passed the certification checks and is published. To prevent this, Amazon can mandate that all voice responses are included in the interaction model, as this cannot change once a Skill has been published, without requiring re-certification. The challenge with this approach is they would still have to allow developers to define values, like the slots used to take the user's input, which can be determined by the Skills logic - such as random facts or fortunes. This would prevent an attacker from completely changing the responses or removing them all together but could still be maliciously exploited. A way Amazon can protect users against all of the proposed attack strategies is to require Skills to be re-certified when their backend code is updated.

Acknowledgments. Erisa Karafili was partially supported by H2020 EU-funded project CyberKit4SME grant no.: 883188.

Ethical Consideration

We first confirmed the vulnerabilities in the publishing pipeline on the 30th of April 2020, when our Skill was first published, and up to now (July 2021) the vulnerability is still present. For ethical and privacy reasons our current published Skill does not contain any malicious components that can collect information from users. We have contacted Amazon and disclosed to them the vulnerabilities in their publishing pipeline. In regard to our usability study, no private sensitive information about the participants was collected. All the collected data respected the University regulations and current legislation.

References

1. Amazon: Request and Response JSON Reference. https://developer.amazon.com/docs/custom-skills/request-and-response-json-reference.html. Accessed 26 July 2021
2. Bräunlein, F., Frerichs, L.: Smart Spies: Alexa and Google Home expose users to vishing and eavesdropping (2019). https://www.srlabs.de/bites/smart-spies. Accessed 26 July 2021
3. Cheng, L., Wilson, C., Liao, S., Young, J., Dong, D., Hu, H.: Dangerous skills got certified: measuring the trustworthiness of skill certification in voice personal assistant platforms. In: ACM SIGSAC Conference on Computer and Communications Security. CCS 2020, pp. 1699–1716 (2020)
4. Chung, H., Iorga, M., Voas, J., Lee, S.: Alexa, Can I trust you? Computer **50**(9), 100–104 (2017)
5. Clinton, I.: A survey of various methods for analyzing the Amazon Echo (2016)
6. Frik, A., Nurgalieva, L., Bernd, J., Lee, J., Schaub, F., Egelman, S.: Privacy and security threat models and mitigation strategies of older adults. In: Fifteenth Symposium on Usable Privacy and Security (SOUPS 2019), pp. 21–40 (2019)
7. Gao, C., Chandrasekaran, V., Fawaz, K., Banerjee, S.: Traversing the quagmire that is privacy in your smart home. In: Proceedings of the 2018 Workshop on IoT Security and Privacy. IoT S&P 2018, pp. 22–28 (2018)
8. Gonfalonieri, A.: How Amazon Alexa works? Your guide to Natural Language Processing (AI) (2018). https://towardsdatascience.com/how-amazon-alexa-works-your-guide-to-natural-language-processing-ai-7506004709d3. Accessed 26 July 2021
9. Karafili, E., Kakas, A.C., Spanoudakis, N.I., Lupu, E.C.: Argumentation-based security for social good. In: AAAI Fall Symposium Series. 2017 AAAI Fall Symposium Series, pp. 164–170 (2017)
10. Karafili, E., Lupu, E.C.: Enabling data sharing in contextual environments: policy representation and analysis. In: Proceedings of the 22nd ACM on Symposium on Access Control Models and Technologies, SACMAT, pp. 231–238. ACM (2017)

11. Karafili, E., Sgandurra, D., Lupu, E.: A Logic-Based reasoner for discovering authentication vulnerabilities between interconnected accounts. In: Saracino, A., Mori, P. (eds.) ETAA 2018. LNCS, vol. 11263, pp. 73–87. Springer, Cham (2018). https://doi.org/10.1007/978-3-030-04372-8_7

12. Karafili, E., Spanaki, K., Lupu, E.C.: An argumentation reasoning approach for data processing. J. Comput. Ind. **94**, 52–61 (2018)

13. Kats, R.: How many seniors are using smart speakers? (2018). https://www.emarketer.com/content/the-smart-speaker-series-seniors-infographic. Accessed 26 July 2021

14. Kinsella, B.: SR Labs Demonstrates Phishing and Eavesdropping Attacks on Amazon Echo and Google Home, Leads to Google Action Review and Widespread Outage (2019). https://voicebot.ai/2019/10/21/sr-labs-demonstrates-phishing-and-eavesdropping-attacks-on-amazon-echo-and-google-home-leads-to-google-action-review-and-widespread-outage/. Accessed 26 July 2021

15. Kumar, D., et al.: Skill squatting attacks on amazon Alexa. In: Proceedings of the 27th USENIX Conference on Security Symposium, pp. 33–47. USA (2018)

16. Lentzsch, C., Shah, S.J., Andow, B., Degeling, M., Das, A., Enck, W.: Hey Alexa, is this skill safe?: taking a closer look at the Alexa skill ecosystem. In: 28th Annual Network and Distributed System Security Symposium, NDSS (2021)

17. Liao, S., Wilson, C., Cheng, L., Hu, H., Deng, H.: Measuring the effectiveness of privacy policies for voice assistant applications. In: Annual Computer Security Applications Conference. ACSAC 2020, pp. 856–869 (2020)

18. Mitev, R., Miettinen, M., Sadeghi, A.R.: Alexa lied to me: skill-based man-in-the-middle attacks on virtual assistants. In: ACM Asia Conference on Computer and Communications Security. Asia CCS 2019, pp. 465–478 (2019)

19. Sgandurra, D., Karafili, E., Lupu, E.: Formalizing threat models for virtualized systems. In: Ranise, S., Swarup, V. (eds.) DBSec 2016. LNCS, vol. 9766, pp. 251–267. Springer, Cham (2016). https://doi.org/10.1007/978-3-319-41483-6_18

20. Statista: Market share of global smart speaker shipments from 3rd quarter 2016 to 4th quarter 2020, by vendor. https://www.statista.com/statistics/792604/worldwide-smart-speaker-market-share/. Accessed 26 July 2021

21. Talebi, S.M.S., Sani, A.A., Saroiu, S., Wolman, A.: MegaMind: a platform for security and privacy extensions for voice assistants. In: Proceedings of the 19th Annual International Conference on Mobile Systems, Applications, and Services. MobiSys 2021, pp. 109–121 (2021)

22. Welch, C.: Amazon made a special version of Alexa for hotels with Echo speakers in their rooms (2018). https://www.theverge.com/2018/6/19/17476688/amazon-alexa-for-hospitality-announced-hotels-echo. Accessed 26 July 2021

23. Yan, Q., Liu, K., Zhou, Q., Guo, H., Zhang, N.: Surfingattack: interactive hidden attack on voice assistants using ultrasonic guided waves. In: 27th Annual Network and Distributed System Security Symposium, NDSS (2020)

24. Zhang, N., Mi, X., Feng, X., Wang, X., Tian, Y., Qian, F.: Dangerous skills: understanding and mitigating security risks of voice-controlled third-party functions on virtual personal assistant systems. In: 2019 IEEE Symposium on Security and Privacy (SP), pp. 1381–1396 (2019)

Handling Meta Attribute Information in Usage Control Policies (Short Paper)

Theo Dimitrakos[1,2], Tezcan Dilshener[1,3], Alexander Kravtsov[4],
Antonio La Marra[5], Fabio Martinelli[6], Athanasios Rizos[1(✉)],
and Alessandro Rosetti[5]

[1] German Research Center, Huawei Technologies Duesseldorf GmbH,
Munich, Germany
`{theo.dimitrakos,tezcan.dilshener,athanasios.rizos}@huawei.com`
[2] School of Computing, University of Kent, Canterbury, UK
[3] European Business School University, Munich, Germany
[4] Israel Research Center, Huawei Technologies Co., Tel Aviv, Israel
`alexander.kravtsov@huawei.com`
[5] Security Forge, Pisa, Italy
`{antoniomarra,alessandrorosetti}@security-forge.com`
[6] Istituto di Informatica e Telematica, Consiglio Nazionale delle Ricerche, Pisa, Italy
`fabio.martinelli@iit.cnr.it`

Abstract. This work builds on top of an architecture and prototype implementation of a novel trust-aware continuous authorization technology that targets consumer Internet of Things (IoT), e.g., Smart Home to introduce a novel trust algorithm and meta attribute evaluation. Our approach extends previous work in two complementary ways: (1) By introducing a novel set of meta attributes that characterize the values of condition attributes such as Time To Live. This set of meta attributes serves as additional information that can be used by the system in order to proper caching attribute values or deciding whether or not to use an attribute already retrieved or to ask for a fresh one. (2) By minimizing the network consumption related to requesting additional and fresh attributes to sensor in IoT environments. Network is the source of major energy consumption in IoT devices, therefore being able to minimize network consumption is beneficial for the whole system.

Keywords: Trust · ABAC · Usage control · Authorization · IoT

1 Introduction

Smart Devices adoption has continuously increased in the last years, they are predicted to exceed 75B in the next five years. As with all new technologies, there

The research reported is part of a Huawei R&D project in cooperation with Security Forge. We would also like to acknowledge the contribution of the following colleagues: Yair Diaz and Liu Jignag at the Munich Research Center; Michael Shurman, Eyal Rundstein, Dror Moyal, Nir Makmal, Avi Halaf, Ido Zak, Daniel Bibi, Ye Zongbo at the Israel Research Center and of Professor Eyal Winter, Hebrew University, Israel.

© Springer Nature Switzerland AG 2021
A. Saracino and P. Mori (Eds.): ETAA 2021, LNCS 13136, pp. 143–151, 2021.
https://doi.org/10.1007/978-3-030-93747-8_10

are risks. According to a recent UK government consultation report[1], there is a large number of consumer Internet of Things (IoT) devices that lack even basic cybersecurity provisions. Smart devices enter our houses replacing traditional ones, changing completely the way we live. Together with an ever expanding network of sensors and actuators, they help interconnect people, appliances and ICT resources in a dynamic environment that pervades our homes. Such an environment is created by means of the continuity of interaction combined with the heterogeneity of devices, information, connectivity and automation. Never before have we relied in so many cheaply and massively produced technological artefacts for so many activities that have such a deep impact in our daily life. For maintaining quality, security and safety in modern living, controlling permissions, access and usage of people, information and resources in such environment is essential. However, traditional identity and access management technologies and models fail to offer an effective and cost-efficient solution.

In this work we build on top of the trust aware continuous authorization model described in [4] to introduce a new model that is able to support external configurations of system and policies. Such configurations are necessary because attributes model different aspects of reality, they can vary with different rates and it is of paramount importance, especially in the case of attributes coming from battery powered sensors to find a trade-off between energy consumption and trustworthiness of provided values. This model is implemented through a modern embedded-systems architecture that has been inspired by adaptive, self-immune security architectures for IoT [13], and open enterprise security concepts originating in service oriented architectures [3], grid and cloud computing [5]. The rest of the paper is organized as follows: In Sect. 2 we report our motivating scenario, background and related work information. Section 3 describes the proposed architecture. Finally, we conclude in Sect. 4 by summarising the main innovations and discussing future research directions.

2   Related Work and Background

In this section we review related work in trust evaluation, access and usage control and highlight how they have influenced our contribution.

2.1   Access and Usage Control

Attribute-Based Access Control (ABAC) is an evolution of Access Control List (ACL) [22] that offers flexibility and generality while being able to support fine granular access management like ACL. For ABAC, access is controlled via policies that are an algorithmic combination of access control rules. Each rule applies on a target consisting of attributes regarding subjects, objects, actions and environment, and contains a condition that needs to be satisfied [24]. Applicable ABAC rules evaluate to an access control decision (typically *PERMIT* or *DENY*) while

---

[1] https://www.gov.uk/government/consultations/consultation-on-regulatory-propos als-on-consumer-iot-security.

the evaluation process may also result in *INDETERMINATE* if some error occurs during the evaluation process (e.g., failed to obtain the value of some necessary attribute). More advanced ABAC models also include actions upon activation of a rule such as Obligations and Advice. A comprehensive reference model of the ABAC paradigm including policy language, evaluation semantics, architecture and administration has been standardized by OASIS in the form of the eXtensible Access Control Markup Language (XACML) [18]. Another ABAC policy language, is the Abbreviated Language For Authorization (ALFA) [19], which is a pseudo-code domain-specific language used to express ABAC policies. ALFA does not bring any new semantics, but rather maps directly to XACML. Usage Control ($UCON_{ABC}$) was first introduced in [20], focusing on the convergence of access control and Digital Rights Management (DRM) and a particularly relevant flavor of Usage Control (UCON) was introduced in [12]. UCON introduces context and continuity of access while conserving a full ABAC baseline model. This is enhanced by adding an authorization context (called *"authorization session"*) and implicit temporal state together with continuous monitoring for updates of the values of mutable attributes and re-evaluation of relevant policy rules upon changes and aims at revoking the access when the execution rights are no longer valid, preventing misuse of resources. Implicit temporal state is captured by classifying policy rules in accordance to their applicability before (*"PRE"*), during (*"ONGOING"*) or after (*"POST"*) granting an authorization.

2.2   Evaluating Trust Level

Understanding, classifying, measuring and assessing the levels of trust have been some of the fundamental research challenges in trust management [11] and focal points in sociology [1], uncertainty reasoning [9], computing [16], e-commerce [6], information security [7], and security risk analysis [15]. Trust fusion from different sources and discounting of a re-commented evaluation based on confidence in the entity conducting the evaluation have always been two focal points in trust management and recommendation networks. Trust fusion has been formalized in Subjective Logic (SL) and used for a variety of applications including multi-source and biometric information fusion [23]. In recent years, the semantics initially attributed to fusion operators in SL, have been the subject of criticism [2] and subsequent improvement in [8] after better clarifying the relationship of SL to Dirichlet distributions and Dempster-Shafer belief functions [10]. Bayesian distributions and networks have been studied for trust level evaluation and recommendation networks [21], for managing uncertainty in relation to trust [14] and for trust fusion [17]. Our current implementation focuses on trust in authentication and follows a trust fusion approach where we combine information from many sources discounted by the trust in each source. Conceptually, the discounting and fusion operations are inspired by subjective logic [9].

3   Trust-Aware Continuous Authorization Architecture

In this section we present our architecture and methodology, which is based on UCON+, a Trust Level Evaluation Engine (TLEE) and ALFA language as they

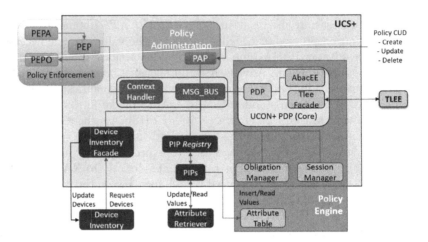

Fig. 1. Architecture with interconnections

were presented in our previous work [4]. UCON+ is implemented according to a message-centric architecture, following the publish/subscribe pattern as shown in Fig. 1. This is a micro-services inspired integration architecture that leverages in-line context enrichment and publish-subscribe protocols to maximize concurrency between policy parsing, attribute value retrieval, trust level and policy evaluation. This maximizes performance and minimizes dependency on low network latency or high availability of computational resources, while improving ability to upgrade or substitute component services and migrate to a distributed deployment if necessary.

3.1   Architecture Component Description

UCON+ provides the core components of the standard UCON enhanced by additional new components as illustrated in Fig. 1 and described below:

`Context Handler` (CH): This is the core component of the framework, acting as message enricher and manager of the operative workflow.

`Message Bus`: This is a sub-component of the CH that implements the publish/-subscribe communication paradigm.

`Session Manager` (SM): This vital component enables the continuity of control. It is a database which stores the information about all active sessions.

`Policy Information Point` (PIP): This component is responsible for interaction with the attribute managers.

`Attribute Table` (AT): This auxiliary component manages attributes and is needed in environments with faulty attribute managers, where there is the possibility that values are not available right away when queried. Whenever a cache is used to store attribute values, avoiding to query every time attribute managers, many question arise on how such a storage is managed during time, how much can attributes be trusted and when should the system clear the cache in order to refresh it. To answer such questions and to enable a flexible and customizable approach to handle each attribute lifetime, a new attribute has been introduced in the system, the so-called Time To Live (TTL).

Attribute Retriever (AR): This auxiliary component is in charge of querying attribute managers when fresh values are needed. **Device Inventory (DI):** Manager of the physical architecture. It stores the list of available devices, specifying which device owns which attribute.

Policy Decision Point (PDP): This component takes as input a request and the corresponding policy. It leverages AbacEE (ABAC Expression Evaluator) and TLEE to perform policy evaluation. AbacEE evaluates former ABAC Expressions, while TLEE evaluates expressions written in TLEE format. Results coming from these specific evaluators are combined together and the result is sent to the CH as one of the following possible decisions: *PERMIT* or *DENY* or *NOT APPLICABLE* when a decision cannot be taken due to semantic reasons, i.e. no rules in the policy are matched; *INDETERMINATE* (Decision cannot be taken since either the policy or the request are malformed).

Obligation Manager (OM): This component handles policy obligations.

Policy Enforcement Point (PEP): Responsibility of this component is to receive evaluation requests (PEPA) and interacting with Context Handler in order to evaluate them. It also sends evaluation result in form of PEPO.

Policy Administration Point (PAP): Creates a policy or a policy set and makes it available to the PDP. The PAP can retrieve, add or update policies.

```
policy <Title> {                                                          1
  target clause                                                           2
          Attributes.<AttributeName> == <AttributeValue>                  3
  apply <CombiningAlgorithm>                                              4
  rule <RuleName> {                                                        5
    target clause                                                         6
          Attributes.<AttributeName> == <AttributeValue>                  7
    condition <ConditionExpression>                                       8
    <decision (permit or deny)>                                           9
    on <decision> {                                                      10
      <instruction (obligation)> <ObligationName> {                      11
        <Attribute> = <Value>                                            12
}}}}                                                                     13
```

Listing 1.1. Structure of an ALFA policy

3.2   Policy Meta Information

ALFA policies for usage control systems have been introduced in [4] and the structure of such a policy is shown in Listing 1.1. In order to include meta attributes in the policy or information related to attributes, such as TTL, ALFA syntax has been enlarged in order to support a policy preamble inside comments. Policy preamble for TTL can be considered as a new profile for ALFA language where meta information related to attributes are inserted. Preamble had following format and each component is analysed below:

$$// <profile\_name>::<attribute\_id>?\hookleftarrow$$
$$<meta\_attribute>=<value>;<meta\_attribute>=<value>$$

- `<profile_name>`: The name of a specific profile where a `<meta_attribute>` has been defined. Only if UCS+ supports such a profile the comment is parsed and evaluated, otherwise it is discarded. This guarantees that the policy would be evaluated by any UCS+ implementation.
- `<attribute_id>`: The id of the attribute for which TTL was defined. Inside a specific policy, each id can have only one TTL associated with it.
- `<meta_attribute>` is the meta-attribute defined in the comment.
- `<value>` is the value associated with an attribute and it can be expressed in many different types or units of measure.
- `<;>` is used as separator for the various meta attributes that can be defined

```
// acm::Attributes.Identity?ttl=60                              1
policy test {                                                   2
    target clause Attributes.role == "admin"                   3
    apply firstApplicable                                      4
    rule open {                                                 5
      condition tlee(BN,Attributes.identity=HOME_OWNER,85)     6
      permit                                                   7
    }                                                          8
    ...                                                        9
}                                                             10
```

Listing 1.2. Structure of an ALFA policy with the TTL function

In Listing 1.2, we present an example of an ALFA policy that includes the TTL following the aforementioned structure. By explicitly stating TTL for attribute, we enable the system to state a validity period for specific attributes, therefore it is not necessary, as long as the attribute is valid, to query external sources to get a fresh value. Other meta information that can be stated can be: attribute source, maximum delay.

3.3   Workflow

Session evaluation has already been depicted in [4], but in order to respect TTL requirements, policy evaluation flow has been altered as depicted in Fig. 2.

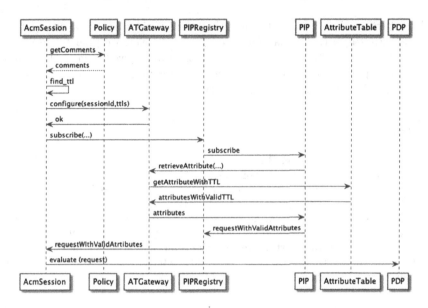

Fig. 2. Policy evaluation flow with TTL

It should be noted that, before starting a policy evaluation, the session config-
ures itself from policy comments. In the attribute retrieval phase, TTL is checked
in order to verify that only valid attribute values are taken into account. If no
attribute value is valid, PIP will retrieve updated values from Attribute Managers and the request will be evaluated by the PDP as-is. If the PDP returns
a result different from *PERMIT/DENY*, the request will be evaluated over the
same policy when an attribute arrives. To avoid starvation or infinite loops, after
a certain number of attempts resulting differently than *PERMIT/DENY*, a session will end up with a *DENY* for timeout or elapsed number of attempts. AT
will not be invalidated for that specific attribute entry because it is still possible
that other policies can consider as valid an attribute with very high TTL because
its freshness is not considered critical by them.

4   Conclusions and Future Work

In this work, we extended our previous work in [4] where we have introduced a
new model, policy language and architecture for trust aware continuous authorization that fulfills the need of continuous multi-sensor authentication, trust
level evaluation and subsequent authorization in a dynamic IoT environment
such as the future smart home. We built on top of the modular architecture
in order to provide the capability of inserting meta-policy information. We presented a use case of such an approach using TTL and how the flow and session
object has been changed in order to support this feature.

As future work, we aim at evaluating the overhead of such an approach and comparing it with the baseline use case. Moreover, we plan to implement additional trust algorithms to be used by TLEE. Finally, we target to the support of additional policy meta-attributes as attribute source and polling times so as to give the policy author greater flexibility.

References

1. Castelfranchi, C., Falcone, R.: Trust is much more than subjective probability: mental components and sources of trust. In: (HICSS-33), Hawaii, USA (2000)
2. Dezert, J., et al.: Can we trust subjective logic for information fusion? In: FUSION 2014, Salamanca, Spain, pp. 1–8. IEEE (2014)
3. Dimitrakos, T., Brossard, D., de Leusse, P.: Securing business operations in an SOA. CoRR abs/1203.0429 (2012). http://arxiv.org/abs/1203.0429
4. Dimitrakos, T., et al.: Trust aware continuous authorization for zero trust in consumer internet of things. In: 2020 IEEE 19th International Conference on Trust, Security and Privacy in Computing and Communications (TrustCom), pp. 1801–1812 (2020). https://doi.org/10.1109/TrustCom50675.2020.00247
5. Dimitrakos, T., Martrat, J., Wesner, S. (eds.): Service Oriented Infrastructures and Cloud Service Platforms for the Enterprise. Springer, Heidelberg (2010). https://doi.org/10.1007/978-3-642-04086-3
6. Dimitrakos, T.: System models, e-risks and e-trust - towards bridging the gap? In: (I3E 2001), Zürich, Switzerland, vol. 202, pp. 45–58. Kluwer (2001)
7. Grandison, T., Sloman, M.: Trust management tools for internet applications. In: Nixon, P., Terzis, S. (eds.) iTrust 2003. LNCS, vol. 2692, pp. 91–107. Springer, Heidelberg (2003). https://doi.org/10.1007/3-540-44875-6_7
8. Heijden, R.W.V.D., Kopp, H., Kargl, F.: Multi-source fusion operations in subjective logic. In: FUSION 2018, Cambridge, UK, pp. 1990–1997. IEEE (2018)
9. Jøsang, A.: Subjective Logic - A Formalism for Reasoning Under Uncertainty. Artificial Intelligence: Foundations, Theory, and Algorithms, Springer, Cham (2016). https://doi.org/10.1007/978-3-319-42337-1
10. Jøsang, A., Elouedi, Z.: Interpreting belief functions as Dirichlet distributions. In: Mellouli, K. (ed.) ECSQARU 2007. LNCS (LNAI), vol. 4724, pp. 393–404. Springer, Heidelberg (2007). https://doi.org/10.1007/978-3-540-75256-1_36
11. Jøsang, A., Keser, C., Dimitrakos, T.: Can we manage trust? In: Herrmann, P., Issarny, V., Shiu, S. (eds.) iTrust 2005. LNCS, vol. 3477, pp. 93–107. Springer, Heidelberg (2005). https://doi.org/10.1007/11429760_7
12. Lazouski, A., Martinelli, F., Mori, P.: A prototype for enforcing usage control policies based on XACML. In: Fischer-Hübner, S., Katsikas, S., Quirchmayr, G. (eds.) TrustBus 2012. LNCS, vol. 7449, pp. 79–92. Springer, Heidelberg (2012). https://doi.org/10.1007/978-3-642-32287-7_7
13. de Leusse, P., et al.: Self Managed Security Cell, a security model for the Internet of Things and Services. CoRR abs/1203.0439 (2012)
14. Liu, B.: A Survey on Trust Modeling from a Bayesian Perspective. CoRR abs/1806.03916 (2018). http://arxiv.org/abs/1806.03916
15. Lund, M.S., Solhaug, B., Stølen, K.: Evolution in relation to risk and trust management. IEEE Comput. **43**(5), 49–55 (2010)
16. Marsh, S.P.: Formalising trust as a computational concept. University of Sterling, Technical repot (1994)

17. Nguyen, T.D., Bai, Q.: A dynamic Bayesian network approach for agent group trust evaluation. Comput. Hum. Behav. **89**, 237–245 (2018)
18. OASIS: eXtensible Access Control Markup Language (XACML) Version 3.0, January 2013. http://www.oasis-open.org/committees/xacml
19. OASIS: Abbreviated language for authorization Version 1.0 (2015). https://bit.ly/2UP6Jza
20. Park, J., Sandhu, R.: The UCON ABC usage control model. ACM Trans. Inf. Syst. Secur. **7**(1), 128–174 (2004)
21. Rafailidis, D.: Bayesian deep learning with trust and distrust in recommendation systems. In: IEEE/WIC/ACM, WI 2019, Thessaloniki, Greece, pp. 18–25 (2019)
22. Shirey, R.: Internet Security Glossary (2007). https://bit.ly/2UP77xC
23. Vishi, K., Jøsang, A.: A new approach for multi-biometric fusion based on subjective logic. In: IML 2017, Liverpool, UK. ACM (2017)
24. Zhang, L., Zou, J.: Research of ABAC mechanism based on the improved encryption algorithm under cloud environment. In: Park, J., Pan, Y., Chao, H.C., Yi, G. (eds.) Ubiquitous Computing Application and Wireless Sensor. LNEE, vol. 331, pp. 463–469. Springer, Dordrecht (2015). https://doi.org/10.1007/978-94-017-9618-7_46

"Ask App Not to Track": The Effect of Opt-In Tracking Authorization on Mobile Privacy

Anzo DeGiulio, Hanoom Lee, and Eleanor Birrell[(✉)]

Pomona College, Claremont, CA, USA
{abdb2018,hlaa2020}@mymail.pomona.edu, Eleanor.Birrell@pomona.edu

Abstract. App Tracking Transparency (ATT) introduces opt-in tracking authorization for iOS apps. In this work, we investigate how mobile apps present tracking requests to users, and we evaluate how the observed design patterns impact users' privacy. We perform a manual observational study of the Top 200 free iOS apps, and we classify each app by whether it requests permission to track, the purpose of the request, how the request was framed, whether the request was preceded or followed by additional ATT-related pages, and whether the request was preceded or followed by other permission requests. We then perform a user study with 950 participants to evaluate the impact of the observed UI elements. We find that opt-in authorizations are effective at enhancing data privacy in this context, and that the effect of ATT requests is robust to most implementation choices.

Keywords: Mobile privacy · Tracking · ATT

1 Introduction

App Tracking Transparency (ATT)—introduced into iOS 14.5 in April 2021—is a new authorization model that requires opt-in user consent for tracking by mobile apps. Any mobile app that collects and shares user data for tracking purposes is required to use the ATT framework to request tracking permission from the user. Users are then presented with standardized permission dialogue (Fig. 1) and asked to choose between allowing tracking and asking the app not to track; Apple's User Privacy and Data Use policy prohibits apps from using identifiers, fingerprinting, or other techniques to track users who ask the app not to track. This work investigates how iOS mobile apps present tracking requests to users and evaluates how observed design patterns impact privacy.

We began by qualitatively coding ATT requests by the Top 200 free iOS apps on June 1, 2021. We found that almost all ($n = 197$) of the apps had been updated since the release of iOS 14.5 and that approximately half of the updated apps ($n = 91$) requested permission to track their users. Using a coding book developed based on experience on personal devices, we also classified each

© Springer Nature Switzerland AG 2021
A. Saracino and P. Mori (Eds.): ETAA 2021, LNCS 13136, pp. 152–167, 2021.
https://doi.org/10.1007/978-3-030-93747-8_11

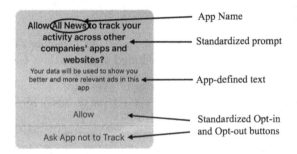

Fig. 1. Example ATT permission dialogue. The format of the pop-up, including the prompt and the opt-in/opt-out buttons, is standardized. The app developer specifies the app-defined text displayed between the prompt and the buttons.

request by the purpose of the request, how the request was framed, whether the request was preceded or followed by additional ATT-related pages, and whether the request was preceded or followed by other permission requests.

To understand the effect of observed design patterns on data privacy, we conducted a user study with 950 participants recruited through Amazon Mechanical Turk. We found that tracking requests for non-advertising purposes were significantly more likely to be granted than tracking requests for advertising purposes ($p = .05$). The framing of the study (positive, neutral, or negative, and with or without the threat of future required payment) had no significant effect on opt-out rate. Surprisingly, the presence of a priming page appeared to reduce, rather than increase, the number of users who authorized tracking, although the difference was not statistically significant.

In a follow-up survey, 67.9% of respondents reported being somewhat or very uncomfortable with tracking, but 60.5% of respondents reported being very or somewhat satisfied the ATT opt-out provided; there were no significant differences in satisfaction between conditions. Moreover, 96.1% of respondents currently running iOS 14.5 or higher reported opting-out of tracking on their personal device at least a few times.

These results show that opt-in permissions are highly effective at enhancing data privacy in the context of tracking by mobile apps. Moreover, opt-in rates were relatively consistent across most conditions, which suggests that ATT is less impacted by dark patterns and other privacy-diminishing UI elements than other preference-setting mechanisms. This suggests that ATT—which requires opt-in consent with clearly defined options presented through a standardized interface—might prove an effective model for managing data privacy in other contexts.

2 ATT Pop-Ups in the Wild

To understand how apps present ATT requests, we conducted a manual user study of the Top 200 free iOS apps.

2.1   Methodology

We developed a coding book based on observed ATT requests during daily use of personal devices. Our coding book included seven distinct features:

1. Does the app request permission to track? (Yes/No)
2. Why does the app request tracking? (First party ads/Third party ads/Ads (unspecified)/Content/Analytics/Other)
3. How is tracking framed? (Positive/Neutral/Negative)
4. Does the app threaten payment if not allowed to track? (Yes/No)
5. Is there a pre-request ATT priming page? (Yes/No)
6. Is there a post-request follow-up page? (Yes/No)
7. How many other pop-up permissions does the app request? (n)

We manually examined and classified the Top 200 free iOS apps (as listed by Sensor Tower [36] on June 1, 2021) according to this coding book. Observations were conducted on iPhone 7s running iOS 14.6 on June 1, 2021.

For each app, one author installed and ran the app. To determine whether the app requested permission to track (1), we then ran the app for a minimum of 30 s: until we observed an ATT request, until it was clear that no request would be made, or until we ran into a roadblock that prevented us from proceeding.[1] If the app required an account, we created a new account for the purpose of this study.

For each app that requested permission to track, we qualitatively coded the app-defined text displayed in the ATT permission dialogue (Fig. 1) for three features: the purpose for which the app requested permission to track (2), whether the request was framed positively (i.e., authorizing tracing would improve the user experience) negatively (i.e., denying permission to track would negatively impact the user experience) or using neutral language (3), and whether the app threatened to start charging for service or features if users denied permission to track (4).

Finally, we classified the context in which the ATT request occurred: whether there was a pre-request priming page (5), whether there was a post-request follow-up page (6), and how many other permission requests were made by the app at the same time (7).

2.2   Results

We found that almost all ($n = 197$) of the apps had been updated since the release of iOS 14.5 and that approximately half of the updated apps ($n = 91$) requested permission to track their users.

The majority of apps that requested permission to track (81.9%) did so in order to support some form of behavioral advertising. Some of these apps ($n = 33$) specified that tracking was needed to support targeted ads on their app (i.e., first party ads) and some ($n = 21$) stated that tracking was used

---

[1] Roadblocks included requests for payment or social security numbers (SSNs).

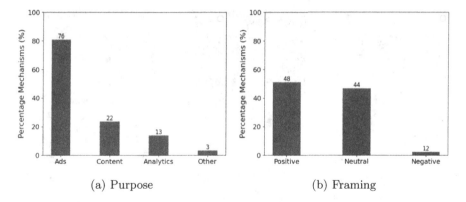

(a) Purpose   (b) Framing

Fig. 2. Frequency of different types of text in ATT requests among the Top 200 free iOS apps that request permission to tracking.

to support ads on other websites and apps (i.e., third party ads); other apps used vague language that did not clearly specify whether tracking data would be used for first party ads, third party ads, or both. The remaining 18.1% of apps requested permission for tracking only for non-advertising purposes; these purposed included improving or personalizing app content, analytics, and other purposes. These results are summarized in Fig. 2a.

Most apps that requested permission used a positive framing that emphasized the benefits of allowing tracking: 51.1% claimed that allowing tracking would allow the app to serve better ads or offer a better experience. Only 2.1% of apps used negative framing (i.e., emphasizing the downsides of opting-out of tracking by claiming it would result in less relevant ads or content); the remaining apps used neutral language. These results are depicted in Fig. 2b.

Other factors we studied were relatively uncommon in the wild. Only 7.7% of tracking requests threatened to start requiring payment if users declined tracking. Less than a quarter of apps that requested permission to track (23.1%) primed users with an ATT-related page before requesting permission to track, and just one app presented a follow-up page when users asked the app not to track.

3   User Study Methodology

To understand the effect of the observed implementation choices for ATT requests on data privacy—and on user's likelihood of opting-out of tracking—we conducted a user study with 950 users.

In the user study, participants installed an aggregated news app called All News on their personal iOS device; they interacted with the app for a few minutes, and then answered a series of follow-up questions.

(a) Home screen   (b) ATT priming page   (c) ATT permission request

Fig. 3. Screenshots from the All News app used in our user study. The priming page was used only in Condition 8. The app-defined text in the ATT permission request dialogue varied between condition.

3.1 App Design and Conditions

All News is an aggregated news app developed for the purpose of this study. It fetches news articles from major sources using the News API and displays them to users. A screenshot of the All News home page is shown in Fig. 3a. When opening the app for the first time, a pop-up identical to Apple's official ATT request appears; it asks the user for permission to track. We varied the app-defined language used in the ATT request between conditions, and each user was pseudorandomly assigned to a condition based on a hash of their IP address. An example ATT request is depicted in Fig. 3c.

The first four conditions correspond to different purposes: first party ads, third party ads, ads (unspecified), and content. The next two conditions vary the framing of the request (from positive to neutral or negative). The next two conditions are variants of the positive and negative conditions that threaten to introduce payments if users ask not to track. Purpose and framing were controlled by adjusting the language of the app-defined text that appears in the ATT permission dialogue between the standardized prompt and the standardized opt-in and opt-out buttons. The final condition introduces a priming page (shown in Fig. 3b) prior to the ATT permission request. These conditions are detailed in Table 1.

Data logged by the application included a unique, randomly generated, 32 character identifier that was assigned to a user upon opening the app. We also

Table 1. The nine conditions included in our user study.

Cond.	App-defined text	Purpose	Framing	Payment	Priming
0	Your data will be used to show you better and more relevant ads in this app	Ads (1st)	Positive	No	No
1	Your data will be shared with our partners to show you better and more relevant ads outside of All News	Ads (3rd)	Positive	No	No
2	Your data will be used to provide you with a better and more relevant ad experience	Ads (vague)	Positive	No	No
3	Your data will be used to show you better and more relevant articles	Content	Positive	No	No
4	This identifier will be used to deliver personalized ads to you	Ads (vague)	Neutral	No	No
5	Selecting "Ask App Not to Track" will result in less relevant ads	Ads (vague)	Negative	No	No
6	Your data will be used to provide you with a better and more relevant ad experience and keep All News free to use	Ads (vague)	Positive	Yes	No
7	Selecting "Ask App Not to Track" will result in less relevant ads and may require us to start charging you to use All News	Ads (vague)	Negative	Yes	No
8	Your data will be used to provide you with a better and more relevant ad experience	Ads (vague)	Positive	No	Yes

recorded which condition the participant was assigned to and whether or not the participant authorized tracking. No other information was collected by the app; the app did not actually receive or record any ATT tracking identifiers.

3.2 Participant Recruitment

In order to include the follow-up questions—and in order to vary the text that appeared in ATT requests, a feature that is not supported by the iOS App Store—we published our app through Expo Go and recruited participants through Amazon Mechanical Turk. The task was advertised as beta-testing an aggregated news app. Participation was restricted to iPhone users who had previously completed at least 50 HITs with an acceptance rate of at least 95%.

Before beginning the study, we informed users about our date collection practices and obtained participants' consent. We then guided them through installing and running the All News app and asked each participant to use the app for a few minutes. After collecting their user identifier in the survey, we asked them a set of follow-up questions about their experience with ATT pop-ups and mobile

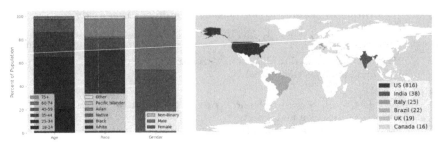

(a) Participant demographics.   (b) Participant location by country.

Fig. 4. Demographic summary of our 950 users study participants.

tracking in general. We also collected basic demographic information. The complete survey is provided in Appendix A.

Responses that did not include a valid app confirmation code (received after the user downloaded All News) or a valid qualtrics code (received after the user completed the follow-up survey) were rejected. Participants were compensated $1.20 upon successful completion of the survey.

We received 2298 preliminary responses; 1348 responses were rejected because they did not include a valid app confirmation code (received after the user downloaded All News) or they did not include a valid qualtrics code (received after the user completed the follow-up survey); we analyzed data from the remaining 950 participants. The median completion time for the user study was 5.4 min.

This study received an IRB exemption from the Institutional Review Board at our institution.

3.3 Participant Demographics

The 54.1% of our study participants identified as woman and 44.7% identified as men. The majority of study participants identified as white (70.5%), 15.2% identified as Asian, and 10.3% identified as Black. Less than 2% identified as Native American, as Pacific Islander, or as "other". 20.6% were 18–24, 44.5% were 25–34, and 21.2% were 35–44; the remaining participants were 45 or older. These demographics of the participants are shown in Fig. 4a. Participants' self-reported country of residence is shown in Fig. 4b (countries with less than three participants were omitted for readability).

We also collected data on participants' smartphone use. 99.3% of respondents used an iPhone as their primary smartphone, and 78.3% of them were running an iOS version 14.5 or higher (ATT enabled).

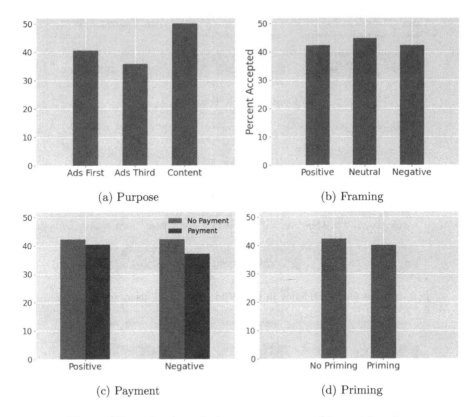

Fig. 5. Effect of various design patterns on tracking opt-in rates.

4   Results

Our user study evaluated the impact of four of the seven factors included in our observational study: (1) purpose, (2) framing, (3) payment, and (4) priming. Due to the infrequency of observed examples in the wild, we did not study the impact of follow-up pages or additional (non-ATT) permission requests. All conditions requested permission to track.

Purpose. We found that users were significantly more likely to authorize tracking for the purpose of personalizing content than for advertising purposes ($p = .05$). This effect was particularly strong for third-party ads: just 35.7% of users authorized tracking for the purpose of third-party advertising compared to 50.0% of users for content purposes ($p = .04$). These results, depicted in Fig. 5a, are consistent with prior work that has found users are more likely to accept permissions if they were essential to app functionality [10, 29].

Framing. Research into behavioral economics and decision theory has consistently found that the framing of a decision affects user choices [25, 37], results

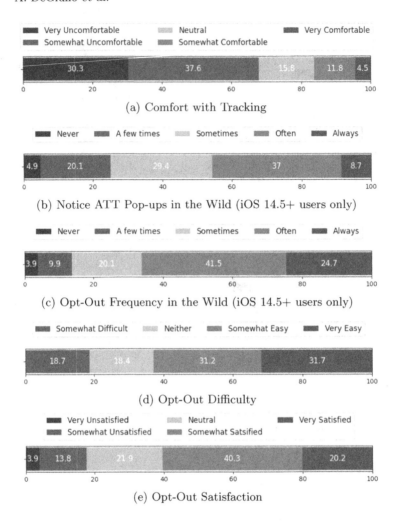

Fig. 6. User experience with tracking and ATT tracking requests.

that have subsequently been extended to privacy interfaces [22] and trust in mobile apps [13]. We therefore expected to find that a negative framing—one that emphasized the potential negative impacts of asking an app not to track—would result in higher opt-out rates than neutral or positive framings. However, we instead found no statistically significant differences between different framings. We saw that positive and negative framings had nearly identical opt-in rates (42.3% vs. 42.2%), both slightly lower than the neutral condition (Fig. 5b). These results suggest that the standardization imposed on ATT requests is sufficient to negate the impact of framing observed in other contexts.

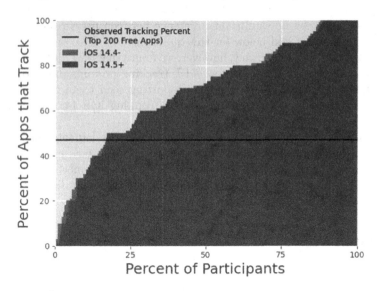

Fig. 7. Percent of apps on a respondent's phone they believe are tracking them

Payment. Prior work has found that most users put a low price on privacy [35], an effect that is amplified by framing effects [3]. We therefore expected users to opt-in to tracking at higher rates when told they might have to pay otherwise. However, we found no statistically significant effect due to payment (Fig. 5c); in fact, the opt-in rates were slightly lower when users were threatened with payment if they opted-out of tracking. This effect might be due to a decrease in perceived trustworthiness when an app threatens to start charging for services if users ask it not to track, or it might be an artifact of the experimental design, in which users interacted with an app that they (presumably) did not intend to continue using in the future.

Priming. Prior work has found that priming can impact users decisions and privacy assessments in the context of mobile apps [5,14]; we therefore expected the presence of a priming page to increase the rate at which users opt-in for tracking. Contrary to our expectations, there was no statistically significant effect due to priming; in fact, respondents allowed tracking 2.3% less often when presented with a priming page before the ATT permission request (Fig. 5d).

User Experience. After interacting with the All News app, we asked each study participant a series of follow-up questions about their experience with mobile tracking. Overall, users reported being uncomfortable with the practice of tracking user behavior, with 67.9% saying that they were very uncomfortable or somewhat uncomfortable the practice (Fig. 6a). However, respondents thought that the majority of apps they had installed on their phone tracked them (Fig. 7), with most users reporting higher rates of tracking than we observed in the Top

200 free apps. We saw no significant difference between users running iOS 14.5 and above versus 14.4 and below for this question.

In a promising sign for privacy, however, we found that 95.1% of users running iOS 14.5+ had noticed at least a few ATT tracking pop-ups prior to completing our study and 45.7% of respondents reporting seen them often or always, (Fig. 6b). We also found that 66.2% of those running iOS 14.5+ opted-out of tracking often or always (Fig. 6c).

After interacting with the All News app, most participants reported that the mechanisms was somewhat or very easy to use (Fig. 6d), and most participants indicated that they were satisfied with the opt-out mechanism provided (Fig. 6e). There were no statistically significant differences in difficulty or satisfaction between different conditions.

5   Related Work

To the best of our knowledge, this is the first work examining Apple's ATT permission system. However, mobile permissions in general, the concept of nudging, and the impact of third-party tracking have been explored in many mobile contexts.

5.1   Tracking

Previous research has highlighted the prevalence of third party trackers in mobile applications. Binns et al. decoded APKs for 959000 Google Play apps to map permissions to domain hosts, finding that 90% apps on the Google Play store had at least one tracker embedded [9]. Liccardi et al. found that of 528000 apps surveyed on Google Play, 46% collected personal data, while Vallina-Rodriguez et al. used ICSI Haystack to examine 1700 apps, finding that 60% connected to at least one ad tracking service (ATS) [28,38]. Razaghpanah et al. developed the app Lumen to analyze device traffic and identify ad tracking domains, finding that the majority of data was shared both within and among organizations [34].

Less research has been conducted regarding third party trackers in applications on Apple's app store. Kurtz et al. found that approximately 40% of 1100 apps they analyzed connected to at least one ATS domain [27]. We found similar results from our data collection on the Top 200 free apps, where 47% of apps requested ATT permission, indicating their use of ATS domains. With such a high rate of third party tracking and low opt-in rates, Apple's ATT policy has a large effect on the mobile application economy.

5.2   Permissions and User Preferences

There is a large body of work focused on how users respond to permission requests. Mohamed and Patel outlined the differences in permission systems between Android and iOS, where Apple is more restrictive of developers access to sensitive subsystems [32]. The introduction of the ATT permission is another addition to these restrictions.

Before Android transitioned from pre-install permissions to ask-on-first-use (AOFU) with the upgrade to 6.0, it was established that users did not pay attention to, or understand the language of permissions requests [8,18,19,26]. AOFU permissions offered some context about how a resource would be used, but were still seen as ineffective [10,39]. We examine the impact of context in our second experiment by stating the purpose of tracking. This allows us to contribute data towards the impact of context, and expand on it by determining if one type of purpose is more readily accepted than another.

Similarly, other permissions work focused on defining the concept of privacy as expectations, where permissions were found to be accepted when they followed user expectations of an app's function. Lin et al. found that users were more comfortable when presented with a purpose for a requested permission, and felt least comfortable when any resource was used for advertising purposes [29]. Similarly, Bonné et al. noted a common reason for denying a permission was that the app shouldn't need it to function [10]. As Apple does not allow developers to remove functionality for users who reject tracking, this work may serve as an explanation for the documented low acceptance rates [23]. Our finding that users accept tracking more often when it improves app content contributes to this area of work.

5.3 Nudging

Previous research has examined persuasive design in a privacy context from a variety of perspectives. Research on framing specifically has returned mixed results. Gluck et al. found that neither positive nor negative framing had an effect on users' awareness of privacy notices, while Adjerid et al. found that the framing of a privacy notice affected how much personal information participants disclosed [4,20].

Johnson et al. observed a significant framing effect when asking users to opt-in or out of a health survey with varying language [24]. They found that users were more likely to participate when presented with a positive frame. We build on this by including neutral language, allowing us to establish a baseline against which we compare positive and negative framing.

Other work on nudging has examined soft paternalism that leads users to better privacy decisions [1,7]. Several researchers have built tools to help guide users through permission decisions, with nudges towards restricting permissions [6,30,39]. Apple's ATT policy is similar, expanding upon their existing permission system to give users more control over their privacy.

While research has focused on helping users improve their privacy, UI/UX is often designed with the opposite intentions in mind. Referred to as dark patterns, these design elements nudge users towards less privacy [12]. Researchers have categorized dark patterns in several ways, most recently splitting them into five categories: nagging, obstruction, sneaking, interface interference, forced action [11,15,21]. Dark patterns have been heavily studied on the web, with previous work examining major platforms including Windows 10, Google, and Facebook [16]. Other studies have cast a wider net, including one that found dark patterns in over 10% of 11000 shopping websites observed [31].

In the mobile context, researchers examined Android apps to determine that 95% of mobile apps contained at least one dark pattern, while 49% contained 7 or more [17]. We observed some dark patterns in the ATT priming pages we documented, falling under the category of interface interference. While we observed some examples, implementing dark patterns is forbidden in Apple's developer guidelines, explaining its low occurrence rate [23]. Similar policies limiting the use of dark patterns have been suggested by researchers previously [2,33].

6 Conclusion

App Tracking Transparency (ATT) introduces opt-in tracking authorization for iOS apps. In this work, we investigate how mobile apps present tracking requests to users, and we evaluate how observed design patterns impact users' privacy.

This work conducts the first observational study to investigate how apps implement ATT requests in the wild. We perform a manual observational study of the Top 200 free iOS apps, and we report on our findings. We note, however, that the behavior of these apps may not be representative of the full app ecosystem; apps that are less popular and apps that charge for installation are likely to exhibit different behavior than the apps we examined. Further work will be required to determine to what extend our findings extend to mobile apps on the whole.

We also perform a user study with 950 to evaluate the impact of the observed designs. Our results show that opt-in authorization is highly effective at enhancing data privacy in the context of tracking by mobile apps. Moreover, opt-in rates (and thus privacy) were relatively consistent across most conditions, which indicates that ATT is less subject to dark patterns and other privacy-diminishing effect than other types of preference settings. Further work will be required to determine to what extend these findings generalize to non-iPhone users and to other types of apps, but our results suggests that ATT—which requires opt-in consent with clearly defined options presented in a standardized format—might prove an effective model for managing data privacy in other contexts.

A   Follow-Up Survey Questions

In this Appendix, we provide the complete set of questions asked in our user study.

1. "What percentage of the apps you have installed on your phone do you believe track you?" (Chosen on scale from 0–100)
2. "If the mobile apps you use employed a permanent identifier to track your behavior across multiple apps and/or to link you to your other behavior online, how comfortable would you be with it?" (Very Comfortable/Somewhat comfortable/Neutral/Somewhat uncomfortable/Very uncomfortable)

3. "How often have you noticed apps you use giving you an option to opt-in or opt-out of sharing a tracking identifier with the app?" (Never/A few times/Sometimes/Often/Always)
4. "How often do you opt-out of tracking on the apps you use?" (Never Have/Have a few times/Sometimes/Usually/Always)
5. (If did not respond "Never" to Question 4) "How difficult on average did you find it to opt-out of tracking on apps you use?" (Somewhat difficult/Neither difficult nor easy/Somewhat easy/Very easy)
6. (If did not respond "Never" to Question 4) "How satisfied are you with the opt-out mechanisms you have used to opt out of tracking by mobile apps?" (Very satisfied/Somewhat satisfied/Neutral/Somewhat unsatisfied/Very unsatisfied)
7. "What sort of smartphone do you primarily use?" (iPhone/Android device/Other/None)
8. (If responded "iPhone" to Question 7) "What version of iOS is currently installed on your device?" (14.5 or higher/14.4 or lower/I don't know)
9. "What is your current age?" (18–24/25–34/35–44/45–59/60–74/75+)
10. "What is your gender?" (Man/Woman/Non-binary person/Other)
11. "Choose one or more races that you consider yourself to be:" (White/Black or African American/American Indian or Alaska Native/Asian/Pacific Islander or Native Hawaiian/Other)
12. "In which country do you currently reside?" (list of countries)

References

1. Acquisti, A.: Nudging privacy: the behavioral economics of personal information. IEEE Secur. Priv. **7**(6), 82–85 (2009)
2. Acquisti, A., Adjerid, I., Brandimarte, L.: Gone in 15 s: the limits of privacy transparency and control. IEEE Secur. Priv. **11**(4), 72–74 (2013)
3. Acquisti, A., John, L.K., Loewenstein, G.: What is privacy worth? J. Leg. Stud. **42**(2), 249–274 (2013)
4. Adjerid, I., Acquisti, A., Brandimarte, L., Loewenstein, G.: Sleights of privacy: framing, disclosures, and the limits of transparency. In: Proceedings of the Ninth Symposium on Usable Privacy and Security, pp. 1–11 (2013)
5. Alashoor, T., Fox, G., Jeff Smith, H.: The priming effect of prominent is privacy concerns scales on disclosure outcomes: an empirical examination. In: Pre-ICIS Workshop on Information Security and Privacy (2017)
6. Almuhimedi, H., et al.: Your location has been shared 5,398 times! a field study on mobile app privacy nudging. In: Proceedings of the 33rd Annual ACM Conference on Human Factors in Computing Systems, pp. 787–796 (2015)
7. Balebako, R., et al.: Nudging users towards privacy on mobile devices (2011)
8. Benton, K., Jean Camp, L., Garg, V.: Studying the effectiveness of android application permissions requests. In: 2013 IEEE International Conference on Pervasive Computing and Communications Workshops (PERCOM Workshops), pp. 291–296. IEEE (2013)
9. Binns, R., Lyngs, U., Van Kleek, M., Zhao, J., Libert, T., Shadbolt, N.: Third party tracking in the mobile ecosystem. In: Proceedings of the 10th ACM Conference on Web Science, pp. 23–31 (2018)

10. Bonné, B., Peddinti, S.T., Bilogrevic, I., Taft, N.: Exploring decision making with android's runtime permission dialogs using in-context surveys. In: Thirteenth Symposium on Usable Privacy and Security, pp. 195–210 (2017)

11. Bösch, C., Erb, B., Kargl, F., Kopp, H., Pfattheicher, S.: Tales from the dark side: privacy dark strategies and privacy dark patterns. Proc. Priv. Enhancing Technol. **2016**(4), 237–254 (2016)

12. Brignull. H.: Dark patterns (2019)

13. Choe, E.K., Jung, J., Lee, B., Fisher, K.: Nudging people away from privacy-invasive mobile apps through visual framing. In: Kotzé, P., Marsden, G., Lindgaard, G., Wesson, J., Winckler, M. (eds.) INTERACT 2013. LNCS, vol. 8119, pp. 74–91. Springer, Heidelberg (2013). https://doi.org/10.1007/978-3-642-40477-1_5

14. Chong, I., Ge, H., Li, N., Proctor, R.W.: Influence of privacy priming and security framing on mobile app selection. Comput. Secur. **78**, 143–154 (2018)

15. Conti, G., Sobiesk, E.: Malicious interface design: exploiting the user. In: Proceedings of the 19th International Conference on World Wide Web, pp. 271–280 (2010)

16. Norwegian Consumer Council. Deceived by design, how tech companies use dark patterns to discourage us from exercising our rights to privacy. Norwegian Consumer Council Report (2018)

17. Di Geronimo, L., Braz, L., Fregnan, E., Palomba, F., Bacchelli, A.: UI dark patterns and where to find them: a study on mobile applications and user perception. In: Proceedings of the 2020 CHI Conference on Human Factors in Computing Systems, pp. 1–14 (2020)

18. Felt, A.P., Egelman, S., Wagner, D.: I've got 99 problems, but vibration ain't one: a survey of smartphone users' concerns. In: Proceedings of the Second ACM Workshop on Security and Privacy in Smartphones and Mobile Devices, pp. 33–44 (2012)

19. Felt, A.P., Ha, E., Egelman, S., Haney, A., Chin, E., Wagner, D.: Android permissions: user attention, comprehension, and behavior. In Proceedings of the Eighth Symposium on Usable Privacy and Security, pp. 1–14 (2012)

20. Gluck, J., et al.: How short is too short? implications of length and framing on the effectiveness of privacy notices. In: Twelfth Symposium on Usable Privacy and Security, pp. 321–340 (2016)

21. Gray, C.M., Kou, Y., Battles, B., Hoggatt, J., Toombs, A.L.: The dark (patterns) side of UX design. In: Proceedings of the 2018 CHI Conference on Human Factors in Computing Systems, pp. 1–14 (2018)

22. Grossklags, J., Acquisti, A.: When 25 cents is too much: an experiment on willingness-to-sell and willingness-to-protect personal information. In: WEIS (2007)

23. Apple Inc., Human interface guidelines (2021)

24. Johnson, E.J., Bellman, S., Lohse, G.L.: Defaults, framing and privacy: why opting in-opting out 1. Mark. Lett. **13**(1), 5–15 (2002)

25. Kahneman, D., Tversky, A.: Prospect theory: an analysis of decision under risk. Econometrica **47**(2), 263–292 (1979)

26. Kelley, P.G., Consolvo, S., Cranor, L.F., Jung, J., Sadeh, N., Wetherall, D.: A conundrum of permissions: installing applications on an android smartphone. In: Blyth, J., Dietrich, S., Camp, L.J. (eds.) FC 2012. LNCS, vol. 7398, pp. 68–79. Springer, Heidelberg (2012). https://doi.org/10.1007/978-3-642-34638-5_6

27. Kurtz, A., Weinlein, A., Settgast, C., Freiling, F.: DiOS: dynamic privacy analysis of iOS applications (2014)

28. Liccardi, I., Pato, J., Weitzner, D.J.: Improving mobile app selection through transparency and better permission analysis. J. Priv. Confidentiality 5(2), 1–55 (2014)

29. Lin, J., Amini, S., Hong, J.I., Sadeh, N., Lindqvist, J., Zhang, J.: Expectation and purpose: understanding users' mental models of mobile app privacy through crowdsourcing. In: Proceedings of the 2012 ACM Conference on Ubiquitous Computing, pp. 501–510 (2012)

30. Liu, B., et al.: Follow my recommendations: a personalized privacy assistant for mobile app permissions. In: Twelfth Symposium on Usable Privacy and Security, pp. 27–41 (2016)

31. Mathur, A., et al.: Dark patterns at scale: findings from a crawl of 11k shopping websites. Proceedings of the ACM on Human-Computer Interaction, 3(CSCW), pp. 1–32 (2019)

32. Mohamed, I., Patel, D.: Android vs iOS security: a comparative study. In 2015 12th International Conference on Information Technology-New Generations, pp. 725–730. IEEE (2015)

33. Narayanan, A., Mathur, A., Chetty, M., Kshirsagar, M.: Dark patterns: Past, present, and future: the evolution of tricky user interfaces. Queue 18(2), 67–92 (2020)

34. Razaghpanah, A., et al.: Apps, trackers, privacy, and regulators: a global study of the mobile tracking ecosystem (2018)

35. Schreiner, M., Hess, T.: On the willingness to pay for privacy as a freemium model: first empirical evidence (2013)

36. Sensor Tower. Top charts: iphone - us - all categories, June 2021

37. Tversky, A., Kahneman, D.: Loss aversion in riskless choice: a reference-dependent model. Q. J. Econ. 106(4), 1039–1061 (1991)

38. Vallina-Rodriguez, N., et al.: Tracking the trackers: towards understanding the mobile advertising and tracking ecosystem. arXiv preprint arXiv:1609.07190 (2016)

39. Wijesekera, P., et al.: The feasibility of dynamically granted permissions: Aligning mobile privacy with user preferences. In: 2017 IEEE Symposium on Security and Privacy (SP), pp. 1077–1093. IEEE (2017)

Author Index

Printed in the United States
by Baker & Taylor Publisher Services